Advance Praise for *American Psychic*

"Fearless and utterly fascinating . . . I have known Marla as a gifted teacher and witnessed her work first hand, and reading AMERICAN PSYCHIC, it's clear she is as good a storyteller as she is a master of her other callings. She makes the 'incredible' totally relatable and the 'impossible' inescapable and divine."

—James Patrick Stuart, Emmy® nominated actor

"AMERICAN PSYCHIC takes us on a journey of discovery and reckoning as Marla details her evolution into one of the most respected and gifted psychics in the country. I'm in awe of her vulnerability and openness as she reveals her personal, intimate awakening and how this pig farmer's daughter tapped into the consciousness of Spirit. Her gifts are profound, and I am excited that she is sharing this inner knowledge with all of us. A brilliant and inspiring read!"

—Ramey Warren, co-creator of
Crossing Over with John Edward

"POWERFUL AND FASCINATING . . . Congratulations to Marla for writing a book that required a great deal of courage and that can help many people."

—Brian Weiss, MD, *New York Times*
bestselling author of *Many Lives, Many Masters*

"A fast-paced story of spiritual and psychic awakening from a brilliant wordsmith."

—Holly Powell: Emmy® winning casting director
and author of *The Audition Bible:*
Secrets Every Actor Needs to Know

"A highly entertaining romp through the hijinks of a success-ful actress turned reluctant psychic who found her way to pro-found forgiveness and atonement. Marla's story shows how in-sight and intuition can guide each of us on our own fabulous journeys—if we don't turn a blind eye to them. I couldn't recom-mend this book more highly."

—Joyce Walker, producer of
The Aware Show and *Being Aware*

"Marla is a force of nature, and AMERICAN PSYCHIC is her funny, eloquent, dramatic and ultimately inspirational account of that forward motion. Hers has been a life brimming with bounceback. All who accept her invitation to share that life will not be disappointed. Renew all hope, ye who enter here."

—Dennis McDougal, bestselling author of
Dylan: The Biography and *Hemingway's Suitcase*

"Marla's transparency in AMERICAN PSYCHIC will crack you open, hold you, and teach you why it's wonderful to be you. Her writing engulfs you in her fascinating story of finding her voice . . . and then using it. She writes about transforming trauma into skill so beautifully and gracefully. Whether or not you be-lieve in psychic ability, you will be mesmerized by Marla's tales and teachings and come away understanding how you can do the same. A MUST READ!"

—Abbey LeVine, Emmy® nominated producer

"Marla Frees's spiritual journey of discovery inspires us to look at our own psychological barriers that hold us back as we come face to face with love and death. Her message is an invitation to gain awareness of the profound connection that all beings, living and dead, have with each other and beyond."

—Joe Whitcomb, psychotherapist and
bestselling author of *Reboot Your Relationship*

"You will love AMERICAN PSYCHIC. Marla shares the unvarnished unfolding of her gifts and gradual understanding of the larger reality in which she lives daily—a reality that is deeper and broader than the one in which most of us live. Yes indeed, Marla is the real deal."

—Thomas Campbell, physicist, consciousness researcher, author of *My Big TOE*

"Marla opens her heart and offers readers not only a fine story, but also the means to inspire a profound change in their own lives. Her words carry depth and power, and her caring about others shines through every interaction she describes."

—Donna Aveni and Keith Warner, MBT Events

"A fascinating read that I couldn't put it down . . . authentic, heart wrenching and moving. Thank you, Marla, for sharing your story with the world."

—Catherine Curry-Williams, founder of Shane's Inspiration and L'Oréal of Paris 2015 Women of Worth Honoree

"Raw, real, exciting, vulnerable, and truly an experience, AMERICAN PSYCHIC is not just a good read, but a journey of healing. Reading Marla's story helped me heal part of my personal story, and I highly recommend it, especially for women who are looking for their voice and want to break through their barriers of fear and begin living a true, authentic life."

—April Hannah, mental health therapist and producer/host of Path 11 Productions

"One of the most unique and entertaining memoirs I've ever read, filled with spiritual depth, profound wisdom, and poignant humor. Marla's journey is rich with adventure, colorful Hollywood stories, and emotional honesty that will inspire you to embrace your own life's journey in a more profound and healing way."

—Minda Burr, playwright and
Writers Mastermind Group facilitator

"Masterful storytelling filled with gut-wrenching candor and laugh-out-loud humor. . . . As Oliver Wendell Holmes stated, 'Man's mind once stretched by a new idea never regains its original dimensions.' Marla Frees's AMERICAN PSYCHIC takes her readers on a mind-bending, perspective-altering, soul-expanding journey."

—Karen Baldwin, Miss Universe 1982,
writer, and spokeswoman

"AMERICAN PSYCHIC has the potential to nudge readers into an awareness of their own intuitive insights. The true gift, however, may be for those who are reminded of their own long-forgotten traumas and inspired to seek support in healing. I highly recommend this book that is so relevant in the American culture at this time."

—Nancy Minister, marriage and family therapist
and trauma facilitator, Meadows Treatment Center,
and certified life coach

"With snark, pizazz, pure love, humor, and sheer magic, Marla reminds us that anything is possible and that there is more to life and death than meets the eye. This is a beautiful, truth-filled story. Marla is a transformational superhero, and after reading this book I feel more like one as well."

—Jenny Karns, healer, speaker, and co-author of
Baby Boy Phoenix

AMERICAN

psychic

A SPIRITUAL JOURNEY FROM THE HEARTLAND TO HOLLYWOOD, HEAVEN, AND BEYOND

MARLA FREES

FOREWORD BY ANTONIA FELIX

Post Hill
PRESS

A POST HILL PRESS BOOK

ISBN: 978-1-68261-572-0
ISBN (eBook): 978-1-68261-573-7

American Psychic:
A Spiritual Journey from the Heartland to Hollywood, Heaven, and
Beyond
© 2018 by Marla Frees

Cover art by Christian Bentulan
Cover photos by Mary Ann Halpin

This memoir reflects the author's present recollections of experiences over time. Some names and characteristics have been changed to protect the privacy of individuals, some events have been compressed, and some dialogue has been recreated.

Post Hill Press
New York • Nashville
posthillpress.com

Published in the United States of America

Table of Contents

Acknowledgments

An acknowledgment is more than thanks; it is a celebration of all the amazing people who have been a part of this extraordinary journey. I am deeply grateful for their contributions in my life and in support of *American Psychic*.

Thank you, Antonia Felix, for heeding the call to guide me. Your encouragement, smarts, heart, and vision for my voice as a writer gave me a safe place to land and the confidence to jump. Your ability to decipher dreams and make them reality held the space for my book to come to fruition. Thank you for your wisdom as a woman, author, musician, friend, and champion of this book.

To my dearest friends, Chris Dane Owens, Rick Miller, Pamela Korst, Bonnie Gordon Patterino, Peggy Beegle, and Maya JB Burrell, who listened, cried, and laughed with me throughout some of the darkest and brightest days of this process. All aspects of your support have been profound. A special thanks to Minda Burr who has consistently empowered me with her maternal/sister love, standing for my voice and encouraging my creativity.

The wisdom and benevolence of Spirit divinely introduced friends and colleagues into my life. Thank you Fred Fontana, Whitley and Anne Strieber, James Van Praagh, Dr. Brian Weiss, Laurie Zaks, Dennis McDougal, Jim Corti, John Shaeffer, Lincoln Bandlow, Eileen Kirkpatrick Tilghman Moss, Pierce O'Donnell, Tom Campbell, Pamela Knight, Donna Aveni, Keith Warner, Kathy Graf, Lisa Braun Dubbles, and Meena Amani.

Thank you to those who contributed their energy, heart, and support: Karen Baldwin, Holly Powell, Catherine Curry-Williams, Tamara Mark, Ramey Warren, Hillary Smith, Cheryl Gutenberg, Suze Lanier-Bramlett, Susan Edwards Martin, Randy Thomas, Rhonda Britten, Mindy Gibbins, Marsha Gaudin, Michael Emanuel, Richard Kuhlman, David Harvey, Richard Baker, Tim Krusback, Lora Jeanne Martens, Birgit Kotler-Balzer, Jim Boyle, Susie Ekins, Jenny Karns, Barbara Deutch, Marty and Jane Rosenblatt, James Day, William Leonard Picard, Joyce Schmidtbauer Walker, Maria Turnhout, Laura Welch, Karen Brooks, Anna Campbell, Robert Fortune, Cheri Miller, Pam Stacey, Diana Donaldson, Lauren Carlin, Anne Windsor, Amy Lynn Stevenson, Richard Blackburn, Colleen McDougal, Shareen Ross, Jeff Hardwick, Joe Whitcomb, Tracy Mays, Abbey Levine, Scott Williams, Cathey Clack Painter, Linda Gray, Tim Krusback, Lee Harvard, Jaimie Artist, Mary Ann Halpin, Clare Henry, Fred and Shirley Ribble, Bob Kotche, Erica Gale, Gerik Cionsky, and Darren J. Cleaver.

I am so grateful to hometown friends for reflections about our lives together: Bette Lu Miller, Deborah Fries, Bob Octavio, Gary and Betsy Ickes, Janice Keys-Leppert, Joyce Layer, Mindy Hillegass, Gail Datesman, Joyce Brallier, and Sue and Mervyn Rose. Special thanks to Michael Herncane for his diligent English-teacher eye and soulful reflection of the love I have for Bedford.

Heartfelt thanks go to the transformational facilitators who guided my healing: Dr. Drue Bogdonoff; Breck Costin and BCC & Associates; Judith Patterson, MFT; and Nancy Minister and the Meadows Treatment Center Survivor Program. Thank you to the authors and teachers who have provided books, podcasts, television programs, and seminars—your dedication to transformation, health, and wellness has been a touchstone for healing: Pia Mellody, Robert Burney, Melody Beattie, Dr. Peter Levine, Jean Houston, Brene Brown, Eckhart Tolle, and Marianne Williamson. I am especially grateful to Oprah Winfrey who by example has taught us that "speaking your truth is the most powerful tool we all have."

My eternal thanks to Nancy Honeycutt McMoneagle and the facilitators of the Monroe Institute. The work we have done together and continue to do in the exploration of consciousness is one of my greatest joys. To the international communities of *Unknowncountry.com*'s "Dreamland" and MBT events, thank you for your support.

My loving gratitude goes to all who are now in spirit. My mother and father, our life together is a testament to the benevolence of God's love and grace. We have moved on in greater consciousness and love because of the work we have done together. Thank you to those who in death found ways through me to connect their love and forgiveness to those still here on earth. Their experience of life after death has taught me even more about life. I am forever grateful for your contribution, sacrifice, and love.

The greatest gift of my life has been the ongoing walk with this Larger Consciousness System, Spirit, God, Jesus, the Voice, Universe, Force, and THEMS. They are my life. Thank you for not giving up on me. May my life be a continuation of the love that you are.

Foreword

Many of us have intuitive hunches that turn out to be beneficial, and we experience synchronicities that are just plain baffling. I am always amazed when someone flashes into my mind and a few seconds later that person calls me. Or when a book comes into my hands just when I need it. Sometimes I've had a sudden change of heart, such as forgiveness, that I can only explain as an act of grace. And many times I've woken from a dream that answers a pressing question or gives me a creative fix for a snag I'm having with my writing. As intriguing as these moments are, it is easy to brush them off as abnormal, or even irrelevant quirks . . . unless one of those hunches saves your life—the light is green, but look to your left!—or the dream of a loved one who just died is so real that you cannot deny the love and comfort warming your heart when you awake.

We love to hear tales of these experiences because they confirm what we know deep down . . . that there is more going on than meets the eye. Life *is* full of mystery, of inexplicable flashes of "knowing," of astonishing connections between us and those we love.

Some seem to have easier access to these extraordinary perceptions than others. Marla Frees was born with heightened abilities, but she did not realize the extent of her gifts until her life got tough. It wasn't a long wait. Those gifts helped her survive, and so did her other talents of acting, singing, and dancing, which led her to a performing career on stage, television, and in film. When I met her, she was reflecting on all the elements in her life and those of her clients that, in hindsight, had to come together to make her life meaningful for herself and others who could benefit from what she had learned. Those heartbreaking, hilarious, mystical, and sometimes jaw-dropping events are found in this book.

I learned about Marla and her work nearly ten years ago while listening to Whitley Strieber interview her on his "Dreamland" podcast on his website, *Unknown Country*. Whitley introduced her as the psychic medium who saved his life by warning him about a medical condition of which he had been completely unaware. He was adamant that if he had not taken her seriously and followed up with a doctor, he wouldn't be alive. His testimonial, along with Marla's upbeat personality, sense of humor, humility, and fascinating experiences, sent me back to my desk to find her website and schedule a session.

Connecting with Marla in that first phone call was a life changer. She relayed a message from my dad, who had died more than three decades earlier. That communication spoke to a difficult situation in my life at that time, something no one knew about or could find on the internet, and hearing it meant the world to me. She also told me to pay attention—close attention—to my gastrointestinal system. You should check it out, she said. I didn't. A few weeks and one excruciatingly painful episode later I had to undergo surgery, a procedure I believe I could have avoided if I had taken action to reverse the condition that Marla warned me about. Lesson learned. Those initial experiences revealed that Marla really can *see*, and that what she sees is significant, or she wouldn't see it in the first place.

In the years that she has been writing this book, Marla has shared her stories with me, many of which are in these pages. These stories have confirmed my belief that we are capable of much more than we think—that the rational mind that we consider the pinnacle of our powers is just a bit player in the larger scheme of things. As a writer who spends a good part of my time using my imagination, whether to dream up scenes or to try to make actual events from the past come alive, I know that our creative reach is endless. And that's where the real action is. We hear hints of this in studies that say that an executive more often makes decisions with her gut than with her head, and that musicians and scientists find breakthroughs in their dreams when their minds are set free. Our knowing reaches far beyond the confines of the familiar waking consciousness that gets us from A to B every day, and Marla has ventured into more levels of this knowing than most.

You are about to discover that Marla's abilities are not limited to sensing ailments ripening in someone's body or bridging communication between the deceased and those they left behind. She can also identify key elements of homicide cases for detectives and successfully scan a house for structural problems without even standing in the building—or being in the same city. Her explorations include training with remote viewers and others leading the way for human adventures in consciousness. But dazzling as they are, these submersions and flights into the "unknown" are only part of Marla's story. They are woven throughout a life that became open to them out of necessity. Her darkest hours led to a vaster perception that not only saved her, but now inspires and teaches us.

I am always struck by Marla's instinct for putting her experiences into a context that holds meaning for others, particularly those who have had similar challenges early in life and are enduring their lasting impacts. Writing this book was often an agonizing ordeal for her, a revisit of too many devastating truths. But like her life, the pain of her recollections paved the way for treasures beyond belief. Marla's adventures of the heart and spirit from the heartland to Hollywood, heaven, and beyond give new meaning to human resilience, transformation, and joy.

ANTONIA FELIX

INTRODUCTION

The Ride

"Life is the train, not the station."
—Paulo Coelho

There was just a glint of sweat on his bald forehead. I resisted the urge to take my napkin and dab it. We smiled at each other as we took a bite of our breakfast cereal and sipped our coffee. We were happy—or at least looked happy—as man and wife. I was glad I'd remembered to have my nails done. We dipped our spoons into the milk again and then started to chew.

"CUT!" a voice yelled. The man and I both leaned over and spit out our partially chewed Cap'n Crunch cereal into a bucket and laughed.

I turned to my pretend husband and said, "Hey, I wish it had crunch berries in it."

"Me too," he said. "By the way, my name is Mike."

"Nice to meet you, husband Mike." We were on a sound stage at Ren-Mar Studios in Hollywood and it was business as usual, spitting out product in between shots for a cereal commercial.

The assistant director removed the bucket and said, "Ok, will our on-set talent, Marla and Mike, please take your positions again?" I picked up my spoon and then the room shifted and blurred. I went blind to where I was. I no longer saw the spoon, the lights, the camera, or the set of the commercial shoot. All I could see now was a bedroom at night. There was a baby crib and a mobile slowly moving over it. Everything was calm and serene in this psychic movie that had started to play out in my head, and then I heard, *"Tell him it's me, Fred, Fred!"*

The assistant director yelled from behind the camera. "MARLA, are you ready?" My mind immediately snapped out of the vision I was having.

"Yes!" I said. "Yes, I'm ready." I sat up straight, adjusted my suit, and got back into my commercial acting mode. I wanted to make an excuse for not paying attention, but in my mind I was being guided into a child's room and I wanted to go back into those images and find out who Fred was.

Mike leaned in, touched my arm and asked, "Are you okay?" As soon as Mike did that, I heard, *"Tell him I watch him read the blue book every night to his son."*

"Hold up," said the director. "We need to reposition the camera. Talent, just sit tight—this will only take a few minutes."

I sat there wondering, should I tell Mike? This talking to the dead business, if that's what was really going on, was something very new to me. I had been highly skeptical of anyone who claimed to be able do it, but I had been forced into dealing with it myself, and here on the set it was happening again. I stared at the Cap'n Crunch floating around in my bowl and felt a surge of love move through me. Then it just popped out. "Mike, do you have a baby boy?"

"Yes, I do," he said.

"Mike, I don't know how to say this since we just met, but I'm one of those people who somehow is able to talk with the dead, and I have a guy here named Fred who wants to talk to you."

His reply was immediate. "Oh, my God, Fred is my dad's name and he died a year ago. What's he saying?"

I said, "Your father shows me a bedroom with a crib. He's pointing to the crib and saying, *I watch him read the blue book every night to the baby.* Does this mean anything to you?"

Mike's eyes welled up. "Yes, I have a newborn son. I've been so upset that my dad wasn't here for his birth. And yeah, I read from a book that's blue! I read the book *Rainbow Fish* every night to my son." We were both in tears.

How did this happen? Did the dead set it up, casting Mike and me together on a national television commercial so Mike's deceased father could communicate with him? Was the love between Mike and his dad so strong that God facilitated this?

These interventions had taken over my life. In fact, they were more deep and meaningful than my day job as an actress. How did my life get to look like this? Me, a Pennsylvania feed salesman/pig farmer's daughter who survived the danger in my home and later in the world of national and international mobsters and then landed in Hollywood and balanced sitcoms, spirits, and a stalker. I was on the ride of my life. Dead people, murder, Hollywood heartthrobs, sex, psychic visions, and UFOs were all a part of it. I found myself catapulted and positioned into situations with psychic awareness and messages from deceased loved ones to assist people from all walks of life—including the most skeptical . . .

"So, what do you think you can do for me?" he asked, leaning back in the chair and folding his arms over his well-defined chest. The word DETECTIVE was emblazoned on the nameplate on his desk, and it seemed that he was doing his best to suppress his skepticism.

I sat up straight and composed myself to convey how sane I was as I explained one of the "unique" things I do. "When it comes to homicides, I like to hold crime scene photos," I said. "By holding the photo, I access information about what happened before and after the picture was taken. Sometimes I experience the events from the victim's point of view, and sometimes I can get inside the head of the perpetrator."

"How did this ability come about?" he asked.

"I've been assessing dangerous situations pretty much all my life. I can feel it, see it. I guess it comes easy to me, even without wearing a badge." I smiled.

"You just hold an object?" he asked incredulously.

"That's one way it works for me."

"Can you read *anything*?"

"Pretty much."

He pulled the left sleeve of his dark blue suit up over his forearm, popped the white cuff of his shirt, and revealed a silver bracelet on his tanned wrist. The bracelet was just as stunning as he was. He smiled and handed it to me. "Ok, what do you see with this?"

The chain was warm and smooth. "I see a beautiful, honey-skinned woman with long blonde hair gave this to you as a present."

"Yes, she's my wife," he laughed.

"I see a white marble bathroom with a separate shower and tub."

"Yes, that's my bath at home."

"You've got a white towel wrapped low around your waist and you're standing in front of the mirror flexing your biceps. Now you're squatting deeply, turning to admire your quads. You're rubbing them hard and then you—"

He snatched the bracelet out of my hands. "That's enough! I have a case for you."

We all have various degrees of psychic, intuitive, empathic abilities—gifts of keen sensitivities, perceptions, and under-standings. These awarenesses go beyond what we can perceive with our minds. They are birthrights. God-given gifts. Some are family inheritances, DNA passed down through neurotransmit-ters and then tweaked after birth by our circumstances and en-vironments. Some gifts are time released, giving us help when we are best prepared for them, and some gifts emerge from dire circumstances, showing up when we need them the most. Yes, answers to our prayers.

Spirit—the collective term I use for God, Jesus, the Holy Spirit, angels, the Universe, the Voice, the Force, and the Larger Consciousness System that has been guiding me for years—put me in specific situations to learn, yanked me out of places in which I wasn't learning enough, and then pushed me into expe-riences that involved strangers, colleagues, celebrities, animals, and friends.

It was a cool, gray L.A. day. It had drizzled. Traffic was sparse because no one in this city likes to drive in the rain. I was stopped at a light when I noticed that the driver in the car next to me was a friend I'd not seen in years. We were both excited as he motioned for me to pull over into the Bed, Bath & Beyond parking lot.

J. Hardwick was a casting director. We'd met ten years ear-lier as judges, of all things, on some high falootin' talent show. We always liked and respected each other's entertainment adventures. I had just gotten over the flu. My face was still show-ing signs of tissue abuse, but I didn't care. I was just happy to see him.

We hugged. "Marla, I haven't see you in years! I've thought of you for various acting jobs, but you never appeared on my casting list."

As he continued to talk I immediately became aware of a presence. A loving golden energy came from around the side of the car and gravitated right beside Hardwick. I heard, "Bud-dy, Buddy!" as if Hardwick's voice was calling the name of this beautiful dog whose spirit had just joined us.

Hardwick looked at me and said, "Why are you smiling?"

I explained why he had not seen me in six years. "I left the business to help people connect to their deceased loved ones, and I see a tan-colored dog sitting right beside you."

Tears came fast as Hardwick reached into his car and pulled out a picture of the dog I had just seen.

Buddy, who had died, was Hardwick's best friend.

I literally saw things from Buddy's perspective and could feel his emotions. I talked as fast as the images came.

"Buddy shows me a hallway leading into a living room. I see another dog. Buddy says he doesn't mind the new dog you res-cued; however, he doesn't like that big black thing in the middle of the living room . . . what is that?"

Hardwick looked shocked and said, "WHAT!? He doesn't like my new black leather sofa?" We laughed with joy.

We all need help along the way, especially when life doesn't seem to be working out the way we want. We seek guidance from friends, teachers, counselors, spiritual leaders, doctors, books, television, the internet, or sometimes someone like me—a person who is "sighted." I had learned to trust the voice of Spirit. Revealing information and solutions for others, I feel what is coming, and hear not only from the dead, but also from the divine—tuning in to the still, small voice that the Bible tells us we can all hear. But when it comes to seeing for me—Marla—it's not so simple. I am still learning.

Learning to see our way through the challenging times of our lives is a journey for all of us. We are not able to see because of fear, denial, or downright stubbornness. We stay blind until we really want to see.

"Blindsight" is a medical term meaning "the ability of a blind person to sense the presence of a light source." Isn't that how we all feel at some point in our lives, blindly searching for a way out of the darkness? Finding that "presence" and moving from the darkness of trauma and drama into the light of transformation is the journey of my life.

PART I

Blindsight

1

The Rumblings

Barn's burnt down—
Now I can see the moon.
—Masahide

I flipped off the switch and watched the water settle around the fountain in front of my sweet little home. The bees were silently moving from one tiny flower of the red apple groundcover to another. I needed quiet to record another radio program. It was a sunny May day up in the hills above Hollywood and I was very happy.

I had left my twenty-five-year career as a television and stage actress to assist others using my intuition. I also talked to dead people.

I was invited by author Whitley Strieber and his wife Anne to be a radio co-host for their popular webcast, "Dreamland." Whitley, famous for his bestselling horror novels and infamous for his experiences with extraterrestrial beings upon which his nonfiction Communion book series is based, thought I'd be the perfect psychic medium expert to join their *Unknowncountry. com* webcast family. My job was to interview credible science, religion, conspiracy-theory, crop circle, UFO, and things-that-go-bump-in-the-night paranormal authors about their experiences and cutting-edge books. I adjusted my notes on the living room table, looked out beyond the deck to the San Fernando Mountains, and waited for the call that would connect me to authors in England. That day I was going to try and make sense of crystal skull folklore.

Chris Morton and his wife, Ceri Louise Thomas, are the authors of *The Mystery of the Crystal Skulls*. No, this was not a *New York Times* bestseller; it's just another interesting fringe element to the wacky world in which I found myself.

"Welcome to 'Dreamland,' Chris," I began. "So, does your book have anything to do with Steven Spielberg's movie, *Indiana Jones and the Kingdom of the Crystal Skull*?"

"Yes Marla, our book has lots of amazing information that movie people are interested in."

I pressed on. "Well Chris, I am particularly interested in the skull you refer to in your book as the 'healing skull' that was used by Guatemalan shamans."

"Oh, yes, that's Max. Max was given to a Tibetan Buddhist healer by a Guatemalan shaman and now is owned by a woman in Texas who travels around the country with him."

"What? Now *that's* a story!" I said.

As Chris and Ceri began to tell my listeners about Max and some of the amazing events that had happened around the eighteen-pound crystal quartz skull, I started to hear in the intuitive way I hear things: *You have to leave your marriage. Leave your marriage . . . come see me.*

I interrupted my interview with nervous laughter and said, "If my talking to dead folks isn't strange enough, I believe I'm hearing from Max. He seems to be telling me to leave my marriage and go see him!" We all laughed. I thought I was being clever adding a flavor that only someone with my sensitivities could. But I thought I heard him. I also thought, being new to the art of radio hosting, that I must have been making shit up. Max the crystal skull talking to me—yeah, it was good radio.

Chris continued, "Yes, Marla, Max is pretty cheeky. He has been known to telepathically get hold of someone, talk their ear off, and give them profound insight into their lives. A healing of sorts that changes everything!"

I was no longer laughing. Which was more disturbing, I wondered, the fact that I thought I heard Max, that Max talked to *other* people, or what Max said to me? *Leave your marriage.* Oh, please, why in the world would I do that? Better yet, why would I listen to a rock?

Eight months later my marriage was over.

I dug out my snow boots and booked a flight to moonscaped, ice-covered Sun Valley, Idaho, to be with my best friend, Maya, who five years earlier had traded in her beach volleyball bikinis for the thermal fleece of North Face. I hadn't been in snow since I moved from Chicago some twenty years earlier, and as soon as I stepped out for my first walk with Maya I decided it was no longer fun. It challenged my footing, made my toes burn, and egged me on as I tried to follow the fast steps of my dearest friend, whose excitement and love of the land reflected the beauty of her mighty spirit. I let her be my guide and strength.

Maya and her boyfriend, Tim, fed me with their smarts, humor, and the most delicious food, along with unfamiliar sounds of bubbling pots of curry, buffalo burgers roasting on the fire, and wine flowing. I hadn't eaten in days. After a few bites I stopped thinking about everything I'd just lost—my home, the love I thought I had, and most importantly, who I was.

Lordy, what happened to me? I had worked so hard to heal so much of my life. I had made conscious choices and gained awareness. I had left a life of pretending. I stopped acting and surrendered my job and my life to Spirit. I had fallen in love and felt secure for a moment. But life never stays the same, and when things go wrong, we react. I went back to an old pattern of going unconscious, choosing not to see, ignoring the red flags, pretending, and hoping.

When I was a child and my reality became too unpleasant to bear, I "hoped" things would be different. Hope was my way of focusing on something in the future that did not exist, yearning for something to change to get me out of the nightmare. I was not capable as a child of doing anything about the trauma in my life, so I acted my way through what I could and prayed for God to change the rest. But I was an adult now, and still trying to cut deals with God. I prayed like a whiney petulant child for things to go my way: Please get me out of this mess. Can't you just make things go smoothly? Can't I get a break? Blah, blah, *blah!* In fact, things were not going my way because they weren't *supposed* to go my way. My prayers *were* being answered, just not the way I wanted. It's just the damnedest thing—we act insane about our agendas instead of seeing the truth and dealing with it.

That is exactly what had happened throughout my entire life. I had prayed for change and gotten it! Spirit was working for me, even when I wasn't.

"Why don't you talk to my detective friend in town?" Maya suggested. "Get your mind on something you're passionate about, like murder. I'll set it up. Hey, maybe he even has a case for you."

She knew me. If I could just focus on working a murder case I'd feel in service. Working on homicide cases had become a passion over the years. I offered my psychic mediumship skills pro bono to law enforcement agencies for any kind of case—missing persons, homicide, and cold cases—as a way to use my gifts of sight as community service. In any city or small town, I'd just walk into police stations and say to detectives, "If you can't figure something out, let me look at it and see if I can help."

I walked into town to meet Steve, a detective, at the corner deli. I scanned the room and saw a man who looked—stealthy. Not in a predator kind of way, but calm, resolved, and yet aware of everything around him. Even though Steve was retired, he still looked like a cop.

His interrogating face met mine and I felt like a guilty accomplice to love gone wrong as I spilled my guts about why I was in Sun Valley.

"I can understand this," he said. "I came home one day to find my wife was gone. Everything was gone. She took it all, along with my son." I was stunned.

"I was half a man for months," he continued, "until I was given a gift. I heard from my high school sweetheart, and we got married just last year. Don't you have an old boyfriend you want to see?"

I wondered about this question—is this how men think? Out with the old, in with the new? I shook my head and said, "Let's put it this way—no. But thanks for asking."

"Ok. But you know, my wife's leaving was the best thing that ever happened to me. Come on, let's go look at a case."

I walked the crime scene in the middle of spitting snow. As I entered the building I felt what happened to the victim. I dropped to my knees and reported, "The victim saw the perpetrator when he came in. She stood to meet him and then he shot her. I can feel life leaving her body as the blood drains." Steve grabbed my arm and stood me up.

"Whoa, how do you know that? You okay?"

"Yeah, I just feel it and see it like a movie. The information still lives in the imprint of this building."

I gave Steve more of my impressions about where and what the perpetrator could have done after the attack. He confirmed some of my intuitive hits and pondered the new information. It was just enough to distract me for a few hours.

Steve and I said goodbye. I sat alone in Maya's apartment in the middle of a blizzard. Why could I see for others but be blinded to what was happening to my life? As the snow squalled, I stared at the Sawtooth Mountains that were so majestic and stalwart and heard, *This is for you. Just listen.*

Maya had arranged for me to work with some people in town. I prayed to be clear enough to hear divine information.

The first three clients didn't come to talk to their deceased grandmother or hear details from a beloved pet—all three women were in tears because their marriages had ended. Great. Spirit's sense of humor, no doubt. So this is what women who have been hurt feel like? It's pretty shitty, but there was a piece missing. Each woman sat and complained about her husband, berating what the man had done *to* her. What was *their* part in the destruction? What had *they* done or not done that would put their marriage in such danger, and why would they not take responsibility for it? These were questions I would inevitably have to ask myself.

That night, under a heavy blanket with a heating pad at my feet, I prayed and heard, *Sometimes you have to feel everything—you must accept this.* I felt a force rip me open from my neck to my gut with a terrible burning that was killing something deep inside of me. Whatever was happening to me was something I couldn't control. I better start listening to the power behind the burn—*You must accept this, Marla.*

My life in L.A. as I knew it was over. I took myself to the Van Nuys courthouse every morning for weeks to learn how to file for divorce without the expense of an attorney. I could barely breathe or swallow. When I did, I ate a shameful concoction of white wine, chunks of French baguettes, and Xanax. I buried my face into the fur of my cat. He smelled of fresh air and earth. He worried about me. I did too.

So many things can happen to end any relationship. The choices, decisions, withheld truth, withheld love, menopause, old family wounds, new family wounds, the toothpaste cap left off. The most damaging wound is the trauma to our souls when someone in our childhood who was supposed to love us—didn't. That wound started for me way before I got married. Our souls are so smart that we pull relationships to us to help us see what we need to heal.

My ego in its blindness was not capable of admitting my own suffering and taking responsibility for it. That's what happens when you're living a fantasy or a lie: God finally calls you out. Spirit wants the best for all of us.

I'd had years of trusting the voice of Spirit. I had learned to listen to its profound guidance, but when I learned my marriage was over and Spirit's words, the first words of clarity I could hear beyond my own cries, *We want you out of this, we want the best for you, trust us,* I was not comforted. I was out of my mind.

I was in a relationship with loss. How I would handle that loss would determine my life. I see now that I was slowly losing myself and yet I turned my head and shifted focus to avoid the loss. I skirted to places that dimmed me, distracted my light, and found ways to numb consciousness. That's what we all try to do, because pain from loss is excruciating. Every day a little death, as Sondheim says in *A Little Night Music.* Well, it was here now, sitting on my bed waiting for me to wake.

Death happens every day. We abhor it, do everything we can to fend it off, but every day we are all touched by various forms of death. How well we deal with the loss is how well we will live.

I shouted from the depth of my soul, *please* shift this pain! Please help me *see, hear, and feel differently*! Then I laughed, realizing that this was what my work and life was all about. This is what I helped facilitate for others. Spirit was very smart.

Within minutes of that plea I got a call from Cindy, a client and friend. "Marla, my German mother-in-law is coming into town and she really needs to see you."

I had not worked for anyone in three months. This was a blessing. I agreed.

I tried to tame my hair, which had started to resemble a rat terrier, cover the dark circles under my eyes, and put some clothes on my bone-hanger body. I opened the door to a well-dressed and attractive woman, Birgit. Her German accent was thick with life as she smiled and uttered, "Hallo." I immediately connected to a deceased man who walked in with her. He was giddy with excitement to be in communication with his ... daughter.

"Birgit, I have a deceased man here that says he's your father, and he's showing me how he comes to visit you in your New York apartment." I moved around the living room carefully describing what this man was showing me. "He says, 'The window where Birgit sits is over here, the stove here, and then there is a calendar on the wall where she writes everything down. She writes everything down!'" Birgit nodded her head in agreement.

At this point I was so grateful. Everything that had happened in my life brought me to this moment for Birgit and her father, to facilitate the opportunity to heal relationships with love, truth, and life beyond the physical.

I took a deep breath, swelled with the love from her father, and said, "He knows how much you adore the opera, and he says, 'Go see the Wagner piece.'"

Birgit's face beamed. "I'd already planned it!"

"Birgit, he keeps showing me over and over again a bridge. He feels terrible about something that happened there and says it's a place that he has had to come to terms with."

With sadness she said, "My father Gerhard was a Nazi SS officer in World War II. He'd been heavily injured in a mine explosion and was held in a French prison camp. When he was released, he had nothing left. He worked hard to try to clear his political past. He became friends with my first husband, who was Jewish, and tried to make amends in the community. But he was a broken man who knew he had fought for a wrong cause. He was desperate to end his suffering, so he ended his life by diving off a bridge."

I was stunned. The horror of what the whole family had experienced flashed in my brain, but in that moment I could feel her father's emotions shift from the grief of his life and death. He wanted to share happier times, to share love.

"Birgit, he wants us to know he's good now. He likens himself to a ladies' man, handsome, full of life and humor. He wants you to know that he visits your mother in South Africa and he knows that she had planted a hibiscus in her garden in honor of him."

"Yes! My God, that's right!"

"He's waiting for your mother to complete her time here on earth. He loves her so."

I could see him smiling and snapping his fingers to the beat of music I could not hear. I found it profoundly ironic that both Birgit's father and my father had fought in the same war, in the same country, on opposite sides, and mine explosions had heavily injured them both. My father spent months in a French hospital and came back to the U.S. imprisoned in a body cast for nearly a year. He struggled for the rest of his life to end the nighttime terrors and daytime shadows that the war cast on his life. He dove into a bottle instead of off a bridge. We were both daughters of broken men.

I felt the excruciating pain that both our fathers went through to try to heal the price of war. Life, love, survival, and death were much bigger than my little problems. Death is not just about the end of our physical life. It is the culmination of something that must change, the end to a certain way of being. Death in its many forms opens a door to a world of loss, and stepping through that door is transformational—if we can embrace the loss.

As I hugged and said goodbye to Birgit, something in me shifted. I said a grateful "Thank you" to the benevolent force that had orchestrated this divine meeting.

That evening memories surfaced of how broken we all were. Remnants of my parents' marriage for which they never took responsibility, which were too uncomfortable to look at. My sobs were not just for me, but also for my parents, who never healed their own pain. The ravages of war in the world, and inside our homes took its toll on all of us.

Is it so intolerable for our souls to live a life blinded that Spirit must intervene? We all have to find our way through love, loss, and forgiveness at some point in our lives. What we resist persists, and with that understanding I began to surrender to what needed to be transformed.

2

The Gifts

"Gifts come from above in their own peculiar forms."
—Johann Wolfgang von Goethe

I was in the kind of shitty mood that needed a dog to brighten my day, so I went to pick up the neglected mail. The mail center was next door to a pet store and grooming salon. I often see dogs with their owners, and occasionally one will hunt me down for a chat (a dog, that is). I hoped to have my mood shifted by a dog's excited wagging tail as he told me about his recent run on the beach, how proud he feels after being groomed, or how much he loves his owner.

As I separated my junk mail from the important stuff and shared my man woes with Sara the mail sorter, a young woman in flip flops sauntered in carrying a little dog in one arm and futzing with a large knockoff Gucci bag with the other. As she walked past me I caught the eyes of her Cavalier King Charles Spaniel pup and heard it say, *"Tell my mommy my bottom hurts."*

I could feel the dog's pain. He didn't have a voice, so I gave him one and said, "Hey, do you know your dog's bottom hurts?"

Without missing a beat, the collagen-lipped gal who never even looked my way said, "Yep, he has hemorrhoids."

Mail attendant Sara, who knew about my intuitive abilities, and I were dumbfounded by her nonchalant attitude. We both stood in silence as the girl dug around in her purse. As I stared at the pup's big brown eyes and began to feel his fear and anxiousness I could not stop myself from blurting out exactly what I heard him say. "Your dog is telling me, *'I am so afraid of what she is going to do to me tomorrow!'*"

Again, without hesitating, the girl said, "Yep, I'm gonna have his balls cut off."

Sara and I were stunned at the girl's insensitivity. Upset about the dog's terrified state and his owner's unconsciousness of it, I said to Sara, "Ya know, sometimes it's just not helpful being psychic."

I grabbed my mail and headed for the door when the girl yelled, "Hey, are you *really* psychic!?"

I turned to her and said, "Oh, my God, girl, how *else* could I know that your dog's ass hurts?"

I went back the next day to apologize to Sara for my edgy outbursts. We both prayed for the pup.

I had become an advocate for those who didn't have a voice, and yet in my own life I struggled to speak for myself. I prayed for strength and help. The voice of Spirit responded, *We will help you, Marla. We will provide.*

And Spirit did. I was embraced and loved by friends and facilitators. I was invited to be a guest speaker at the Women's Jonathan Club of Los Angeles, where I talked about my work and then gave numerous readings to the lunching club members. After that event I flew back to Idaho to be a guest speaker and presenter at the Sun Valley Wellness Festival. Just four months earlier I'd been stuck in the blizzard of my world falling apart, but it was now spring and I could feel the budding of all sorts of possibilities.

Going back to the glorious nature of Idaho, seeing my girlfriend Maya, and giving talks and demonstrations about my work was an incredible gift that helped me begin to feel . . . normal.

The SyFy network hired me to join homicide detectives revisiting cold cases for a TV pilot called *Soul Evidence*. It was a dream come true. The nerve-bending anxiety of painful loss heightened my "sight" and my psychic abilities were on fire.

When working for law enforcement it is never my job to "solve" anything. I am another investigative tool for them to gain a different kind of insight to their ongoing investigation. I offer information that often corroborates what they already know or I provide a new piece of information. Sometimes I get psychic impressions or information from a deceased crime victim. It's a collaboration.

The production team drove me to an empty parking lot. I was handed a crime scene photo of the same parking lot where a murder had occurred thirty-three years before.

I like to touch things to "know." As I child I always had to touch food before I could eat it and touch people before I could trust them. Holding an object or photo links me to information about the object or what happened before or after a photo was taken. "Movies" of places, feelings, thoughts, and words can flood into my head. This ability, called "psychometry," is odd, but it works.

The photo they handed me of the parking lot included a single car parked under a tree. I walked to the same place the car was parked, stood under the tree, and immediately felt transported back to the night of the crime. I began to see and feel what happened to Janet, the victim. "Janet was here in the front seat of the car," I told the detectives. "He had her neck pressed up against the driver's door. She was raped and strangled at the same time."

I then repeated what I heard Janet tell me: "'I was there for days. It took so long for them to find me. Please tell my family I'm fine now. I don't want them to be upset again; I don't want them to remember me like this.'"

Detectives corroborated that Janet lay there with a broken neck for many days, paralyzed, and then she died.

Perhaps Janet knew that I, too, had suffered a similar scenario some thirty years ago in the front seat of a car. I had been more fortunate than she.

Janet's murder was a cold case. Law enforcement had not arrested anyone for this crime. It was my job to provide information that might lead detectives to the perpetrator.

Later we got ready to film a segment in the police evidence locker. The room's high ceilings with towering metal shelves held hundreds of boxes with names and dates, all pieces of evidence that had been used in investigations. Silent messages from the dead, just waiting to be spoken. The police, in conjunction with the production company, had prepared a series of evidence bags from the cold case we were working in Garden Grove, California. I knew that if I just held a bag of evidence I could probably ascertain more emotional and visual information for the case.

Michael, a husky African-American homicide detective who had been more than irritating in his skepticism of psychic mediumship abilities, was slated to work with me. Sam Korkis and Mike Nichols, the reality show directors, were up in the rafters watching as the cameras started to roll. I picked up one of the old, brown paper evidence bags and images of the victim walking flooded my head. "These are her work shoes," I said.

I put the bag down and picked up a smaller one. "These are the keys to her car. He made her drive to the place where he raped her. I can still feel her fear."

I looked at the table again and before I picked up another bag I heard, "Hey! You've got my DNA in there!" I pointed to the table where the bags of evidence were lined up. The voice I heard came to me like I always heard the deceased, but this time it came *out* of me. I realized I was actually starting to take on part of someone else's personality. This was not the victim. This person felt gruff. I took my boots off, making myself shorter. Oh my God, I thought, I think I'm connecting to the perpetrator, whom we had not yet identified, but who could also be dead. I looked at Michael and said, "I think I have the perpetrator here—I can feel that he is willing to talk. Ask me questions— challenge me as the perpetrator and let's see if we can get more info out of him."

Michael's eyes were popping out of his head as I said, "Look, I've never done this before, but I'm able to feel that the man who killed Janet wants to talk, so help me!"

Michael started his interrogation and questioned the perpetrator like the professional detective he was.

"Have you ever raped or killed before?" he asked.

"Heck, yes, and I'll show you what I've done!" I said. The perpetrator was pompous, but I could feel that under his bravado was a man who felt remorse for having killed someone. I grabbed two sheets of yellow paper from the pad I always carried.

"Here's the kill," he said. I could see my hand drawing a star on the paper, and then some lines that somehow I knew were roads and a freeway.

"But here's where we got sloppy and here's one I did by myself (pointing to other locations). Here's one that was fun, and this one we should never have done." He had just revealed key pieces of info about whether one or more men had committed the crimes. What ended up on that paper was some sort of a map.

Then I told the production crew that I had to stop. I was overwrought. I'd just experienced the most unique moment I'd ever had when working a case. Mike the detective gave me a bottle of water and asked, "You okay?" I nodded.

"That was pretty fuckin' weird," he said.

I agreed. Sam came over and said, "You know the bag you were pointing at when you yelled, 'You have my DNA in there?' Well, in that bag is a piece of the car seat that, in fact, has the perpetrator's DNA on it—semen."

Tim Krubsack, the producer in charge from Universal Studio's television division, sat with me to make sure I was okay. "Just to be on the safe side, I'm going to have a psychiatrist call you tonight, to make sure that your personality is back together," he said. I was fine, but making sure of that was important. I had a nice chat with Doctor B. on the phone about the odd dissociative ability I found I now had with this capacity to experience both victim and perpetrator.

The next day Detective Elaine Jordan of the Garden Grove Police Department took the map that had been drawn 'through me' by the perpetrator and placed it over a map of Los Angeles County. The roads I had indicated lined up with the freeways near the Garden Grove crime. The other marks I had drawn as the perpetrator were all locations of the unsolved rape cases in the same area. Where my hand had drawn the star, the area the perpetrator called "the kill," was the scene of the unsolved Garden Grove murder case we were working on. We were all dumbfounded.

Yes, we would have loved it if the perpetrator had said, "Yeah, it's me, Jack Smith!" but that is not what happened. And as is common in television, the pilot was not picked up. I knew that Spirit had other things in store for me.

It was now my birthday month, and I remembered that the year before I had made a birthday promise to face my fears. I chose issues brewing in my soul that I knew I needed to take action on. Within weeks of that promise, I secured a writing agent to support the potential book inside of me, stepped into the world of the paranormal to host a radio show, and embraced my work as a psychic medium on TV. That promise also unwittingly revealed the deep fear that I'd repressed, like my marriage ending. I was beginning to learn that the truth of 'consciousness' is beautiful, despite how ugly and unpleasant it can seem.

In a meditation that previous year I heard God/Spirit ask me, *"Marla, what would you do if I gave you the gift of a shiny red apple for your birthday?"*

"Well, God," I responded, "I would be grateful for such a delicious gift. I would be delighted in its beauty."

"But what if the apple was bruised, decomposing, and filled with worms?"

I paused, furrowed my brow, and said, "Well, I wouldn't consciously pick that, and I'd wonder why you would give me such a gift."

"Just because it is in transition, is it not still beautiful? The worm thinks so, and the seeds that will soon fall will produce another great tree that will bear delicious fruit and bring shelter and shade to all I have created."

"But God, why would you give me that?"

"Marla. Just understand that if I give you a gift of a bruised apple you are to see the truth of what I give you, and find the beauty."

The apple, a symbol of truth, knowledge, and wisdom, is our intuitive birthright. Perhaps the serpent of the Garden of Eden story represents fear and unconsciousness, cloaked in seduction. So here I was a year later, reminded that I had been given the gift of truth. Now, how would I find the beauty?

I was beginning to feel better, my humor was coming back, and I was deeply in awe of how intimate my relationship to Spirit had become. When people asked me about what God, Jesus, Spirit, the Universe, my guides, and angels were telling me about my own life having been so tenderized by loss, I replied, "Oh, THEMS? Well, they are here and workin' their magic." This was my special way to lovingly include all the amazing support I was getting for these very hard lessons. As soon as I came up with that name I heard, *If you use the term THEMS, then you better know what it stands for: The Heavenly Eternal Message System.*

I and my dismantled ego were tired as I surrendered to what was coming next. I heard THEMS say, *We're sending you a gift.* Oh Lord, now what? But resistance makes the situation much worse, so I surrendered with, "Ok, bring it on!"

Within a week I received a message on Facebook. "Marla, I have never stopped thinking about you. I am so sorry I was not capable of expressing how much I loved you many years ago. I am riding my bicycle across the country from Florida and would like to see you when I get to the West Coast. Will you see me? Love, Bill."

I had buried my college ex-boyfriend so deep that I'd nearly forgotten him. Why was THEMS resurrecting Bill Bonnard and encouraging him to peddle across America to see me?

My mind jumped to my freshman year at Miami University of Ohio—our late-night innocent longings as college sweethearts, eating pickles, watching rain storms, dry humping on the floor of Bill's off-campus apartment, my hair entangled with all the germs and beer nuts stuck in the green shag carpet while *The Best of Bread* crooned, "Baby I'm-a Want You." Rich memories of our frustrating on-again/off-again love affair.

I wondered what could have happened to Bill after all these years. Maybe THEMS had found him and smacked him up the side of the head like they had done to me. I wrote back a cautious, "Call me."

It was great to hear the timbre of his voice. Part of me was home—my body started to relax as we laughed and talked for hours. He said he never married, that he left his job of seventeen years and decided to get away from the Florida lifestyle. What did that mean? What had he been doing since heading up a top technology company? I had two weeks to find out everything I could about him before he landed in L.A.

I studied his Facebook page. Postcard snapshots of new friends along his bike ride, roadside diner specials, lizards crossing railroad tracks, and blown-out tires needing to be fixed. There were photos of a man who started out twenty pounds heavier, now scruffy, but in a Forrest Gump kind of way and full of life. I could not wait to see him. Could Steve, my retired detective friend, and THEMS be right? Maybe this was just what I needed for my first holiday season after my marriage ended, an old boyfriend.

Late one night after a long, delicious phone conversation, I had to ask Bill the question that had been looming behind all others. "Bill, how do you think your mother is going to handle you coming to see me?"

I was hoping he'd say, "Oh, Marla it's been twenty-five years, for God sakes." But instead he laughed and said, "Well, we will just have to see."

He registered himself and his bicycle at a local hotel, but didn't stay there long. My body craved his. His aquiline nose, blue eyes, and bowed lips on his six-foot-one frame were beautiful. He still looked like Michelangelo's David, smelled like rolled oats, tasted like butter, and felt like heaven. That incredible chemistry was still there and our age had seasoned it. My body melted with his familiar banter, wit, and smarts. With every newspaper he read and every thrust between my legs, I felt alive again. My body told me that it wasn't menopause that had dried me up or hormones that had buried my sex drive. What a gift to remind me of that.

Bill kept his Facebook travel updates filled with tales of our wonderful new adventures. He was surprised that I no longer acted, but he embraced my spiritual path and joined one of my mediumship groups. He watched me download information and hear messages from deceased loved ones and wrote about it to his friends in emails like this one:

> Who'd have thought that my girlfriend from college could talk to dead people? Tonight, Marla had a psychic mediumship session with six guests, including me. Bits and pieces of personalities from those on the other side began to unfold with names, dates, details, and visuals for those of us in the room. Even my dog, Scout, showed up. Marla was able to feel and see what Scout showed her. Marla even drew a map of our back yard, indicating where the dog house had been and what it looked like.

Bill was proud of me, interested in my work, and unfazed about sharing it with the world. That made me smile.

The next morning he poured a glass of orange juice and crawled back into bed. My former college boyfriend reclined against my satiny soft sheets. Hair and skin golden, his blue eyes still dreamy from our night of passion, he was a package my body found difficult to resist. I pinched myself that THEMS had sent this gift. His cellphone rang. Bill looked at the number, clicked it off, and said, "That was Mom."

I crawled in beside him. "I hope after all this time your mother is supportive of whatever you do with your life and is happy you're with me."

As he held me in his arms I took a sip of his orange juice. The vapor of vodka flooded my nose. "Jesus, Bill, you can't possibly want vodka at nine in the morning!" I choked out.

Bill didn't resist, but said, "Hey, it's not a problem. I can stop."

I had perhaps just tasted the truth of his last thirty years.

I believed him, so I took the glass and cheerfully walked into the kitchen. "*I'll* make you a drink!" I said as I grabbed Dr.

Bo Wagner's Garden of Plenty, a ground-up concoction of every green plant pulverized into a powder mix. I blended the mix with crushed ice and soymilk. He grimaced at the sight of it, but trusting me, smiled and drank. I poured his early morning Absolut screwdriver down the drain, and with this gesture started to tremble. I was no longer in my L.A. kitchen, but back into my thirteen-year-old self, standing by the wash sink in the basement of my childhood home ...

I was looking for gold spray paint. I'd collected a batch of pinecones and was about to make my neighbors, Mr. and Mrs. Bachelor, a holiday wreath for their front door. Poking around the cubbyhole of my father's basement workbench, I came across a small bottle. I opened it and took a swig—whiskey. The burn in my mouth made me spit. Did he hide this, or was it tossed aside from some hunting trip? I poured it out in the sink, but wondered, *If he is hiding this, is there more?*

I started in the laundry room and found a pint in his tool box, then went through every knotty pine closet of the basement with feverish intent, digging in his hunting clothes, pulling apart his long johns, moving twisted branches of the wood pile, and rummaging through his filing cabinets, desk drawers, and shotgun case. By the time I finished scouring the entire house, I had twenty-three bottles.

Mother was in the kitchen making dinner as I carried in a coal pail and wash bucket filled with the semi-spent fifths, pints, and flasks. My breath heavy from all the excitement of finding betrayal in my house and getting ready to expose it, I said, "Look what I found!"

It was one of the very few times my mother and I were on the same team, and she handed me the gauntlet. "What are you going to do?"

I didn't even blink. "I'm going to confront him."

Mother grabbed a chicken leg, smacked it into the flour, pounded pepper and salt into the skin, and dropped it the frying pan. The oil popped. Her disgust was as hot as that Crisco. "You know he's going to be upset."

"I don't care!" Digging for all the evidence had given me plenty of time to think about all the time I had spent as a child sitting alone in the car outside of the bars waiting for him to finish a few drinks and drive me home impaired.

I walked into the den and found him asleep in his rocker recliner, mouth open and bristly grey mustache vibrating as he snored. He looked like a giant beached otter. I wanted to have an impact—my family had an alcoholic in its midst, and by God I would shame him into compliance with my preteen wrath. I was tired from the adrenalin surging though me, but giddy in the power of what my buckets held. I didn't know how to express the emotion I felt so I just dumped the stash on the floor and wailed, "Look what you are doing to our family!"

Mother came in to watch me. She stood there and for once was void of anything to say.

My father said, "It's not a problem. I can stop."

I believed him.

Bill said that he might have been drinking too much on his cross-country bike expedition. Who was I to judge? I'd been so rattled by my marriage falling apart that I too had been substituting wine for water and air. Sobering us both up was the right thing to do.

We spent our days hiking the canyons, enjoying breakfasts and alcohol-free lunches with friends. And daily we'd collapse in a surprised heap, gasping for air and asking, "My God, how did we forget about this kind of sex?" We watched the puffiness disappear in his hands and welcomed the return of a well-balanced digestion. He no longer needed his acid reflux meds, and within a few weeks he dropped ten pounds. I felt great, no longer needing to numb myself. I was finally on the road to recovery, strong enough to test for my red belt in Taekwondo.

Bill and I lovingly sorted through the painful parts of our six-year attempts at a relationship. We forgave each other for past transgressions and started to broach some of the deeper problems that twenty-five years did not erase. This reunion that THEMS had set up was an astonishing revelation that love can transform any aspect of loss into forgiveness when we are willing to face our pain. I wondered what this was all leading up to. THEMS had a plan and I just had to let it roll out.

I had a few phone chats with his mother, Sharon. I had always loved her, but we both loved Bill. The fear of losing that love made us both less than our best at various times during my relationship with Bill. I thought for sure that with her energetic, spunky personality she would have ignited all sorts of possibilities for herself over the last twenty-five years. In Sharon's witty way she veiled disappointment and shared that she, too, had suffered what many women of her generation were experiencing with their husbands who came back from war. Medicating the painful past was a coping mechanism that permeated the lives of almost everyone I knew. The emotional disconnect between husbands and wives and children created chaos and its survival mechanism of codependency.

This is a cycle, a pattern with twisted roots deep in the family tree. I had begun to unravel this in my own life with highly skilled facilitators, but apparently I needed a refresher course.

The holidays *had* been a wonderful gift. As much fun as Bill and I were having, it was time for me to get back to my life. Bill left to see relatives and traverse Indonesia, Australia, and Africa. I prayed for the next phase of my new life to teach me more, and if that included Bill, I was sure THEMS would let me know.

The first leg of that new phase began when I was hired to appear as myself on the reality show *Harry Loves Lisa*, reading celebrities Harry Hamlin and his wife, the lovely Lisa Rinna. When I was an actress my job was to walk on a set and deliver my lines. As a psychic medium, I had no script except the messages from Spirit and dialogue from the dead.

Cameras started rolling. I knocked on the big wooden door of their Hollywood Hills home. Harry and Lisa excitedly invited me in. As I walked into the front foyer, my heart began to hurt. A deceased man came to me and shared that he was Harry's father, so I started to talk. "Harry, your father is here. He tells me he died of a heart attack."

Harry did not invite more conversation about his father, so I pulled out my yellow pad and, without having seen much of the house, drew a diagram indicating structural compromises that needed to be fixed. Harry had another agenda. "I want to know about our business," he said. "We have a clothing store called Belle Gray."

I couldn't control the information I received from Spirit or Harry's father. I was there to do a job, and even though this was reality TV and hyped-up drama, I needed to stay true to the integrity of the information I was given. I was frank. "You need to let go of the store—you have bigger fish to fry. If you don't let go, I see you losing a substantial amount of money by October." That certainly didn't sit well. By the time the show aired they had cut out the parts about Harry's father, structural compromises, and my "read" about losing money. National news and the tabloid media would later report that their store was robbed three times in October and closed a few months later. Harry and Lisa did have bigger fish to fry after letting go of Belle Gray. Lisa launched her own collection at QVC and Harry became one of the founders of Tri Alpha Energy, Inc., a company created to develop fusion power.

Bill came back to the states and called me from Florida. The Florida Panhandle, the place he left, the place where he ended a seventeen-year career and launched a bike trek across the country. The Pan held secrets.

"Marla, I want to come see you again, but I have to tell you that I feel resentful from our last visit. I was not really being who I am."

What was this about? Maybe he was still in love with his on-again/off-again Floridian nurse whose bedside manner he had briefly shared with me, so I said, "Well, what do you mean?" He sounded like a very young man as he cleared his throat and said, "I am resentful that you tried to control my drinking."

"Wow, I guess you really didn't like Dr. Wagner's concoction," I said. Bill chortled.

"Why do you feel I was controlling you?" I asked.

"You asked me to stop."

"Bill, you had a vodka orange juice at nine a.m. I thought that was odd, and you said you didn't have a problem with not drinking it."

"I guess I did have a problem. The point is, I want you to know I like to drink. It relaxes me, and I am going to drink." He was clear.

As I sat on my white cotton sofa staring out the window at the birds squabbling for food in the bamboo, I asked THEMS what I should do and heard, *Let him come.* I took a breath and said, "Okay, I guess we can see how it goes when you're here."

He reiterated, "I just want to make sure you know how I feel."

"I hear you." I said.

At the airport I held up a little sign that read "Bonnard," as if I were a chauffeur with a town car waiting out front. He came down the escalator. Oh my God—somewhere between Bali and Zimbabwe he had taken a turn and morphed into a glazed-eyed, disheveled Rodney Dangerfield.

I heard my father's voice again as my mind returned to the morning after I ambushed him with the witnesses of Jim Beam and Jack Daniels. "It's not a problem, I can stop."

There I was, thirteen years old again. "Daddy, we need to have a talk."

He sat down with his big coat and Stetson hat, and I said, "Daddy, you are an alcoholic."

"Oh Marla, now . . ." He couldn't finish his sentence.

I was a precocious child taking my father to task, like I knew what I was doing. "Daddy, who leaves a child alone in the car while he goes into a bar and drinks, and then drives home? Who keeps bottles of booze hidden everywhere in the house?"

"Well, your mother gets upset when I drink and she always checks the liquor cabinet to see if I've been drinking."

My throat ached with sadness for this man I loved. What could I say? He was a war hero who had seen and experienced things I could never imagine. He was wounded, beaten down, and we were both fearful of Mother. I had no skills here. I couldn't see what to do, I was way out of my league, and there was no one to stop this family from dying.

"I can stop, Marla. It's not a problem. I can stop tomorrow."

I just sat there and cried.

Now, watching Bill stumble off the escalator, I knew I had my hands full.

When we got back from the airport, Bill said he wanted to go out for dinner. I thought I'd throw in a load of laundry before we left, and I opened up his carry-on case. Instead of any dirty laundry from his month-long trip, his case contained a 4.5-liter bottle of Absolut vodka with only an inch left in the bottom. I put it on the kitchen counter and said, "So, you didn't want to pay for booze on the plane?"

He laughed, but something horrible was happening to me.

Just like my mother with my father, I began to watch every move Bill made. I went from being a loving and adoring old flame to a scrutinizing, fault-finding fanatic. I couldn't think about anything else but his drinking. I tried to ask him about his exciting African adventures, but was more riveted watching him down two, three, four doubles of cranberry juice and vodka in an hour.

"Bill, I don't understand. You were here for fifty days and you weren't drinking like this. You were so happy and healthy when you left—what changed?

"I like to drink."

I was heartbroken, and then I heard, *This is why he left Florida; it was killing him.* Oh dear God, and THEMS sent him to *me*? I'm behaving like I did as a child when things were out of control and I thought I had to fix them. Flashes of my father, relatives, men on whom I relied who didn't feel reliable filled my mind. This made me hyper vigilant because since they would not be responsible, I tried to control everything. Everything around me was out of control. This was the codependent crazies.

The deep familial wound, the trauma of the alcoholic history of my father and my mother's wrath, all came crashing in. This is a gift? CRAP.

My love for Bill now morphed into fear as I smacked him like a velvet hammer, reacting like a fearful codependent, caretaker, lover. I took him to every doctor, facilitator, meeting, and friend who had lived this. My love could not change him. I couldn't control this. I had to let go.

This is what THEMS wanted me to see and feel.

God grant me the serenity to accept the things I cannot change, the courage to change the things I can, and the wisdom to know the difference.

I had cast myself as a lifeline to try to save another beautiful, wounded man before he drowned and floated away like my dad. The addiction that consumed two men I had loved was a traumatic, deadly pattern that, when I broke everything apart, had infiltrated almost everyone I knew, both living and dead.

Once you pick a bruised apple, how do you find its beauty? Oh my God, I've got a broken picker! I thought.

Bill kept saying, "Accept me for who I am."

The truth was, I was having problems accepting *me* for who I was. I had spent the last ten years working on my intuitive abilities to assist others, but became unconscious of what I needed to face. These experiences with Bill were teaching me that the truth will set you free, if you face it. That perhaps the only way to move forward is to actually face the past . . . that we can't help anyone unless we are willing to help ourselves. Hiding in the depths of our pain is a wounded child that needs to be loved. Medicating the pain away with alcohol or drugs or exchanging one relationship for another isn't the answer. We are all bruised and we have to do the work to find a way to love ourselves.

Spirit/God/THEMS had orchestrated these amazing events, these excruciatingly beautiful gifts to help us *all* heal.

With painful endings come new beginnings. It was a very difficult separation for Bill and me, but necessary. Bill went home, his mother died a few months later, and after a deep period of grief Bill began a life of sobriety and a profound walk with Spirit that included helping others. The power of love gives way to forgive. Not just each other, but ourselves—that's the beauty of the bruise! God works in mysterious ways.

We come here to learn, to experience life and the mysteries that come from being human. We all need help along the way, and throughout every part of my life in which I felt frightened and blinded, Spirit had always guided me to see. My prayers were always answered, not the way I wanted, but exactly how I needed. Yep, that's how it had been, perhaps even before I was born.

3

The Inception

"The wound is the place where the light enters you."
—Rumi

I was hovering, a spirit on reconnaissance, checking out the town where I was to be born. I could almost touch the lush, velvety green tops of the rolling mountains that defined the small, quiet town below. *Marla, this is the perfect place for you to grow up, the perfect fractured family to teach you things you need.*

The heavenly council decided that it was time for me to be born again.

Would this family welcome the new child who was coming to ignite all sorts of possibilities? I snuggled in and allowed myself to grow. I could hear muffled voices in anticipation. The laughter that came from deep inside the belly of the woman who was to be my mother was not heard often enough. She had prayed for something to change her life. I thought I could make a difference.

There in the womb I could feel my mother's anxiety. The memory of who I'd been and what I knew before was fading. I wanted out. The cord wrapped around my neck twice was squeezing the life out of me. I kicked and kicked. Oh, my God, get me out of here—I'm going to die before I'm ever born!

No, it will make you stronger. It wasn't normal, those forty-two hours of labor and then the light so blinding.

My mother was born in Washington County, North Carolina, to Inez Victoria Chesson and Benjamin Snell in a year that constantly changed according to how sensitive my mother felt about her age. Mother's family were Carolina landowners and farmers. Genealogy tells the tale of a shipwrecked French sailor who propagated his way up the coast. His descendants married the English and Scots-Irish and retained the Native Americans and those of African descent as concubines and sometimes wives. Inez named her baby girl "Reinette," which in French means "little queen." Reinette's great-grandmother, Mary Ann Armstrong, was one of those 'sometimes wives.' A photo of Mary Ann dressed in her mid-1800s Sunday best captured the beauty and curiosity of our mulatto heritage. The other element of our North Carolina genealogy were the contributions of the "free colored," a version of slavery in which men, women, and children of African descent worked the small farms side by side with their masters.

Reinette, dirt poor and built like a 1940s pinup gal, longed for a dashing military officer to rescue her from the small North Carolina Mill Pond Road tobacco farm on which she grew up. Those were the war years where demands of life, American liberty, and the pursuit of a husband kept Reinette busy. When Harold Jacob Fries (I changed the spelling of my birth name from Fries to Frees, to reflect proper pronunciation) met Reinette, he was a radiant young man with strength and agility.

My father's paternal side were farmers fresh off the boat from Germany in 1738. His maternal side of the family, the Mellotts, were French Huguenots who fled France when it was persecuting Protestants, and settled southern Pennsylvania in 1663. They were frontiersmen who served in the Revolutionary War. Among them were traitors, rumored horse thieves, founders of Baptist and Lutheran churches, those who married Indians, and those who were attacked, captured, or killed by Indians. My father's great-grandmother was a first cousin of Ulysses S. Grant, the eighteenth president of the United States and commander of the Union army during the Civil War.

This is the tumultuous mix of my parents' DNA. A grab bag of some who fled religious persecution and then founded churches, of slave owners as well as slave liberators, and of rebels who fought for war and worked against the system, all doing their best to survive, love, and thrive. Yellowed, dog-eared photos tell the story of how my Northern father beamed beside my Southern mother. She expressed an uncertainty of life, yet glimpses of her humor, charm, and gorgeous legs attracted Fries. He'd be the last of a long list of suitors. Not the bad boy type, he offered Reinette fidelity and a ticket out of her department store job. Fries was drafted and they married the same day he began active service in WWII. This was Mother's foray into her dream of being an officer's wife.

Unfortunately, "Fries," as my mother called him, barely survived the war. He was a captain in the Forty-Second Rainbow Division of engineers, penetrating and destroying a section of Hitler's Siegfried line. When he and three other men driving in the Haardt Mountains were blown up in their jeep by a landmine, his driver was killed, another man lost his legs, and Fries was thrown far. He came back to the States in a body cast. He was commended for his outstanding courage and resourcefulness that had contributed to the success of his battalion and was discharged with a Purple Heart and two Bronze Stars. A fraction of the healthy, virile man he was before the war, Fries went back to his discouraged wife and became a feed salesman, settling in the quintessential small town of Bedford, Pennsylvania.

By the time I was born, my parents had weathered much: the war, my father's injuries, the death of both sets of parents, the loss of a pregnancy, and the end of his military career—my mother's dream. Even with building a new colonial-style home and rearing an eleven-year-old daughter, Deborah, my mother was unhappy. The role she wanted to play was not working out in the second half of her life. I was a surprise she didn't want, but the hope that she had prayed for.

Mother's dis-ease crept into my earliest memories. In one, I am on a big, colorful flowered quilt, resting from eating sand and tackling my first ocean wave. A blue umbrella keeps me shaded as I pick at the edges of the quilt while sucking my thumb. I can see each member of my family. My father bobs alone in a wave. My mother stands watching him, poised with hands on hips, her feet seemingly stuck in wet sand. My sister, reading with her back turned, casts a long shadow beside me. I am just shy of turning one, and even at that young age I have made my first "psychic snapshot," a moment of physical, visual, and emotional information to which I am supposed to pay attention. *There is something wrong in my family.*

In another early memory, birds are chirping between the flapping of sheets drying in the sun as I lie on my back in the grassy yard, looking up, always looking up into the blue. What was beyond the sky watches me, and as long as I have the sun to warm me and someone to feed me, I think I will be safe. "Marla, it's time for a nap," my mother calls. I lie in her arms on the sofa, pulling on her loose elbow skin while she lights Marlboro cigarettes over and over again with a shiny silver lighter. I wait for the "daytime stories" she watches all afternoon on TV and make her happy. I wait for my sister to come home from school. I wait for something to happen, because it always would.

It was a summer afternoon when light was no longer noontime bright in the kitchen. Mother had just gotten up from a nap. There was no one else in the house. It was time for me to eat. Mother picked me up and shoved me into the highchair. Her roughness made me cry. Little hands that would pat the tray for food were now grabbing at the air, begging Mother to hold me. "Mama, Mommieee!" I cried as my mother tightened the strap on the chair that cinched me in. She went to a drawer and got herself a spoon. I whimpered and struggled to get out of the highchair.

"Now, don't you act ugly!" my mother commanded, shaking the spoon in my face. She opened the cupboard, reached to the spice shelf, and poured a pile of blackness onto the spoon. This was not the happy airplane that delivered mashed carrots and peas into my mouth. This airplane was sinister with a cargo that exploded upon landing. I choked out, "HOT HOT HELP ME!" in bloodcurdling screams from a mouth that must have done something horribly wrong to deserve a spoonful of pepper.

I came into this life filled with joy despite the actions of others. I ran through sprinklers, explored flowers and bugs, and waited in the back yard to be old enough to spend time in the outside world with neighbors. For a while, I was the youngest of the sons and daughters of a circle of families in Meadow-brook Terrace, a new housing development on the edge of town carved out of the foothills of Pennsylvania's Evitts Mountain.

We spent winters sledding down the steep neighborhood hills, roads, and driveways and summers flying on swings, play-ing kickball, selling Kool-Aid popsicles on toothpicks, and watching our 1960s parents medicate themselves with Marlbo-ros and martinis.

The signs of trauma were already being passed down and acted out on the smallest. I didn't mind that the older girls would hold me down, tie me up, put a wreath of thorns on my head, and leave me in the yard until my dad drove up the hill and noticed a smaller version of Jesus lying on the lawn. I was used to being hit by the yardsticks, flyswatters, hairbrushes, and hands my mother wielded at home, so I would put up with the abuse just for the chance to play with those kids.

Years later we are all Facebook friends, sharing the terrors we endured in the circle. It's too bad we couldn't prove the secrets of our small town, like satanic cults, the Ku Klux Klan, or that all our houses were built on Indian burial ground like in the movie *Poltergeist*. No, there were other reasons some parents beat and abused their children; we just didn't know what they were.

The choices my parents made a few years after I was born set in motion a chain of events that had dire consequences. Mother and Daddy could not simultaneously manage a toddler and my sister Deborah's adolescence. They decided to send my sister, eleven years older than I, away to prep school. Mother's explana-tion was, "Your sister is book smart and she needs to be some-place where some goddamn boy isn't going to distract her."

Mother's decision was perhaps based on a combination of reading a *McCall's* magazine article or advice she got at the beauty parlor, or maybe it came from the uncomfortable suspicion that she was not capable of facing her own unresolved issues that had been activated by motherhood. To her, getting my sister out of town seemed like the best thing to do, but it wasn't. With Debbie far away Mother was unable to control her. That triggered all of Mother's fears, along with intolerable anxiety.

Medicating with magenta pink Darvocet and Valium, Mother would retreat to the sofa, trying to cover her private hell like her soap opera stars did or seek out closed-door confrontations with Daddy, who had no clue how to handle a toddler and what was happening with my sister so far away. Those verbal fights didn't relieve Mother—they just fueled her rage. She would systematically wait until she and I were alone and then release that rage on my body and soul. I prayed to be rescued by someone or something, even aliens in a spaceship.

Since that didn't happen, I had to intuit ways to survive.

The 1960 wood-paneled Zenith television in the corner of the den was my babysitter and best friend. It was a powerful wooden box that commanded Mother's attention all day and then gathered us together in the evening. I wanted to crawl into that TV box to be one of Lawrence Welk's shiny-bright beautiful ladies, singing songs and wearing powder blue chiffon; show up as one of my mother's favorite soap opera divas; help Lucy Ricardo get out of a jam before Ricky found out; or be one of those ladies between the TV shows that convinced us that happy households use Palmolive because it was the best dish detergent and Pine-Sol because it was the freshest cleaner.

If I could be one of those women on TV, then my parents might be happy and Mother would love me, not hurt me.

I was a confident five-year-old, wearing a cowgirl hat and boots and riding a stick pony when I climbed up on the stage in the social room of Trinity Lutheran Church to sing "On Top of Old Smokey" to entertain the Rotary Club. I heard cheerful applause for my efforts and saw my mother's face finally lit with joy. I would find my way into that box.

Never without lipstick, Mother would dress up her Playtex-model figure with tailored shirts, girdles, skirts, and pearls and be the most beautiful and charming person in town, if she wanted. A camel coat with matching pocketbook and gloves completed her outfit when she went to see Dr. Reginald Myers, our family physician. She took me to his office every other month, whether I was sick or not. A taller, thinner version of Alfred Hitchcock, Myers waddled like he had an invisible broom up his butt and was proudly cleaning the floor behind him with every step. He was the one who'd pulled me out of Mother after a forty-two-hour labor, freed me from the cord wrapped twice around my neck, and cracked my ass into the blinding light of life. He was smart, and Mother liked that—Mother liked doctors.

It was important for me to sit still on the examining table as the doctor looked me over. His breath was heavy as he pressed the thingy with the light and plastic cone into my nose to examine my mucus membranes. I wanted ever so badly to pluck the illuminated errant hairs that grew like weeds on the top of his nose.

After the exam I was shuffled off to sit alone in the waiting room. I thumbed through *National Geographic* and *Esquire* magazines, looking at naked savages and other things I wasn't supposed to see. I organized the magazines on the shelf to pass the time as I waited and waited for Mother to appear from behind the door of Dr. Myers's dark office, which was lit only by a green lamp on a desk.

Mother trusted Myers. Perhaps she was in there sharing her fear that God was punishing her because I almost died at birth and then again at sixteen months. Dr. Myers no doubt listened as he wrote out a prescription for her guilt. Maybe he encouraged her how to care for my chronic tummy upsets and bronchial distress with sound medical advice—"Stop smoking, Reinette." But Mother instead would take her own advice that enemas, frenetic genital scrubbing, paregoric, Fletcher's Castoria, spoonfuls of scotch, and something called "ipecac" that made me vomit until I passed out would be good for me. Whatever Dr. Myers said, or didn't say—helped. Mother would emerge from his office happy and relieved.

She was also delighted when company came, even though most of the time that was just the housekeepers. When Daddy married Mother and moved her north of the Mason-Dixon line she brought with her some "post-Depression" Southern traditions. Good manners, good food, and the strange social expectation of white women sitting atop an imaginary pedestal, a powerless symbol of authority that, like her soap opera stories, became her reality. Part of fulfilling that role was enlisting women to do the work Mother didn't want to do. Putting herself in that role subjugated not only the women who came to work for her, but also Daddy, me, and ultimately herself.

Millie was the first "colored" woman I remember. She was tiny, round, warm, and happy. Her coffee-colored skin smelled like the fresh linens that hung on the clothesline, and when she laughed her face beamed. I learned to walk by following around Millie's good nature and sweetness all day. Sometimes she let me carry her bucket. I loved her. One day, Millie didn't come, but Greta did.

Greta was skinny, dark-chocolate colored, and what my mother called "ornery." She was the finest ally a six-year-old could ask for. I followed Greta around, too, learning to clean bathtubs and other things my mother never did.

It was a sunny May morning and I had just finished first grade. Greta was in the living room reaching up under the outside of the windows to clean the glass. I went around the front of the house to talk to her while she washed the windows. I peered into the window well below—the place where creepy-crawly things lived along with my secret family of pet toads.

"How many you got in there?" Greta asked.

"There's a mom and dad and two babies." I said. I kept watching her work and I "knew" the way a deeply sensitive child would know that Greta did not want to be there washing windows for my mother. I was going to help her.

"Lemme help you wash this window, Greta!"

"No Marla! Now you go back inside and eat your lunch. Don't stand on that edge!" she scolded.

Ignoring her warning, I took a rag and straddled the rim of the window well.

I didn't feel myself slip as I hit the steel—the corrugated steel that tried to split the middle of me. My right leg fell into the window well and my left leg stayed outside on the flower-bed dirt. In the shock of pain I lifted myself out, and all I could see was the reflection in the front glass door of a little girl in a white sailor dress, hair pulled back from her face with a bow, little white socks and tennis shoes, running to the door with bloodcurdling screams.

Greta was there to embrace me, rid me of my dirty clothes, wrap me in a towel, and hold me tight as Mother whisked us away in her car.

"OH, DEAR GOD, IS SHE BLEEDING, IS SHE BLEEDING?" Mother screamed as she drove us down the hill to where our neighbor Dr. Gordon lived.

There are appropriate ways to teach a child not to touch a hot stove or cross the street. A child is supposed to learn from her parents what is safe and what can be trusted through their own healthy boundaries. But mother had no boundaries of her own and was afraid of everything she could not control—pandemonium was her normal.

I found myself in the Gordon's white and powder blue bathroom. I didn't know what I was doing there. Mother ripped off the towel. I had no strength, no voice as I stood naked in front of our neighbor.

"MARLA! Lay down and let Dr. Gordon look at you!"

There would be bad consequences if I didn't do what she wanted.

Doctor Gordon had delivered most of the Bedford babies, but not me. He had never examined me or seen me naked. He was stocky with rolled shoulders and a short neck. He owned antique cars and when he was in a good mood, he was very good. He would pile us kids into his 1926 Rickenbacker and drive around the neighborhood as we stood on the running board, hanging on for dear life. He erected a huge swing set, monkey bars, and sandboxes to keep us kids occupied and out of trouble. He generously plowed our driveways in the winter, laughed loudly as he drank gin martinis in summer, screamed at his children and hit them with a razor strap, and was now scrutinizing my privates. I hoped he wouldn't hurt me. Instead, he gently laid me on the fluffy white bath mat.

"She's in shock, Reinette," he told Mother as he looked me over. "It seems she already has some scar tissue here from some other trauma."

I turned my head away and left my body on the bathroom floor. In my mind I flew outside, up the hill to our house, and down into the window well where I had fallen. I searched to see if I had accidentally smashed one of the toads when I fell. The wet crumpled leaves and rotting smells of earth made me feel safe. I could barely hear the voices in the bathroom as I hunted for my toads. Words echoed like they were in a pool, underwater.

"Other trauma? Oh, yes . . . years ago she had an accident on a little toy school bus that she was scooting around on," Mother said.

"Well, this fall contused her . . . If she can't pee by tonight, we will have to take her to the . . . hospital," Dr. Gordon said.

"OH, DEAR GOD!" Mother's cries snapped me back into my body and her drama.

Greta left us soon after that, pregnant with her last baby. Years later her baby girl, Janice, and I shared stories about our mothers. Janice acknowledged that it was my mother who taught her mother how to cook fried chicken, corn pudding, and peach pie. I was happy Mother had shared her Southern gifts of cooking with Greta and her family, but saddened that she had segregated her own family and others by playing the role of an entitled Daughter of the Confederacy.

Many years later I would learn that "leaving my body" was a coping mechanism that allowed me to disassociate from trauma. I continued to fly and leave my body when things were done that should not have been. It was also the introduction to my ability to see things remotely as a psychic.

As the Civil Rights movement swept across the country, Mother chose Pat—robust and Anglo-American pink—as our next housekeeper. Pat stayed for forty-two years. She needed us and we needed her. I loved the early winter mornings when her husband Don would drop her off at the house. I heard the back door open and there would be a burst of muffled laughter under my bedroom in the kitchen, laughter that was never there until Pat came. She brought out a joy in my dad that I never saw before she came. They shared stories and jokes, brief moments of what happy normal families might sound like.

Late in the afternoon I would sit on the kitchen counter as Pat ironed everything, including my underwear. We played guessing games. As Pat pounded the iron trying to steam away the Fries family wrinkles she'd say, "I spy with my little eye . . ."

"I bet it's orange," I'd say.

"That's right!" Pat would confirm. Then I'd scan the room and intuit which orange thing she was thinking about. All of these games were highly entertaining and I was really good at them. Meanwhile, Mother lay on the sofa in the den just a few feet away watching her favorite soap, *The Doctors*, and getting riled up before dinner. "*Whose baby is it, Nola? Colin's or Jason's? Tell me! Oh Nola, your whole life up to this point has just been a lie!*"

Mother bonded with her soap opera characters' vengeance as she smacked her hands together, punctuating the last line of the show and yelling out loud, "You tell her, Althea, that Nola is just a bitch!" It was just enough of a victory for Mother to bounce off the sofa happy and laughing as she headed for the kitchen to start dinner.

On the days that Pat didn't come I pretended to be whatever I needed to be to keep Mother from hurting me.

Legs still too short to touch the floor, I sat in Daddy's rocker as a captive audience and armchair therapist while Mother reclined on the sofa like an Allegheny Mountain Cleopatra on her Naugahyde throne. There she would stare at her soap operas while ruminating over whomever or whatever had "done her wrong." I waited for some glimmer of hope that she would find her way out of her pain. I listened, nodding like I understood and silently giddy with relief that she wasn't attacking me. Once in a while she would reveal some strange truth about her life before I was born. Wistfully digressing into her past, she spoke about how much she loved her mother, hated her father, adored her old boyfriends, and also shared provocative memories of the men she'd "known" before Daddy.

My father told no one how he ached from his emotional or physical war injuries, but sometimes he woke screaming from nightmares and his body was obviously wracked with pain. He never mentioned any girl he'd known before Mother. There probably wasn't one. He didn't know what to do with my sister, me, or Mother. He sank his heart into being a good provider, expanding his job from a feed salesman to a top Landrace hog breeder. What was left of his soul after the war overseas and the battles in our home he poured into hunting the woodlands of Pennsylvania and a shot glass.

Daddy's Sunday ritual began with dropping me off at the back door of the Trinity Lutheran church. While I donned my choir robe and scanned the congregation for cute boys, he made his way to the Village News Stand. This little establishment in the heart of Bedford sold girlie magazines and big-city newspapers.

Wafts of cherry pipe tobacco and fresh newsprint welcomed patrons as they opened the door. Off to the side of the counter was a place no child could enter. Two swinging wooden doors, just like the ones gunslingers barged through in Westerns, held back ghosts and secrets that only war veterans could understand. While I sang "Onward, Christian Soldiers" my dad and his brotherhood fortified themselves with Canadian Club and prepared to press on with life. A brown paper bag filled with red licorice for me and *The New York Times* for Mother would be in the front seat of the station wagon when he picked me up.

On Sunday afternoons I cozied up to Daddy on the sofa as he read the funnies out loud. We both laughed because every character he read sounded the same. Mother eagerly scanned the *Times*' fashion section, looking for something to buy that might make her happy.

"Look at this fur, Fries!" she'd say to my father, slapping the Sunday paper around so Daddy could see what she thought was so exciting. My eyes bulged at a full-page photo of a naked woman wrapped in a glossy black mint fur: *"What Becomes a Legend Most? Blackglama."*

"Uh huh," he would say. She didn't like that answer, so she snapped the paper back around even harder.

At the beginning of the month it excited mother to secretly take Daddy's monthly military pension and me to the whopping metropolis of Cumberland, Maryland, thirty-two miles away. She'd drag me from one store to another to try on clothes and parade me in front of the saleswomen. These strangers' approval gave her joy, which taught me that looking nice was important because it made Mother happy.

"Hey there, Marla, come on down to my house," said Bruce Allen on the phone. "I went huntin' and got sumptin' to show you."

Bruce and I were neighbors and fourth graders together. He'd just become my real good buddy during my tonsillectomy, carrying my homework and cards from classmates up the hill. The handsome Allen boys were all sports stars and hunters. Hunting was a rite of passage for boys in my hometown, and also for a few girls like me who needed to bond with their fathers. I had been shooting guns from the time I could squeeze a trigger and won BB gun contests in the basement of the Presbyterian church. It made Daddy happy when I could shoot better than him at such a young age. I preferred paper targets and tin cans to the hunting, but I'd risk the grief of killing just to be with Daddy.

Bruce sounded excited. My throat was almost healed, so I put on my coat and sneakers and ran down to his back yard where he sat beside a pile of dead squirrels. I watched as he peeled the skin off the meat with the tail attached. I thought, *Well, it's not mink, but that fur might look real nice on my Barbie—it's even got sleeves. Mother would think that was real stylish.* "Hey, can I have that?"

"Well, my family was gonna eat it," he said.

"No, I just want the fur, with the tail."

Bruce wrapped it up in a paper bag. I ran home, sewed up the rough edges with dental floss, and slid it over my naked Barbie. It hardened in a day and I was never able to get it off. I ruined a perfectly good Barbie trying to be fashionable for Mother.

I was always overjoyed to see my sister whenever she came home from some school far away. She'd crawl into bed and hold me, making me feel safe and happy. She brought music, art, movies, and the magic of intuition into my life. The cover of one game she gave me for Christmas asked, DO YOU HAVE EXTRA SENSORY PERCEPTION *(ESP)?* Kreskin's ESP game came with cards not like the ones my mother used for bridge, but with all kinds of shapes on them.

"Hold the card with your eyes closed and guess what the shape is," my sister would say to me. I was fascinated that there was such a thing as ESP and that Debbie and I could find it together.

Valerie, who lived down the hill, was my part-time partner in the paranormal. In the middle of the summer we'd retreat to the concrete hollows of Valerie's dank basement. Next to the washing machine and in the midst of laundry piles we'd sit at a card table and try to conjure dead folks. With five kids, Valerie's mother was endlessly doing the laundry, so between the wash and spin we never got a good grip on a dead soul.

By the time I was ten I got to hang out with my gorgeous, older next-door neighbor, Paula, a walking advertisement for *Seventeen* magazine. Organized, smart, and statuesque, with a long mane of beautiful chestnut hair, Paula was my substitute older sister and my mother's substitute favorite daughter. I ran across the street and knocked on her back door. Ann, her mother, was fixing stuffing for a Thanksgiving turkey. "Paula's not back yet, but come on in—wash your hands so you can help me tear up this bread."

Ann was a Catholic who married Lee Cohn, the only Jew we knew. Lee was the first man I remember, other than Daddy.

His sweet, pale face with dark hair and bushy eyebrows would come to my crib with big smiles. There was something about his energy I loved. His long hands held me gently and his soothing voice made me happy. He gave me a little pillow from his downtown store, Maurice's. Rubbing the edges of the crisp, white cotton tickled my fingertips as I hugged the pillow and sucked my thumb, which calmed me. I kept the pillow as my "binky" much longer than I should have. Dragged all through the house, various incarnations of my pillow were soiled with dirt, snot, saliva, and tears. Mother said it was embarrassing, but my pillow would make me feel good when nothing else could. Lee got sick with cancer from WWII radiation poisoning and died, leaving Ann a widow in her forties who had to raise their three girls by herself.

On this particular day Ann plopped a bowl in front of me. "Here, take this bread and break it up." It was nice to be invited into her kitchen to help. In my house, the kitchen was Mother's domain and I was just in her way. Both Ann and my mother liked to show off. It was a silent rivalry that manifested in better cars, clothes, accomplishments, and mistakes. They'd continue to one-up each other over the years, with their daughters used as poker chips.

The bread was dry and easy to pull apart. I thought it was a fine way to pass the time as I waited for Paula. Then it happened—my mind went blind to the bowl of bread. A movie started in my head that showed me Ann's boyfriend, Les, with another woman in a parking lot. As the images flickered, I felt Les's anxiousness of wanting to be with this nurse and spend money on her, not Ann. Then the movie stopped and words just blurted out of my mouth: "Your boyfriend is seeing a nurse at the hospital—he wants to break up with you before Christmas so he doesn't have to buy you a present."

Ann stood at the kitchen sink and didn't move. There was silence and then whoosh, she appeared right in front of my face. "How do you know that?" she demanded.

"I'm sorry, Ann. I just see it."

She glared at me, but I could see that she believed me, as if I had confirmed what she already knew. "Go home, I'm calling your mother."

And that was that, except I heard she broke it off with the boyfriend and then years later married him. It was a brief moment of confirmation of a new reality that had begun inside me. My psychic snapshots were now movies.

Mother thought it was funny at first, only because she delighted in the creepiness of her daughter telling her rival a prophecy. But she didn't like it later when other people found out.

I had one more public display of "sight" when I was invited to read people's fortunes at a festival held at the Church of the Brethren. I didn't really know what people wanted me to do, but I remembered an episode of *I Love Lucy* in which Ethel wore a turban and wrapped herself in a tablecloth to become a fortune-telling Madame. She looked convincing, so I threw on one of my mother's flowered table coverings and some bangle earrings, darkened my beauty mole, and wrapped my head in a towel to become the mysterious Madame Marla for the night.

Mr. Hawksworth, the high school's skinny, quiet, social studies teacher, stepped into my makeshift tent of tie-dyed sheets and candles. I held his hand and a scene flashed into my mind. "There's a woman who you will meet at a different church and by summer you will marry her."

He nervously laughed and said, "Well, I will look forward to that." Word got out here and there about my predictions, and Mother wasn't happy about it. When Mr. Hawksworth was married a year later in the middle of June to a woman from another church, people talked. Mother scolded me for being talked about over this "weird stuff," and although her anger discouraged me, it didn't prevent my further "sight."

4

The Slaughter

"Every day was a question mark."
—*Alice Sebold,* The Lovely Bones

By the end of that 1970 summer I found a bigger thrill than a new Barbie or my fascination with the paranormal. I joined a girlfriend from church for a Saturday matinee of the remake of *Wuthering Heights* at the Pitt Theatre in downtown Bedford. There was no parental code to warn that a powerful, dark, and brooding Timothy Dalton as Heathcliff could seduce eleven-year-old girls in a passionate tale of doomed love. I even bought a poster.

It was a good summer for movies. I felt like a grown-up when my sister took me to the Moonlight Drive-In Theatre one warm Friday night. I was mesmerized by the gigantic images of a handsome, dark-haired man pulling a naked woman out of a bathtub, thrusting his mouth onto hers, killing an intruder, and kissing another woman who gets painted gold and then dies. Is this what men did with women? Who was this gorgeous, powerful James Bond, and where could I find him?

When the movie *Splendor in the Grass* with Warren Beatty and Natalie Wood was released on TV, I watched it every time it played. The character Bud, who was more handsome than any of my mother's soap stars, was in love with Deanie. Driven by his wicked hormones, Bud kept making the same mistake every time the movie was on, ending up on a farm with chickens in the kitchen and a baby on the floor. Deanie kept saying "No" to Bud's sexual advances. She wanted love instead of sin, and when Bud had sex with the school tramp Deanie had a nervous breakdown and was sent to a mental institution. She eventually got healthy and married another patient who became a doctor. Every time I watched the movie I hoped Deanie and Bud would work things out and get back together. Life looked so complicated. I had been imprinted by these seemingly powerful men.

The first week of September that I became a seventh grader the fog rolled in and frost started to age the corn. I was lost in wonder of what would happen next as trees changed colors, pumpkins morphed into Jack-o-lanterns, and my body stirred with the thoughts and smells of boys. Without a junior high school to ease us into young adulthood, the seventh through twelfth grades pooled together in Bedford High like different breeds of fish swimming around one another, sensing who would be the first to spawn.

Mother had no choice but to let me go, yet she made certain to capture as much of my life as she could. She promised to pick me up after school in her dark blue Oldsmobile Delta 88 Royale with white leather interior and drive me the .04 miles back home. Not four miles, .04 miles. I could have walked home more quickly than it took mother to pull her squeaky-clean Olds out of the carport and drive down the hill.

"I'm not going to waste any more money on lunch tickets," she would say. "You don't eat anything anyway, so you can buy your own damn lunch." Mother laughed and "frapped" me with her hand, her signature gesture that combined something she found funny with a slap. Laughing and smacking her coral pink lips, she opened up her purse and handed me a buck fifty. I liked it when she laughed. It gave me hope.

I had no idea what to do, how to be. I was ever curious but in no way prepared to step into the foray of what the halls of the high school offered.

They came on buses, the future football, wrestling, and basketball stars. Sinewy muscles defined their T-shirts and jeans. Their hearty laughs and cow's-milk white teeth sauntered the halls in search of their sophomore girlfriends, whom they quickly categorized by breast size and hairstyles.

Those girls in their short skirts and tight sweaters were my real teachers. They knew how to walk, slow and deliberate, confident of what was under those books clutched to their chests. My daydreams of *Splendor in the Grass* scenes became real. I was enamored of this brave new world and excited about what had to happen before I, too, could beam when spotting the face of a hunk who thought I was cute. I had a bit more than raisins on a bread board, but it would not be my figure or mousy brown hair—which my mother had lightened from the time I was six—that would be bait for a boy. I believed it had to be my sheer willpower.

On my first day of seventh grade I was introduced to my locker, homeroom, God-awful-one-piece gym uniform, and the loud, bustling cafeteria. I didn't recognize anyone as I stood in line to pay for my ice cream sandwich and potato chips.

"Hey, your dad has the hog farm, right?" I was surprised to hear this out of the girl in the white shirt and red plaid skirt in front of me.

"Oh, yes!" I said. "What's your name?"

"Mindy," she said. "My dad makes hay for your dad—you have the buckskin horse."

We actually lived "in town" in a mini version of a *Gone with the Wind* kind of house my father built for my Southern mother, but Dad also bought a farm thirteen miles south of town so that he could prove the quality of the feed he sold for Wayne Feeds Company. The farm also gave us a respite from Mother. Dad, his herdsmen Gary, and our Hickory Hill farm were becoming famous as American Landrace hog breeders. My father's humility kept the ribbons and trophies in his office shoved behind bills and paperwork. Gary was the one who posed in the newspaper with the fat, pinkish white Landrace winners. Now in the lunch line, I was a tangential part of their popularity.

Anyone who knew about me, my horse, my dad, and the farm had to be from the "valley"—a thirty-mile stretch of Route 220, the two-lane highway between Bedford and the Maryland state line called the Cumberland Valley. Homes with big porches, large green lawns, and fields filled with corn and hay peppered both sides of the road.

I didn't think anyone really noticed me down there. The farm was my private world where I gathered black walnuts, caught chub fish from the creek, daydreamed in the hay loft, chewed raw oats, and thundered up the state game land roads on my horse, her hooves spitting gravel like buckshot. I was safe there, away from the hands of my mother. I made friends with just about every tree, stone, and trail of our land.

My lunch-line conversation made me wonder what girlfriends I was missing in the valley, so I followed the plaid-skirted girl with her tray of meatloaf and mashed potatoes through the cafeteria and asked the obvious: "Do you live down in the valley?"

She gestured for me to take a seat with three other girls. "Oh, yeah, we're all from the valley."

I sat down directly across from a tiny, tow-headed, blue-eyed girl who looked much younger than most of the kids. She had a precious smile and said, "I'm Kelly Jo Brallier, and I live on Buck Falls, off Teaberry Road."

I knew Teaberry. It was a single-lane back road that ran parallel to our farm. "You live on the other side of the ridge."

She nodded, "Yep, my dad knows your dad."

She was sweet as she munched on a little sandwich she had brought from home. Another girl said, "I'm Jeannie; we all live down the road from each other."

Kelly Jo piped up and said, "We're gonna have a new baby any day."

"Is that your first sister or brother?" I asked.

"Oh no, I'm the oldest of six, soon to be seven, and I take care of all of 'em."

I knew it was important for me to sit and chat with Kelly Jo that first week of school, but I didn't know why. I couldn't take my eyes off her. Her little shoulder-strap pocketbook, dirty from wear, stared at me as it hung on the back of her chair. Her wisps of blond hair were thinner than mine. I wanted to protect her. I took one of my "psychic snapshots" to capture her innocence, a moment of physical, visual, and emotional information I was supposed to remember.

From that very first week I had my eye on a boy. I calculated any way to get closer to Harvey, a blond, smart, funny kind of guy with a wicked laugh. He was sitting with some noisy boys directly across from the chatty girls from town at lunch. So on the second week of school I moved away from the valley girls to the table with the townie girls, just to be close to Harvey. I could still see Kelly Jo and Mindy and we waved at each other.

The first varsity football game of the season was Friday night with rival Everett High, just eight miles away. I was sure my dad and I would go, and probably everyone else from Bedford. Any possibility of being near Harvey in the halls, classes, and at a football game captivated my daydreams that whole week—

that, and wondering what I'd get for my birthday the following Tuesday. Life was amazing and distracting all at the same time.

I don't remember which team had the most touchdowns. I was scouting out the area, positioning myself in and behind the stands and taking numerous trips to the snack stand (though one could only drink so much pop and hot chocolate) just to run into Harvey. Overwhelming happiness surged through me when I thought about him, saw him, and stood next to him. For the first time I felt as alive as a girl could possibly feel. I was in love.

I looked forward all week to the delicious treat of sleeping in on Saturday morning, but early the next morning the telephone rang me out of that bliss. I could hear my father down the hall in his office: "Oh no, that is just terrible, just terrible. Oh, my God, yes, thanks for calling, Gary."

For my father to say "Oh, my God" was serious. He didn't seem alarmed, but whatever Gary the herdsman from our farm was telling my dad, he could do nothing about it. Like something was over and that was that. I listened closely to what was and wasn't said.

"Uh huh. Okay, yes, I'll be down this afternoon." He hung up the phone and his swivel chair squeaked as he got up. I could hear him go into the hall, his leather slippers padding him down the steps through the den and into the kitchen, under my bedroom, where a muffled conversation between he and my mother started.

I grabbed my robe and followed. Mother was sitting at the table in her nylon pajamas and robe with the Saturday morning paper in front of her. My dad stopped talking when I walked in. I looked at him. He was pale.

"What? What happened?" I asked. My mind flooded with images of my horse dead or hurt with a broken leg. Maybe they had to put her down or she got stuck again between two trees like she did as a colt, when she rubbed her flanks raw and was scarred for life.

"WHAT?!" I demanded. I could feel something really bad had happened between the "my God" on the phone and the way my father looked at me now. I had never seen my father like this. He grabbed me and squeezed tight; it was a big hug with tears and unexpected words.

"Oh, I love you so much, Marla."

This was so unfamiliar to me. I had only seen him cry once, sitting in the dark on the edge of a hotel bed after my sister got married. But now it was a sunny Saturday, emotions had found him, and he gave in to the unknown sensation of feelings.

I wiggled out of his arms to watch him shake his head as he said, "One of the families down in the valley has had a terrible thing happen. A young girl was murdered last night. They found her body off Teaberry Road. She was a Brallier."

He knew the family, but what he didn't know is that I knew who he was talking about. I had been sitting with her for a week. The sweet face I watched munching that little sandwich talking about homeroom, teachers, and family.

I quietly said, "Kelly Jo," and then burst into tears. I hadn't told my parents about my lunches with Kelly Jo or my love for Harvey, but I did that day, over and over again.

The safe, quiet town of Bedford, where newspaper headlines are usually the scores of the Friday night football games or the details of who crashed their truck into a mailbox to avoid hitting a deer, now told the story of how David Cruthers, twenty-two, of Cumberland, Maryland, who cleaned and put away the linens at the Bedford Springs Resort, often drove down Teaberry Road to see a friend of his. But on Friday night he came across Kelly Jo, who was walking to Jennie Keefer's house for a ride to the football game. He decided to make her vanish.

When she didn't show up to Jennie's house for her ride to the game, neighbors went looking for her. On the side of the road they found the blanket she was carrying to keep her warm on that September night. A few yards down they found a little pocketbook and a bloody trail that sent searchers 160 feet across a field and up the ridge to a patch of bushes where David Cruthers "sexually molested her" and then beat both sides of her head in with a ball peen hammer and a rock. She was twelve years old and weighed seventy-five pounds.

I was sick with the unfamiliarity of grief, frozen by thoughts of things that can happen to little girls just down the street from their houses. I wanted to be consoled. Did it hurt? What happens when you die? Did angels come and take her before she was cold in the rough, dry grass? What did he do to her? Did she cry for help? Did anyone hear her?

Instead I spent the weekend overhearing my mother on the phone constantly discussing the details of rape and other unspeakable things that were spoken.

Kelly Jo was buried on Tuesday, my twelfth birthday. I couldn't stop thinking about her murder. The only thing that compelled me to go back to school was seeing Harvey. No one talked about it, there was no service at the school, and no one had the chance to get to know her. Everything went on like nothing happened—except the valley knew and grieved.

My dad and I didn't talk about it either. Everything in my world was different. Gone was the sense of wonder in the woods. I started to look for dark, dirty men hiding behind trees who would rip me off my horse, take me away, and hurt me. What would I do if that happened? I started to plan my escape. I stopped wanting to go to the farm and found excuses. I went to Hershberger's art store and stocked up on oil paints and brushes. I made my own canvases and scoured *National*

Geographic magazines for exotic pictures of faces from other countries. I controlled my world, hiding in the basement with my jukebox and easel. And I had to find a way to protect myself from my mother.

Spring came and my dad said he had a surprise for me down in the laundry room. There in a large box were three fuzzy yellow baby ducks. It was a good way to coax me back to the farm: give me little animals to love.

They were a funny bunch. The tall, skinny one that jumped for lettuce I named Heathcliff; the wide, knock-kneed one was Gertrude; and the round little baby became Gladys—all named after television comedian Red Skelton's wacky seagull characters. I was delighted for a while to cradle their wispy down bottoms, but really, all they did was eat and poop. Within four months they were big, white, constantly honking, and not so cuddly. I could not stand that they were caged—I wanted them to be free!

At the same time, a worm-infected calf named Crimson that my dad and I saved from a slaughterhouse and nursed back to health a year before had also lost his cuddly cuteness. When we first got him into a stall and started to brush and cut out his crusted mats of hair, a russet-crimson color emerged, hence his name. I gave Crimson as much love as I could with bottles of milk, feed, and Concord grapes from the vine. That animal loved grapes. Now a huge bull, Crimson seemed to have forgotten how I took care of him as he made it his mission to mow me down every time I tried to enter the corral. No amount of brushing could change his nature. That was another harsh lesson of the farm—don't love what doesn't love you back. It was hard not to take it all personally.

Since Crimson was on the warpath, I didn't want my ducks anywhere near him, so Daddy suggested we take them to the Beachwood Inn, a little gas station and coffee shop just two miles north of our farm that had a big pond out back.

Mary and Marguerite, proprietors of Beachwood for thirty-two years, were the oldest women I knew. They dressed in faded housecoats that covered their massive drooping breasts as they served hot turkey lunches to travelers on 220.

Beachwood was open all hours. Through the storefront windows at night I could see shadows of black-and-white TV images dancing on Mary and Marguerite's chubby orthopedic hose-covered legs. Cranked up in La-Z-Boy recliners, they'd wait behind the open door to the back room for the occasional late night customer. A bell would ring when the inn door opened. It was usually Mary who came out with a smile, scoop up a whopping vanilla ice cream cone for me, tell Daddy a dirty joke, and then go back to watching Johnny Carson. I liked Beachwood much better than my father's usual reward for a day at the farm—a bar called "Dad's" where I'd sit alone outside in the car and wait for him to knock a few back, tell a few stories, and prepare to face my mother. I made up games trying to intuit when he'd finally come out and reward me with a bag of pork rinds or beef jerky.

Beachwood was the perfect place for my ducks. The big pond had lots of nooks where all three could enjoy the safety of the marsh, tall grasses, and cattails. Marguerite and Mary were delighted when we drove up and took out the crates. Patrons said Marguerite could make change "faster than a Vegas dealer" from the money purse she had strapped to the inside of her thigh. It must have been the purse that made her waddle as she came out the back door for the unveiling.

"My goodness, Harold," Marguerite said, "those are some big ducks! And they're so white—they blind my eyes!"

Mary was the one with a sense of humor. She came busting through the back door eyeing Gladys. "Ooh, this one looks pretty tasty, Marla."

I knew she was kidding, but I tugged on the cage harder to get them away from the inn and to the pond's edge.

"We have plenty of bread crusts for snacks, don't you worry, Marla," yelled Mary.

I opened the crate door and the ducks ran out honking and flapping like they'd just been released from prison. I wanted them to be happy and safe. I spotted a picnic table and thought that would be a nice place to sit if I came by for a visit.

But I didn't want to stop and visit. In fact, I didn't ever want to stop at Beachwood that whole summer. A dark, silent weight that settled in my gut every time I thought about the place kept me away. I just shook it off and trusted that the three ducks were swimming around that pond, teasing Mary's palate as she looked out at them from her kitchen sink.

It had been just over a year since Kelly Jo was killed. I wanted to mend my fears when I agreed to join Dad for a brief stop at the farm. It was cold and rainy, just on the verge of a snowy Thanksgiving Day, when we came upon a family of five in an old, beat-up station wagon. They had run out of gas a hundred feet from the entrance to the farm.

"Go get the red gas can from the tool shed, Marla," Daddy urged.

Pellets of sleet stung my face. I had no hat or gloves, but these people were in trouble and we had to help. My dad just took control, filled the can from our pump, and said, "This will get you all the way to Cumberland, Maryland."

The man, who was soaking wet, started up the car for his freezing family. He tried to pay my dad, but my father said, "Oh, no, no, no. It's Thanksgiving, for goodness sakes."

The man turned to me and asked, "Well, can I give your daughter a dollar for being so nice?"

My heart melted and Daddy said, "Sure." This was who my dad and I were, sensitive souls who wanted to make a difference when we weren't defending ourselves against Mother. I saved that dollar for years.

As we drove past Beachwood I looked and looked to see any flashes of white on the pond. Nothing. I was worried for my ducks' safety and hoped Mary had not served them up for dinner.

The next afternoon Daddy informed me that Gertrude, Heathcliff, and Gladys had all crossed the road at the same time and had been hit by a semi-truck. And Crimson was now in our freezer, stuffed into dozens of white paper packages stamped with his name on them.

I was devastated. Goddamn it, when will people ever tell the truth in this family? I had been so worried about my ducks, and even though I tried to trust that they were okay, I *knew* something was wrong, that danger was coming. And even after Dad told me the news, that dark grip still welled up in my gut when I thought about Beachwood. For some reason I would not go near the place. Something was coming.

Death was on my mind that first week in December when a skinny, dark-haired stable boy turned up at Beachwood. Tidbits I heard from valley folk went like this: Mary took pity on the scruffy boy when he showed up after lunch and asked him, "What you gonna have to eat today, son?"

He replied, "Nothin'. I don't have any money."

But Mary brought him some food anyway, along with a piece of pie and a scoop of that delicious vanilla ice cream. Twelve hours later, in the middle of the night, he came back with a stolen pistol and shot Mary between the eyes with a single shot and leveled Marguerite with three more slugs. He ransacked the place, took a stash of dimes from the cash box, and left them dead. He must have missed the special place where Marguerite hid all the money. George Butler was a dark, dirty, twisted pyre of evil that burned its way into our town.

Fear cut an even deeper hole in my life. The valley was now a scourge and my home was a waystation for unhappiness. Instead of paying attention to my budding intuition, I fluctuated between being deeply sad and filled with anger from all the injustices. No one could explain the slaughter.

I shifted my fear into a bravado that began to call the shots. I was ready when Terry Munson stole some pigs from our farm. Taking my cue from many nights of watching *Mission Impossible* and *The Wild Wild West* I told my dad what to do: "Get him into the front seat of your car, and get him to confess." Dad went for the idea. Terry didn't know that I'd stuck a microphone under his seat and caught his confession on tape to keep as insurance if he didn't make restitution. Terry spent the next summer cleaning out the pig stalls where he'd perpetrated his crime.

5

Twirling, Boys, and Jesus

"Twirling is the physical parallel of revelation ... the throwing yourself up to God. It's a pure gift, hidden from Satan because it is wrapped and disguised in the midst of football."
—Jane Martin, Twirler

Mother controlled everything, including my friends. She preferred the girls who came from Bedford's "best" families, the daughters of successful businessmen and doctors. But when Lynn Speirs invited me to her sleepover birthday party, I didn't care what Mother thought. I was excited.

The Speirs family lived down the hill in a sweet little house that always smelled of wax beans and harbored a stash of decomposing Easter candy in the attic. I never knew what Lynn's father did, but her mother was a smart, tough English teacher at the high school.

Lynn was funny and wild. I enjoyed her zest of life and that she didn't care when she got into trouble. Lynn also had a very pretty older sister who loved to twirl batons.

Mother was relentless in her disapproval of me attending the birthday party. "Well, if there are boys and beer there, your dad will come and get you! Remember, sex and alcohol are the two worst things God ever created!" She had me terrified. As I went out the door with my orange sleeping bag, she yelled, "There better not be any boys or beer at this party—you don't know what's going to happen!"

Down in Lynn's basement the music blared, lights flashed, and fourteen-year-old girls jumped around in a chaos of straight-haired girls gone wild. The room spun around me. I began to shake like the dizzying lights and flying hair. The overload of unfamiliar, disturbing frequencies struck me down with a terror of the unknown. I was so enmeshed with my mother that I was not my own person, I had no voice, and I could not explain what was happening inside of me. My fits of anguish were so strong I had to vomit. I lasted half an hour.

I was filled with shame that I could not control my body, that I was not mature enough to be a girl gone wild. Did my mother know me so well, or did she expertly mold me into a terrified child and joystick my every move? Who knows what happened later? There could have been boys and beer.

I may have had no voice against my mother, but I started to take action against her abuse. It took Kelly Jo's rape and murder for me to set some boundaries and no longer allow her to come into the bathroom and do things to me that she should not have done. I learned to keep my mother out of my bathroom by opening up the closet door all the way so it completely blocked the main door. If she did try to come in she would bang the door into the closet door, chipping and scraping up the paint, something she would never tolerate. Now that I had stopped her from coming into the bath she no longer had access to my body.

I was too terrified of Mother to risk any private moments at home with Harvey. But young love and joy held no bounds, so

Harvey wrote me letters . . . long, sweet, and as meaningful as he could write.

Once in a while I was allowed to visit Harvey out at his home by the river. "I'll pick you up in three hours," Mother said when she dropped me off. "And don't you dare fool around with that boy."

I loved Harvey. His laughter and smell made me feel warm and cherished. However, the dreamy wet kissing and afternoon fumbling on a blanket was not enough for him. He needed more, and like Natalie Wood in *Splendor in the Grass*, I said, "No."

Harvey grew sullen. Whatever was going on, the more Harvey tried to love me, the more uncomfortable I felt. So I pushed Harvey away and turned to twirling and Jesus.

From the time I was a toddler bundled up and standing on a curb watching Halloween parades I was overwhelmed by a band's drums that beat inside my chest. The flashing silver sticks tossed high and the snappy white boots captivated me. I couldn't stop talking about the majorettes and I started to twirl batons that were as big as I was. I did the prerequisite work of playing the trombone in the marching band until tenth grade, when I finally became a Bedford High School majorette. I found freedom and a different kind of wild expression twirling those long metal wands that I could point and toss and point again. When I was later selected as head majorette, I got to wear white, blow a whistle, and lead the band.

At the same time I found a much older born-again Christian boy. Josh was a smart, tall, athletic, and talented bright light with esteemed virtue who lived life filled with joy. "Getting to third base" was a term he only used in softball.

Josh said I had to find Jesus and be *saved*. I thought I already knew Jesus. I had spent most of my life in the Trinity Lutheran Church, starting with my baptism, then Sunday School, confirmation class, Bible study, singing in the choir, going to all the Halloween parties, and starring in the church plays. What did I have to be saved from?

Josh explained, "If you don't want to go to hell, but want to get into heaven, and if you want your prayers answered, you must be 'born again' and accept Jesus as your personal savior to be *saved*." Lordy, I hoped I didn't have to reenact my birth. Josh continued, "You will be special, and only those who are born again will get into heaven."

Well, I *had* been a little disappointed that my prayers were not being answered the way I hoped, and I would do anything to solve the problem of my mother. But why didn't my ministers know about this special born-again club? Maybe this was the answer.

We were parked in a green Bronco beside the high school track. Josh leaned in close. I thought that this might be the moment his hand caressed my face and his lips met mine, just like in the movies. Instead he reached behind my seat and handed me a present—a Bible. He was bold and confident as he prayed with me for Jesus to come into my heart. I was fifteen years young when I accepted Jesus as my personal savior. "Remember," Josh said, "Jesus only wants you to have sex when you're married." I believed in Jesus *and* Josh.

That night I did feel special, even though Josh didn't kiss me. I woke the next morning with the excitement of being born again, saved, and going to heaven, and to top it all off, Jesus would solve my problems with Mother.

In appreciation to Jesus for all the work I knew he had cut out for him, I donated all the money I had made selling my art and teaching guitar to Billy Graham's crusade. I read my new Bible as I listened to my transistor radio every night, tuning in to ministers as far away as Ohio to hear them proselytize to listeners to repent. I spent Wednesday nights in choir practice and weekend evenings rehearsing church plays. I went to Bible study, carried a Bible, and used the Good Book as a sword from the almighty, a protective weapon standing between me and my mother and the wicked feelings that came with growing up. I expected miracles just like the ones Moses/Charlton Heston made happen after he talked to God in *The Ten Commandments*, but Josh dumped me for a college girl and I fell back in love with Harvey.

Those last two years of high school were confusing as one by one classmates and Bible study friends who were lucky enough to find true love had to explain to their parents and everyone else how they got pregnant.

But Josh had told me that I not only needed to retain my virginity, but that it was my duty to save people from going to hell by getting them to accept Jesus as their personal savior. I loved Harvey and I wanted him to love me too. I felt pressured to do something that would keep Harvey happy and save us both from burning in hell as a punishment for having premarital sex.

One night, while Harvey and I were steaming up the windows at the Moonlight Drive-In Theatre, I was trying to catch glimpses of the Woody Allen movie so I could make sure my mother knew we had watched it. Our sticky love felt so right, but so wrong. So I grabbed hold of that part of Harvey that demanded my attention and rhythmically pleaded for him to accept Jesus as his personal savior. But Harvey's, "Oh, God, yes, yes, yes," was not the conversion I was hoping for.

I was crushed when Harvey found an older, much more mature girl who didn't care about hell.

It had been three years since Kelly Jo and the Beachwood women were murdered. I was finally feeling better about being down at the farm, but my dad knew I was still leery about riding in the woods on my own.

"So, do you want to go for a ride with me and Blaze?" he asked.

I wanted my dad to be proud. "Nah, I think I'll go for record time on a ride by myself. Let's see if I can make it back in an hour."

"Okay, but it looks like rain. You sure you don't want me to ride along?"

"Thanks, Daddy, but I'll be fine."

I knew this route with my eyes closed. First we'd trot up past all the hog barns to an opening in the fence by the field. Then we'd canter up the hill to ride the small ridge, wind around the thick old maple trees, trot through a mountain stream to a spot where ferns mingled with pine trees, and then run through the tall grasses before coming out onto the state game land road that led to Route 220. The entrance to the farm was about a half mile away.

It was around noon and the sky was getting dark. Daddy was right—there was a storm brewing. I loved storms and had no fear.

I never had a problem controlling my buckskin half-Arab/half-Quarter horse, Flicka (she came with the name). We had just turned onto 220 when lightning struck with a clap of thunder and she took off. I wasn't scared—I knew what to do. I had already thought about this scenario a number of times.

Flicka was a roping and cutting horse, so she could turn fast and stop on a dime. I would normally grab one of the reins and pull to one side or the other, making her spin out, but that day the hackamore around her nose and under her chin was loose. I could not control my frightened horse. I was now on the highway and it was beginning to rain. Semi-trucks buzzed by to my left and a barbed-wire fence stood to my right. There was no place to spin. I pulled on the reins with all my might to slow her down, but it had no effect.

With the farm in sight she was running to the safety of the barn. I knew that a huge pile of sawdust used for the stalls stood inside the barn, a pile so high that if she decided to stop I would most likely fly into that pile. My brain focused on landing in that pile, and then I heard a voice . . . *NO!*

The voice, alone and clear, spoke with purpose and authority: *There is no pile—dig your heels deep into the stirrups and hold on.* I did as I was told.

I got to the shale-covered area in front of the barn and saw that the voice was right; there was no pile. I screamed, "Daddy, help me!" Two farm workers ran to try to grab the out-of-control horse. As soon as Flicka got inside the barn, she dug her back hooves into the concrete floor. I flew forward, but my right foot was lodged deep in the stirrup just like the voice told me to do. I spun to the side of my horse, hit my tail bone on the ground and then watched the swallows in the roof rafters fly as the back of my head hit the concrete floor.

I woke hours later to the smell of hot dog vomit in my hair. I was in the Bedford County Memorial Hospital with a bad concussion. Mother sat beside my bed all night. She was terrified and angry that Daddy had bought the damn horse in the first place. She tried to feed me my favorite Lipton chicken noodle soup that she'd smuggled in. We both cried. The Voice had saved my life. Was that Jesus?

That summer I had no short-term memory. My typing teacher gave me a generous C in summer school. I dropped my batons more than normal, and I broke up with Harvey again. My brain had been scrambled and my whole system stunned from such a blow.

Life moved on. Classmates talked about college. I wasn't like my sister, who loved learning and got superior grades. After my horse accident, it became a challenge for me to keep up with my As. I didn't want to go to college, but I certainly didn't want to stay home.

Because I had painted, drawn, and sculpted my way through school, everyone expected that I would major in art in college. It was a ruse. I could list a host of sound support for a life as an actress. I had Lucy Ricardo and Ethel Mertz, the crazy divas of mother's soap operas to babysit me, and Carol Burnett to remind me that life could be funny. Movies and television programs showed me how to handle life outside of Bedford and three angels in the form of schoolteachers gave me flight.

Bette Lu Miller, my second grade teacher, was attractive, strong, funny, and smart. She made every book and story come alive, making me believe I was sitting in the barn with Wilbur the pig, watching Charlotte spin her web. Mrs. Miller believed in me. She treated all her students with respect and honesty and she was *real*, not a character on TV, but a gift from God who *had* character. She not only supported my talents, but her unconditional love helped me find parts of myself I didn't even know I had. Bette Lu—along with Blodwin Replogle, the grade school music teacher who always stood at the piano to pound every note into my head, and Arch Stewart, the quiet, smart, chain-smoking musical wizard at the high school—helped hone my heart and the talents brewing in my spirit. They all wrote letters of recommendation to colleges that wanted to know about the Marla they knew.

I gave Miami University of Ohio, one of the schools listed in the library's college catalog, two stars for being too far away to be a comfortable drive for Mother and three stars for not listing math as required freshman subject. But as an out-of-state applicant I couldn't just get in with my B average—I had to impress them with something special. So I took pictures of every drawing, painting, sculpture, knick-knack, and doodad I had crafted. They accepted me as an art major, not exactly what I wanted to do.

At the same time I was making choices about how to escape from home my dad made a unilateral decision to replace the award-winning Landrace hog operation with cattle. Continental Grain, the company Daddy worked for, promised that raising cattle on a new feed they had developed would be extremely successful. This spun my mother into a fury, but my father got cocky about it with a confidence bolstered by one of his whiskey bottles. He got a big loan and started to convert the farm to handle his newly purchased five hundred or so cattle. He was hopeful that the cattle, like the hogs, would be an award-winning example for Continental Grain. During the gloomy summer of 1975 beef prices plummeted and my father went bankrupt. We had to sell the farm and auction off everything I loved, including my horse.

I sat in the barn on the back of our red pickup, which had been freshly cleaned for the sale, and watched the crowd gather. They parked their cars, trucks, and trailers and filed in with sun-worn faces, humidity-frizzed hair, and plaid short-sleeve shirts, ready to bid.

My throat ached with sadness as I watched the auctioneer hold up my horse tack and saddle with the yellow and red Navaho print blanket that came with Flicka the day my father surprised me with her for my ninth birthday.

"Okay, we have a saddle, blanket, and bridle. Let's start the bidding at thirty, gimme thirty-five, forty, do I hear forty-five?"

"FIFTY-FIVE!" shot a voice from the back.

I tried not to cry as I dropped my head down and stared at the place where my head hit the concrete the year before, remembering the Voice that saved my life.

What *was* that Voice—Jesus, come to save me?

Despite my father's financial ruin, he promised he would send me to college. I guess I was going whether I wanted to or not. I marched out of Bedford's heartland sheltered, battered, and naïve, with a Bible in my suitcase and a Voice in my head that I thought was Jesus.

6

The Push

*"When you follow your bliss, doors will open where you would
not have thought there would be doors, and where there
wouldn't be a door for anyone else."*
—Joseph Campbell

Miami University of Ohio is the picture-perfect Norman Rockwell college campus out in the middle of the vast cornfields of Ohio. I moved into my dorm, "The Pines," and looked around to see where I'd fit in. The born-again Christian groups wanted us to stand on boxes and "witness" to kids on campus, but no one wanted to spew Bible verses, let alone listen to them. We were all away from our parents, groping along as young adults and driven by wicked hormones. Why Jesus would give us hormones was another question. All I wanted to do was spend time with a boy named Bill Bonnard who seemed to like the word "no" more than I did. I was away from my mother and feeling great joy for the first time in my life.

I was hooked by my first art course, seamlessly emulating the exquisite lines and curves of the nude models with all the varieties of charcoal and lead that a college student could afford. But the frustration of silkscreening and other art projects I hated gave me the excuse to change my major to theatre.

Why not follow my bliss and audition for a role in the university musical? I did and was cast in a lead role—the naïve virgin Polly Peachum in *The Threepenny Opera*. For some of the juniors and seniors of the theatre department, a freshman getting cast as the ingénue lead of the coveted annual musical might have seemed unfair, but I was ready. Not for Julliard or Broadway, maybe, but evidently for the lead in a musical at a college out in the middle of a cornfield and revered for finance, marketing, and football. I was a naïve virgin from a small town in Pennsylvania who wanted a powerful man to save her and whose mother had visions of grandeur, but was so desperate she'd sell her daughter and her soul for security. I *was* Polly Peachum.

The morning of opening night I awoke so very happy. I was not flunking out, I had learned to do laundry, and was starring in the university musical. I also had a new family, a tribe of talented, fun, creative theatre friends. But by lunchtime I started to feel the same way I did at Lynn Spears's home, full of the same sense of chaos and upset of that "girls gone wild" night. It was so unsettling that I couldn't locate the same joy I felt when I woke up. By four o'clock that afternoon, four hours before showtime, a force I could not see shoved me out of my dorm room door and set me off on a brisk pace toward the theatre. As I walked across the field to the performing arts center, I realized I was running, my skin bristling. I was upset and didn't know why. I "knew" something was terribly wrong.

There was hubbub on the stage but the rest of the building was quiet. I went downstairs to my dressing room. The door was unlocked. I flipped on the switch and thought, "This is so dumb—why am I so upset?" I shook my head at the silliness. Everything looked in order, but my body said something different. I felt pushed to the closet where my costumes hung.

The first thing I noticed was my white blouse for my first-act entrance. I ran my hand over the ruffles; it was beautiful and pristine. "Ooh, they did such a nice job of ironing it," I thought. But the top button was missing, and the second, third, and, oh my God, all the buttons were gone! My blue blouse for the third act revealed the same thing. I felt an impulse to run out and grab whoever was on stage and report the wardrobe vandalism, but then the Voice came into my head. *Investigate further.*

The fasteners were snipped off my skirts, my first-act boots were replaced with another pair way too small, my white satin wedding boots were replaced with 1960s white patent leather shoes, and in place of my black tights was a pair that would only fit a troll.

Calm came over me as I realized that I had been warned of a coup to sabotage me, the same kind of calm that is now so familiar to me as a psychic. I went into the large costume storage room and grabbed safety pins, pulled out period shoes that fit, found another pair of adult-sized tights, and stuffed it all in a bag. I took care of business and then rested in quiet furor.

Aside from that near-miss sabotage my opening night went off seamlessly, with all the pins and hooks necessary.

On Monday morning I went to the dean of the Theatre Department, Donald Rosenberg, and told him of the plot to disarm or disrobe me. He listened intently and said, "So, you say they did this to you deliberately?"

"Why else would all the buttons and hooks be cut off and my shoes replaced?"

He looked ready to dole out punishment to someone, probably the director of the costume department, I thought, when he picked up the phone. It was a cordial chat, and then he wrote down an address on campus where I was to go: Roudabush.

"Where is that?" I asked.

"That's where the school psychiatrists are located."

He clicked the cap back onto his pen and handed me the address. I was stunned. "You're sending me to have my head examined?"

"Perhaps the Theatre Department isn't where you belong," he said. "Maybe you're not cut out for this."

I wasn't crazy. I was becoming psychic and being guided by a force that knew better than I did.

It was an easy decision to begin to close the door on my college of choice. I found out Daddy was selling timber off our not-yet-sold farm to pay for schooling I didn't want in the first place. That was the deal breaker for me. I finished my sophomore year taking all the classes in which I knew I would excel, landing a solo in the "Hallelujah Chorus" with Miami's Choral Union, and leaving with a nod on the dean's list.

In my naiveté I thought I would just follow my bliss, move to some city, get a job, start auditioning, and maybe get cast in another musical. But first I had to go home, resume my lifeguarding job at the Bedford Springs Hotel, and wait to see where I'd be pushed.

"Oh dear God, you blew up!" Mother screamed. I brought home an extra twenty pounds on my normally 104-pound frame.

"Well, we're gonna fix that!" She was out of control. I came home fat and soiled her world, like someone had stepped in dog shit and tracked it all over her carpet. For the first time, no one could see my hip bones or ribs and I'd grown a full set of boobs.

"If you don't exercise, you won't lose that weight," Daddy said.

My father's out-of-character concern for my appearance was disturbing.

I thought he was taking me out for one of our "father-daughter drives" through the lush dairy farms of Bedford, but instead he drove us to one of the steep trails off the state game land road and pushed me up the hill with a powerwalk to try to help me sweat off the embarrassing poundage.

No one thought my weight gain might have been the unnecessary estrogen Mother made me take *before* I left for college. So as I trudged up the hill I remembered the appointment Mother had made for us to see Dr. Myers. I will never forget our standoff that morning in his office. Mother sat on one side of the room and I on the other. Doctor Myers, our family physician, refereed. He was emotionless sitting between us with his big bald head, translucent skin, and errant nose hairs. "Put her on The Pill!" Mother demanded.

He looked at me and calmly asked, "Marla, do you have any intention of having sex?"

His inquisition was easy to answer. "No, Dr. Myers, I am a born-again Christian."

Hearing that, he wrote a prescription for birth control and instructed that I had to take them every day or I could end up "in trouble." The only trouble I was worried about was Mother as we climbed into the car and she remarked, "Alcohol and sex are the two worst things God ever created, and don't you forget it!"

Now, as I huffed up the hill, my father called out behind me, "You know your mother is only looking out for your best."

"No, let me clue you in, Daddy, it's for *her* best. It always is."

Pushing me out of town would assuage whatever shame my mother felt about me dropping out of college and losing my stick-model figure.

Mother sat on one leg and rocked with the other as she pressed the phone into her cotton candy hair and told my sister Debbie, "Well, if she's going to leave college to go anywhere, she better go live in the same town as you!" Where do you go when you leave college for a bigger, brighter future as an actress? Milwaukee.

The city actually had a well-known summer stock theatre called Melody Top. I figured I could start there, audition, and maybe get my first professional job. After all, I'd just had the lead in a college musical.

Mother pointed her crooked finger in the air and commanded Debbie, "Go find her a cute and safe apartment!"

I was uneasy about the strange partnership of Mother and Debbie working together on my behalf. Mother lived on fantasy, illusion, and small-town dreams that became *National Inquirer* stories. Debbie heeded Mother's demand to me a find safe home, but what kind of place could she find that would be exciting enough to satiate mother's tabloid-sensibility need to live through me?

Debbie called to say she'd found the perfect spot.

Mother sat in Daddy's rocker and reiterated out loud what Debbie was saying on the phone. "Oh, it's a cute little studio apartment with a Murphy bed and kitchenette . . . in a beautiful East Side Art Deco-style hotel, and it has a little Italian restaurant on the bottom floor called Bugs. Oh shit," Mother giggled, "Snug's." My mother was now rocking in a frenzy. She was happy.

After scouring the hip East side of Milwaukee near the lake, my sister found me the only place she could hold for me without signing a lease. My new home was The Shorecrest Hotel, a well-known Milwaukee establishment owned, operated, and occupied by the Milwaukee mafia family, the Balistrieris.

7

The Family

*"Happiness is having a large, loving, caring,
close-knit family in another city."*
—George Burns

By the time I was four, Debbie was in boarding school, and later she went to college. I longed for Debbie to come home, and when she did, she was coerced into babysitting me. That might not have been great for my sister, but it was really good for me.

The sweltering heat of the Pennsylvania summers pushed Debbie and me to retreat to our knotty pine-paneled basement, complete with a 1951 Wurlitzer jukebox, big fireplace, dozens of records, and a wet bar. We used the basement as an art studio and dance floor. I loved dancing in Debbie's arms. She'd pick me up and I'd wrap my legs around her waist and lay my head on her shoulder as she danced "the stroll" to the lull of The Four Tops and The Temptations. We'd get out paints, mess things up all over the wet bar, and create what I thought were masterpieces.

Debbie's passion for poetry imprinted me with rich images and words. Her reading of Lewis Carroll's "The Walrus and the Carpenter" was my favorite. The fat, curious little oysters who naively scrambled to walk beside the walrus and the carpenter were doomed—innocents seduced to the slaughter. The oysters blindly followed the walrus and the carpenter, whom the oysters thought were nice. But their companions turned out to be pathological and thoughtlessly cruel, systematically eating them all. I was terrified but curious as Debbie read and brought the oysters' plight to life. An older sister's early warning of the danger that lurked in our home and the danger in the world.

But I had already begun to feel that danger when I was tied to the high chair. Survival came with a price.

I got out of my sister's car in front of Milwaukee's Shorecrest Hotel just in time for Snug's outdoor café to be all abuzz, serving up its famous mozzarella marinara and chilled Chablis.

The dark hall to the hotel's front desk had high ceilings, Romanesque paintings, black marble trim, and an occasional naked statue on a pedestal. Light from the lakeside windows bounced off the polished floors, making things seem cheery in a Mario Puzo kind of way.

The building had charm—my room was serviceable with a purple and green tile bath and a bed that flew up into the wall. No lake view, but high enough over the restaurant parking lot that I couldn't smell the rotting veal Parmesan in the garbage bins below.

I dropped off my bags and went to my sister's house for dinner. Debbie's husband was big, bossy, and overly charming as he showed off their new home. He reminded me of Mother.

We settled in for dinner. "So, you like the Shorecrest?" he asked. "Well, you know about the Balistrieris; they're the mob." He laughed this weird Curly (of Curly, Moe, and Larry) kind of laugh. Sucking the life out of his Marlboro cigarette and tossing my cooing baby niece around, he added, "Yep, everybody knows 'em. Frank, the father—jeez, he's done some scary shit. Then there's Joe, the oldest, and John—they're the sons, both attorneys, good guys. Hey, you know they live at the Shorecrest?"

I didn't know that, but now I did. Deft pieces of important info since I was now living with them. Thoughts of Marla the "mob moll" briefly rolled through my brain, but I had more important things to think about. I was not cast in Melody Tops' summer stock season, so I had to get a job. Why not get one at the little Italian restaurant downstairs?

Geno Frinzi, the maître d' at Snug's, was sweet and funny—an odd cross between Redfield, Dracula's minion, and an older Al Pacino. We liked each other immediately. It didn't seem to matter that I had never waitressed before because Geno said, "I just have to get the approval of the boss."

The whole mafia thing sounded weird to me. I had no reference other than Hollywood's *Godfather* movie. I'd been in town a week and didn't see any guns, shoot-outs, car bombs, or people on their knees kissing rings.

Geno and I were sitting at the bar when he entered. He was dressed in a black suit, white shirt, no tie, but a thin gold chain that rested in the hair of his chest. He was walking confidence. I couldn't move.

"Mr. Balistrieri, this is Marla. She wants to work here."

He smiled and took my hand and said, "Hi, I'm Joe."

His cufflinks were gold and he smelled like nothing I had ever known. He was completely captivating.

"So, you want to work for me?"

I stood. My high-heeled sandals put me eye to eye with him. I wanted to melt, but instead I stammered, "Yyyes, sir."

"You're hired. Put her on with Paul, and let him train her." He turned on his heels and left just like, well . . . Dracula—poof.

"That was easy," I said.

Geno smiled. "He likes you."

I'd been working for a week and felt happy and excited about my new life. I would start setting up for dinner at four p.m., polishing silver, positioning wine glasses in the main dining area, and buffing water stains with a seltzer-dampened linen napkin. Then one day the hair on the back of my neck prickled up.

The staff scurried the way birds and small animals react when they sense a predator. A smallish, thin man in a light grey suit, jet black hair, pasty white skin, and impeccable posture slithered through the tables watching everything and nothing at the same time. He moved right past me as I flashed my happy smile. His lips never parted but he modestly acknowledged me, then went straight to the only table with a phone in the corner, a red phone, and made a call.

I walked back to the comfort of Paul, the bartender. "That's him," he said.

"Who's him?" I asked.

"*The* Boss, Frank."

Paul handed me a cup, "Okay, go give this to him and get out of there fast."

My stomach felt queasy, but I did as I was instructed. I put everything in place and turned the handle of the cup so he could pick it up easily. He nodded, and then I left.

Frank Balistrieri was Joe's father, the real life "Godfather." You know how you get a piece of information that changes how you think and feel about everything? Like when you learn there's no real Santa Claus? When you realize people do go to jail, men do beat their wives, and there really are men who have other men killed? Well, welcome to Snug's.

I sucked as a waitress. I'd screw up orders regularly, but my charm and naiveté saved me. When Joe and his "friends" from Chicago would come in for dinner, I'd hear, "Marla, take that apron off and sit down with us." So I did.

"What do you want to drink, honey? Pauley, get her whatever she wants."

I wasn't used to this kind of attention. I had an idea of what they wanted, but I was uncomfortable as a dessert.

I did not come to Milwaukee to serve food. Geno understood that. He knew the head of the Milwaukee Opera Company and promised to put in a good word for me. Within a week I auditioned and was hired. My first paying job as a performer had me taking the bus to a funky rehearsal space downtown across the river from the Ambrosia Chocolate Factory, where an elevator with a big gate delivered me to the rehearsal studio. It was a joy to be with professionals. I would also be cast in productions with the Skylight Opera and the Great American Children's Theatre. This is why I came to Milwaukee.

My waitressing shifts changed with my new job. I no longer had to be at Snug's when Frank would slither in at lunch, get on the phone at the table in the corner, and do some business. I was learning more about Joe, though, and he seemed far different from his old man.

The residents of the Shorecrest knew that Joe had a ritual on Sunday mornings *sans* church. He'd throw open the windows that faced the lake, put on an opera recording, and belt out all the words. French, Italian—whatever the language, he knew them all. Needless to say, when Milwaukee Opera hired me, Joe was thrilled.

I made out with Paul the bartender one night. When news got back to Joe, Paul was put on lunches. I felt things were getting a little too familiar with my Shorecrest family, so I decided to get my first apartment with a partial lake view, just a few blocks south of the hotel at the Quarles Apartments.

The bus from downtown was not as reliable as Joe, whose two-toned maroon Bentley would just happen to be coming up Prospect Avenue when I was walking home from a rehearsal. He'd pick me up and drop me off, making sure I got to my waitressing job on time.

There was a package in the mail from Mother for my twenty-first birthday. She liked giving her daughters what she wanted us to have. Debbie's birthday and mine were a few days apart. We had years of comparing the disparagingly odd gifts Mother would give us, projections of what she thought of us. One year it was a vacuum cleaner for Debbie and a gold lamé jumpsuit for me. I'm not sure which present was worse. I had trepidations of what waited for me in that box.

Bette, my new friend from across the hall, came over to see the contents.

"Open it," she said.

"Hmm," I said. "Two pairs of white socks, five pairs of white, no-sex-for-sure granny-style underwear, a check for a fifty dollars, and under that a bunch of old *Cosmopolitan* magazines! Yahoo!" I was thrilled.

Mother pretended *Cosmo* was a girl's guide to fashion, but it was really all about sex. Sex was in everyone's life except mine. It was all over television, movies, and magazines, and even politicians and religious leaders were having sex before marriage and with other people while married. I decided turning twenty-one would be the time to lose the proverbial virginity. I was tired of wondering what all the hoopla was about. It was time to get this over with.

Bette and I read that *Cosmo* front to back, hoping to pick up much-needed skills. The *Cosmopolitan* bachelor of the month, Bennett Gordon, looked like a good place to start.

"Oh, Bette, he's so cute," I said. "A redhead, successful businessman, skydiver, lives in Los Angeles, and looking for a long-legged, sexy girl who looks like Miss America and likes Italian food. Well, at least that last part fits me."

"Write him!" Bette demanded. "What could you lose, except your virginity?"

We were in hysterics, girls gone wild in Milwaukee. I tossed the magazine on my table and decided to stay close to home and start my sexual exploits with John Smith. Yes, that was really his name. Smith was a tall, robust, Brad Pitt-looking kind of guy who lived in my building.

We went out on a few dates and ended up floating in a dingy off the shore of Lake Michigan, where I declared he would be my first. My unrequited love with college boyfriend Bill had been too tangled up between his mother, Catholic guilt, my born-again status, and other excuses to be more intimate. I was sad that we had not consummated our young love that had started at the end of my college freshman year. Unlike my childhood, I would now be in control of who touched my body. I had no role models other than movie sex—people looking really good up close, and then afterward everyone being happy.

I planned it like I was setting up a dinner party. I carefully picked out new sheets, bedspread, and the perfect mood lighting. After a Saturday night dinner by the lake and not much conversation, we went back to my apartment. John was slow and tender, but there was little chemistry, certainly not the kind of chain reaction when everything feels right, when body touches and smells tell body parts what they are supposed to do, that strange and wonderful imprinting of young love.

I hoped to feel something while Smith's 200-pound frame was between my legs. Perhaps that is why mother scrubbed the feminine life out of me, to deny me feeling, need, or desire. Smith could not satiate the emptiness inside me.

There was never any real explanation or memory of how my hymen broke as a child, leaving no proof I was still a virgin. I had no evidence of the rite of passage into the world of sex that night, just the satisfaction I took in having a nice ambiance.

Monday I had a day off, no opera or Snug's. I met my girl-friend Bette at the Coffee Trader. We were schmoosing details of my night with Smith over coffee and chocolate cheesecake when Stan entered and stood at our table. A Friday night Snug's regular, Stan the man was probably in his forties, tall, with brown hair parted on the right, and dressed in a brown suit. He would tip me a twenty just for bringing him two scotches. He never really talked to anyone, but people seemed to know him.

"Bring us a bottle of champagne for the birthday girl," Stan called to the waitress.

Wow, champagne? That was so grown up and extravagant. But how did he know it was my birthday? With that gesture, we invited him to sit down. We had a fine time chatting, but Bette had to leave. I walked her out to say goodbye, and when I returned, Stan stood up and pulled out my chair like a wonderful gentleman. I finished my glass of champagne. Then it started to get dark, and I didn't feel well.

Things began to slow way down as I stared for the longest time at the fork on my plate. The next thing I knew Stan was guiding me out of the restaurant. He opened the passenger door of a burgundy car. *That's nice.* I thought. *He has his car parked right in front of the door—how'd he get such a good parking space?*

"Don't woooory," he said, "I knowww where you live, I'll take you hoooome."

I was woozy as lights blurred in the darkness. When I came to, I realized I was on my back in the front seat of the car, the top of my head hitting the driver's door with a thump, thump, thump. A yellow neon motel sign illuminated the dashboard and steering wheel.

"Nooooooo!" I tried to say, but I could not hear myself. I could not feel myself, or my body.

"Don't worry," said Stan the man, "I've had a vasectomy."

"A vasectomeeee?"

During this living nightmare, I flew in my mind into the motel sign above, just like I had left the pink bathroom of my childhood home, hovering over the town, thinking of warm and safe places below, waiting for whatever my mother was doing to my genitals to be over.

There on my back in that sedan I thought, who will help me? Where is Daddy? Images of my daddy and me at the farm flashed in my head.

On cold winter nights when the sows were giving birth, my father and I would sit together and wait for life to come. A rush of hot moisture split the cold air with the delivery of each baby pig. My job would be to clean them off and gently place them on the straw under the warmth of the heat lamps.

Sometimes I had to oil up my arm and reach into the sow, feeling for the tiny one who didn't want to be born. With just a tug, I could pull him out, warm, raw, and squealing with life. But there was another barn where boars had to be prepared for market. It took the strength of two men to hold the metal noose around the front two tusks of each boar. Once snagged, they'd naturally back up and try to pull away.

"Marla!" my father yelled, "go grab the bucket of disinfectant. When John gets a hold of this boar, I'm gonna take my knife make the slits in the testicles and rip 'em out. I want you to swab the open wound with the sponge that's in the bucket, okay?"

I was a terrified accomplice, doing what I was told to make Daddy proud, trying not to slip in the blood, shit, and antiseptic as I ran to try to help the screaming injured. The sounds were deafening, the smell overwhelming. It was devastating.

I lay on my back in the front seat of the burgundy sedan. I could not move or speak over the silent screams in my head as Stan the man pressed his face into mine, whispering again, "Don't worry, I've had a vasectomy."

I woke up at two-thirty p.m. the following day. I couldn't remember how I got home or ended up naked in my own bed. I had missed rehearsal and called in sick at Snug's. I studied my body. Things seemed to be intact. I was sore, but I was alive. It was raining, and as night fell, I just sobbed.

Stan left a message on the answering machine. "I had a good time. When can I see you again?"

What—had a "good time?"

I slept for another day. Nothing seemed right. I had made a mistake. Could I have stopped this? What happened between taking my friend to the door and coming back to finish my glass of champagne? No one spoke about date rape in those days, or the drugs that render a girl numb and unable to talk. But this was wrong. I saw what he did, but I didn't feel it. I heard what he said but could not intervene. I wasn't a victim, but a witness to a rape. How could I talk to the police if there was no victim?

I was riddled with terrible feelings of guilt and shame. The perpetrator had moved out of my bathroom, out of Bedford, and into the world ... no place was safe.

Sadness followed me everywhere, and there was no one I could tell. I prayed to forget about it. Where was Jesus? Had he left me because I worked for the mob and had sex for the first time? All I told my sister was that I went out on a date and drank too much. She was a direct link to Mother, and I would not give Mother the satisfaction of having been right, that *sex and alcohol were the two worst things God ever created.*

In the aftermath of that night, I buried myself in work. Late one night at Snug's I was cashing out when Joe came in. He asked me to sit with him. "So you called in sick and you don't want to work Fridays?"

I didn't know what to say. I was frightened to tell him, and worried not to tell him. I wanted someone to protect me and take the pain away. I stared at the stained glass behind the bar as I told Joe what happened. All I heard was the muffled sounds of pots and pans way back in the kitchen. Joe got off the bar stool and put his arms around me.

He held me close and said, "Don't worry."

I could not let the memory of my twenty-first birthday be ruined by a mistake. I didn't realize at the time that I had choices, ways to care for myself, professionals to seek out who could help me with my experience. I was upset and wanted those memories to be replaced. Stan never showed up again at Snug's. I never heard anything more about him. I still ached to be held and told that everything was okay. I wanted what I had been missing for a very long time . . . love.

I turned my attention to the stack of old *Cosmos* Mother sent me, scanning the pages to find something that might expunge what I'd been through. No article, fashion spread, or tidbits on tantalizing sex eased my pain—except the confident smile of a *Cosmopolitan* Bachelor of the Month, Bennett Gordon.

I had nothing left to lose, so I sent him a picture and a letter.

I came home from a rigorous day of singing opera in a Milwaukee mall. The men had sported cheap tuxes and we girls wore red polyester dresses as we belted out selections from the musical *Kiss Me Kate*. The audio was bad, the audience unappreciative. The mall echoed with the screams of babies and badly behaved children. I stepped to the microphone to sing my solo, "Till There Was You," and thought, *Get me the hell out of Milwaukee.*

I had gone from being thrilled about landing my first professional job to singing in front of a cheese store in a mall. Our little Milwaukee Opera company sang our hearts out to drum up an audience of mallgoers and hand out flyers. Evidently, the company's publicity campaign was not well thought out.

When I got home from the mall I plopped down on my sofa with a bowl of Rice-A-Roni, just in time to see the only man who had been in my apartment since the one night with John Smith. Peter Jennings, the television anchor from *ABC World*

News Tonight, was my smart, dashing evening companion who would tell me what was going on all over the world. He was just getting to the U.S. news when the phone interrupted us.

"Is this Marla?" I didn't recognize the voice. "This is Bennett Gordon, the *Cosmopolitan* bachelor of the month." I was stunned. "Do you look as good as your picture?"

I laughed and told him I had just had it taken a few months ago and thought it still looked like me. My heart was pounding.

"Tell me more about you," he said.

This was too good to be true. He was sophisticated, gorgeous, well-traveled, and much more successful than any man I had ever known. And he was interested in me. He said he felt coerced by *Cosmo's* owner, Helen Gurley Brown, to be the bachelor of the month. "I had no idea that so many women would be interested, let alone write," he said.

Of course I felt very special that he read my note and called me. We began a late-night phone relationship that made my heart skip, just like the shimmering light of the moon on Lake Michigan outside my window.

"How would you like to go to Jamaica, Marla? I'll get you a ticket and we can meet in Montego Bay the first part of November."

I was giddy. What a wonderful surprise, no more one-night stands, mafia, or Stan the man. Though this had only been a brief courtship so far, I had a generous, exciting invitation from a prominent and well-respected man—he was in *Cosmo*, for God's sake!

I started picking out what would be suitable to wear on a Caribbean island date. Bette suggested a diaphragm. She was right, a *Cosmo* girl had to be prepared.

I was not well versed in pelvic exams when I sought help from a free OB-GYN clinic. A very unattractive doctor with maybe twenty hairs left on his head asked, "Well, do we want to go on the Pill?"

"No, we don't," I said. I didn't think it was necessary to tell him my history of being force fed The Pill by my mother and packing on twenty extra pounds. None of that was half as upsetting as what my mother would do to me if I got pregnant.

"Well, it's best to be prepared, so I suggest the diaphragm," he assured me.

This was before STDs were on the rise or AIDS had entered the conversation. He dug around in the examining room drawers and said, "I hope you don't mind me asking, but do you work on TV? I feel like I have seen you."

"No, I haven't been on TV yet. Do you like opera?"

"Yes, my wife and I have season tickets to the Milwaukee and Skylight Opera Companies." I smiled, wondering if she had heard us in the malls.

He got down to business and held the little rubber dome in his hand. "Ok, so this is the tricky part. You have to fold it like this, and then . . . oh dang."

The diaphragm sprung out of his hands and skidded across the examining room floor, coming to rest under a cart. He bent over to pick it up, dusted it off, and said, "See, that's what I'm talking about. It is really tricky. Just take it home and practice inserting it and getting it out."

"I'll take a new one, if you don't mind," I said.

Spermicide and rubber domes all sounded like such an ordeal, but I was a *Cosmo* girl and had to be prepared.

I heard no resistance from the Voice when I lied and told Geno I was going home and told the opera company I was going on a family vacation. I told my sister the truth, and she in turn told Mother, who took out a life insurance policy on me. I didn't care. I was going on a date with the *Cosmopolitan* bachelor of the month to Jamaica. So there.

8

Cosmo

"Good girls go to heaven—bad girls go everywhere."
—Helen Gurley Brown

I went through my closet, tugged at too-tight clothes, and settled on wearing a white shirt, beige blazer, Candies sandals, and a pair of jeans that would make me look hot—if I could lie down flat enough to zip them up.

I puffed, primped, and pinned up my hair so that when I arrived in Jamaica and pulled the pin out, my hair would look just like one of the ads in *Cosmo. You too can feel incredible and sexy on the way to meet your date!* However, the flight was six hours long, and when I got off the plane I couldn't feel my feet, my tight jeans cut off all my circulation, and when I released the pin, my hair just drooped.

I was nervous and self-conscious going through Jamaican customs. I wanted to be attractive, cool, and more mature than twenty-one. What was I so nervous about? He was in *Cosmo* for God's sake—he has to be who he said he was, and more.

I saw him at the bottom of the escalator, sitting in the waiting area. Oh, yes, he was a ginger all right, attractive, dressed in jeans, a dark blazer, and a crisp white shirt. I was diggin' the attire. Oh good, he's reading—*Playboy*? Oh my God. Okay, maybe he just reads it for the articles.

Playboy was something my next-door neighbor, Norm, or Mr. B., read. He gave me an old one that I kept in my nightstand to share with neighborhood girls—until someone's mother called my mother. My mother stormed into my bedroom. "Marla, why the hell do you have this magazine? Don't you know that if you look at this you'll become a lesbian like Mr. B's daughter who lives in Maine?" I didn't know what a lesbian was, and I didn't want to move to Maine. *Playboy*, I learned, is what men think girls should look like, but it's shameful and should not be kept in a nightstand, let alone read in public. I bought into those ideas, and at twenty-one still believed them.

Bennett Gordon stood and kissed my cheek. He wasn't as tall as he professed to be in the magazine, but had all the confidence in the world. From behind his aviator glasses he said, "Marla, you look as pretty as your picture."

I had just spent the last six hours on a plane. Was he being kind, or was he used to lying? I dismissed that thought as soon as the warmth of Montego Bay's soft breeze caressed my face.

This was a welcome change from Milwaukee's wet, chilly fall. We threw open the balcony doors of our hotel room to find the beach and a stunning sunset view. We both sighed. This was just what I needed. We went for a brief swim, and then to dinner and dancing on the beach. He glided me through the first night as a gentleman. We talked into the night and feel asleep to the sound of the waves.

The next day we soaked up the sun. He wanted to know all about my acting and opera career, and I didn't tell him about the shopping malls. Between the rum and sun we started to explore other parts of each other. We were quite comfortable, but not enough to be more intimate. When he leaned in close to rub oil on my shoulders, he said, "I have a friend back in the States who wants to get a relative out of a jail. They apparently put him in jail for drugs." I listened intently. "I need to talk to the authorities tomorrow morning," he said.

Bennett was calm and confident. I wasn't sure what it all entailed, but he seemed to know what he was doing. I felt safe as I lay beside him. Calypso drums lulled us to sleep. I woke to a nasty sunburn and note on the dresser: "I'll call you when I am finished with business."

I took a swim and sat in the shade by the pool. I had a subtle nag of a feeling that I should let people know where I was, so I jotted off post cards to the parents and Bette, letting them know I was better than okay. Insurance, if something went wrong. A porter ran over to me. "You have a call, Miss." It was Bennett, and he was curt. "Marla, pack our bags, everything, and take a cab to the Montego Airport. There's a ticket waiting for you to go to Kingston."

"Kingston?" I was dumbfounded, but could not get a word in edgewise. "Marla, the plane is going to leave in forty-five minutes. We don't have time to talk."

I asked the desk clerk where Kingston was.

"It's a hundred miles across the other side of Jamaica, lady."

No time for a shower, so I threw everything into the bags. Not wanting to irritate the sunburn, I put on the least amount of clothes I could pull together, a yellow tube top, white shorts, and tennis shoes. I didn't get to ask why I had to bring all our bags. We were supposed to be in Montego Bay for a week. I wasn't careful packing—I hoped he wouldn't mind. The flight was only a half hour long.

Bennett ran to greet me. "So glad you made it—we just have a few minutes before the plane to Havana leaves."

"What do you mean, Havana?" I asked.

"I was cleared to go see that American prisoner in jail, and there's only one flight a week." Bennett hailed a porter and asked where we could pick up the bags from my plane.

"No, man, there be a work embargo," said the porter. "No work for baggage men. You can't get 'da bags off 'da plane."

Bennett ran outside to the plane from which I had just disembarked and yelled, "Hey, I've got to get my bags off this plane!"

A tall black man dressed in what looked like a gardener's green shirt and pants said, "You can yell all you want, but we not going to work, man."

"Just let me look and I'll get them myself," Bennett pleaded.

"Okay, the belly of da plane is open. You can look."

Bennett literally crawled up into the plane. He came out empty handed and said, resigned, "Okay, we're just going to have to leave with the clothes on our backs."

I was simply caught up in the moment of this adventure that had now taken a detour to Cuba. A "friend," a relative? An American in jail—in Havana? I wasn't worried about the diaphragm, toothbrush, or reasonable attire I was leaving behind. I just hoped I would come back to the States in one piece.

A golf cart whizzed up beside us. The driver said, "Mr. Gordon, the plane is ready to leave. You must go now!"

Bennett handed me a ticket and said, "This is your visa. It cost me a box of cigars and a promise."

I hoped he would explain, but we were whisked off on the golf cart to a four-propeller Mexicana airliner. No words were exchanged, just the flash of our papers to let us climb the stairs.

White mist wafted in as we made our way through the aisle. On the plane to Havana were five Russian soldiers, two men who looked like Cuban police, Bennett, and me in a tube top and shorts. The stewardess, dressed in an old blue-and-white pants suit, casually passed Cuban rum and tonics to us. She sat and drank with the soldiers.

"Marla, it's difficult to get visas into Cuba. I had to make some concessions. You will be considered my fiancé, and we'll say we are Canadians on holiday. You might have to have these papers stamped when we get there. Don't worry, you're safe with me."

I prayed he was right.

Hidden deep in lush vegetation below were grey barns, the hangars of Havana's airport. Everything down on the ground was carefully concealed, except us. Bennett's red head and bleached white jeans and my blonde hair, short shorts, and a tube top with spilling breasts screamed LOOK AT US! WE'RE CANADIANS ON HOLIDAY!

After being escorted into the hangar where guards were waiting, we shuffled through customs. There was a flurry of Spanish about the visa paper Bennett had given me before I got on the plane, and we were held. Bennett didn't look anything but confident as the tall, mustached men in green fatigues yelled back and forth over my head. I pulled my tube top higher. Hands were waving, papers flapping, and then I was given a "special paper" that I apparently had to deal with later. They all calmed down and ushered us through.

I was still in shock over the invite-me-on-a-date-to-Jamaica-and-then-hijack-me-to-Cuba turn of events as we flagged down a cab. But as we rode through the city, I began to pay attention to my surroundings. Havana was an impoverished city. Dilapidated villas, the former homes of well-to-do families, were now occupied by dozens of people. Pre-revolutionary 1950s American cars, vintage heaps in need of paint and parts, were the only models that lined the streets. Armed soldiers stood watch on every other block.

A room at the seaside Riviera Hotel awaited us. Everything looked like a throwback to the 1950s. I watched as people dressed in modest attire scurried around us, staring. We were an out-of-place couple. I said to Bennett, "I have to get something else to wear."

"What do you need?"

"From the looks of women around here, no one is blonde and they don't wear tube tops and shorts. I need something that won't draw too much attention."

The little tourist gift shop was empty of other customers as we thumbed through the racks of gaudy, expensive, gold-studded costumes for tourists. Bennett pulled out a dress and said, "Could you live with this?" We burst out laughing. He held up a puffy white cotton dress with off-the-shoulder short sleeves. An embroidered bodice with the colors of the Cuban flag—red, white, and blue—topped the white, layered skirt. I imagined it was a costume that some fabulous Cuban dancer had deliberately left behind in a hotel room.

I took it into the little dressing area, pulled it up and cinched the back. It was the most outrageous thing I'd ever tried on; however, it did strap down the boobs, and maybe that was a good thing. I walked out and Bennett said, "You belong on top of a Cuban wedding cake."

We doubled over and out came all the suppressed emotions from the time he left me in Montego Bay. My laughter quickly turned to tears, and he held me close and kissed my cheek.

I had always been knocked over when a boy I liked, liked me back. It was my Achilles heel, someone filling my void of not feeling loved. This was the quest that ruled me all through school and stopped me from focusing on my own life. So when Bennett picked me, I wasn't thinking about whether or not he was best for me. I was just overjoyed that he had chosen me. I didn't realize at the time that the validation of my worth ultimately had to come from me. It would take many more lessons and years to figure that out.

We got the thumbs up from the sales woman who was as round as she was short. "*Es muy bonita*" (It's very pretty).

Bennett picked out two t-shirts that exclaimed VIVA CUBA. We grabbed toothbrushes and toothpaste marked *Made in Russia*. In fact, everything in the little store was stamped in Russian. I selected a pair of flat shoes, a flimsy bathing suit, and the dress. I understood that Bennett's Spanish was about as bad as mine when he pulled at the top of his underwear and asked the sales woman, "*Dónde?*" (Where?) to find out where we could get some undies.

"*No los tenemos aquí.*" (Not here). She drew a little map that could lead us to another store.

Bennett suggested that we make the most of our evening. After all, this was supposed to be a date. I got gussied up in our hotel bathroom with soap that wouldn't lather my hair and towels that looked and felt like scrub cloths the housekeeper used to clean the toilet. But when I was ready, I actually felt attractive with my skin turning gold in my off-the-shoulder Cuban wedding dress. I was thrilled to be on a date in a foreign country with Mr. Cosmo.

Our first stop was the Tropicana. Orange and rose tones colored the dancing girls dressed in purple shorts, midriff tops, and 1960s go-go boots. I thought for sure Ricky Ricardo would come out beating his congas and singing "Babalu." The rapture of drums and brass stirred the patrons, sweeping us up in the sensual soul and passion of Cuban music. The audience drank the no-label Russian beer and tapped the beat on the tables and floor. Bennett pulled me up to cha-cha and then whisked me out and into a cab.

Bennett took command, *"La Bodeguita del Medio, por favor."*

We were off to one of Havana's finest restaurants. The atmosphere was filled with music, tinkling glass, waiters' voices, and laughter. We walked past lovers who sat close, fed each other, and smiled as we approached our table beside a chalk blue wall where visitors had etched their names, along with the signatures of Hemingway and Pablo Neruda.

Bennett poured copious amounts of Russian white wine, and my dashing, smart, quirky date started looking better and better. Guitars strummed us into a dinner of pulled pork, green plantains, and *con gris*, black beans and rice. With every spoonful I fell more for Cuban cuisine and Mr. Cosmo.

As we stepped out of the restaurant, the Caribbean breeze brushed my hair in a moment of calm and bliss. I loved that I had taken a risk, and now the caution I had thrown to the wind was reminding me that all was safe. Bennett's hand caressed the back of my neck and his lips moved to mine. His other hand wrapped tightly around my waist and pulled me close. A lovers' movie moment.

The slam of a car door broke us apart. The headlights of a brand new Mercedes-Benz flashed as two distinguished men quickly got out and said to us in perfect English, "Let us escort you back to the Hotel Riviera."

"No, thank you, but we'll wait for a cab," said Bennett.

The men moved close, opened the back door of the Mercedes, and said, "Get in."

A bottle of Johnny Walker Red, still in its box, lay in the back seat. I climbed in first and Bennett sat behind the driver. The man in front of me said, "So you are Canadians on holiday?"

Shit, I knew that story wasn't going to fly.

Bennett said, "Yes, well, we are Americans, but, uh . . ."

Bennett grabbed my hand. He was interrupted before he could find more words.

"We want to show you our Havana," said the man sitting in front of me. They drove us through town and pointed at Castro's home and various touristy places, showing off in the way family members boast for out-of-town guests. Bennett intermittently squeezed my hand as the conversation continued.

"You must go to Varadero. We have the most beautiful beaches here. Why not stay a week? We will put you up in one of Castro's villas."

We laughed nervously. "Are you Cubans always this hospitable?" Bennett asked. "And who are you?" Bennett's voice squeaked with anxiousness as he tried to make light of our situation. Our companions did not share their names.

I felt a wave of danger move through my body, and then the electrical prickling, like the storm I felt as a teenager right before I was thrown off my horse. I heard the Voice say, *tell them you're sick.* I didn't wait to confirm what I had heard. "Excuse me, but I think I'm getting car sick. Could we go back to the hotel?" I pinched Bennett to let him know I was fine.

The man sitting in front of me said, "Of course. We would love to have a drink with you at the Riviera."

We had no idea what was going on. I looked to Bennett, who was just as confused as I. There was some relief as we made it back to the Riviera; people would see us, know where we were. We were escorted through a door draped in beads that led to the Riviera bar lounge. The light dimmed and we all morphed into the same lounge lizard orange, our faces erased, and our escorts' features were now defined by just a few tufts of black hair.

"We will bring some drinks," said the one who drove us. I carefully watched for any slip of the bartender's hand while he poured. Stan the man taught me that it was possible to render a girl paralyzed. If things get bad, I thought, this time I would fight for my life. They ushered us to the back of the lounge and sat on an L-shaped sofa. Bennett sat right in the middle. I was on his right, and we were bookended by the Mercedes-Benz men.

In a well-orchestrated move, two other men from across the room put down their drinks and stood at the door, keeping others out and us in. Another, who was much darker than any of us, came out of the shadows and sat down across from us. I had seen him in the lobby of the hotel when we first arrived. He complimented me on my dress. I laughed nervously, and then we all laughed. It broke the suffocating tension.

They introduced themselves by title. The taller one who drove said, "I'm the Ambassador of Afghanistan." He introduced the others. "This is the Ambassador of Iran, and the one who was your tour guide in the car is the secretary of the Palestinian Liberation Organization."

They were terrorists in the making.

"We knew who you were before you landed in Havana," said the PLO man.

They had been waiting for us. I gritted my teeth, thinking, *Canadians on holiday, Jesus, Cosmo man, what were you thinking?* Bennett sat stonefaced as the secretary of the PLO asked, "So, you took a meeting at the jail?"

"Yes. I'm a businessman trying to help a friend."

"Cuban jails are not good places for Americans," PLO man responded.

He smiled and then looked at me. I turned to Bennett and silently begged him to do something. Please, God, get us out of this. I felt a hand slip inside my skirt and touch my leg—it was not Bennett's.

PLO man leaned across me to Bennett and gestured with his wallet, "Here, look at pictures of my family." I nodded.

"We accommodated you by giving Marla a visa while you try to help that friend of yours in jail. Now we want you to accommodate us. We want visas into the States."

Bennett kept his cool and said, "I'm not sure what I can do for you from this end."

The PLO man made himself clear. "Well, you will have to think about this and get back to us. We told you before, we'd like you to stay."

PLO's hand now caressed my thigh, right under Bennett's nose. I stood, an involuntary reaction to being touched inappropriately. It was the message to end the night. Bennett followed my lead.

"We will see you later," said the man from the PLO.

The Ambassador of Afghanistan departed with, "Good luck at the jail."

The two men who guarded the door paused for a moment and let us go by. We went straight to the elevator.

As soon as the elevator door closed, Bennett turned to me and said, "There is no way I can help them get visas. Only people with a lot of power and money have cars like that."

We were in danger, but for the moment we were thrilled to have gotten away. We opened up the door to our room and locked it. The white wedding dress collapsed to the floor as we stripped each other naked. Danger had made our attraction even stronger; the night's peril pushed us to devour life and each other. Bennett's tender mouth passionately unlocked the secret that had been silenced between my legs. I was taken over the top in an ecstasy that surged through my body for the very first time. I gasped as though I'd taken my first breath.

This was what had been stolen from me by my mother, shamed beyond exploring, scrubbed into denial. This is what my mother feared and missed, or knew and destroyed: the carnal, overwhelming truth of life.

I lay there in awe. My body in its twenty-one years had never shuddered in this way. The physical elation rendered me spent. It was so powerful. I had to learn much more about . . . the awe.

He held me and apologized for not telling me everything. Bennett wanted to see this American prisoner and hoped to help him. "I'm sorry I didn't tell you sooner, but I'm going to the jail in the morning," he said. "I have to try for the sake of the family, and I know you have to do something about those special papers from the airport. Will you be okay alone?"

After what I just experienced, I felt like I could rule the world. "I'll find us some underwear!" I said confidently. He laughed and rolled over to kiss me.

Bennett went to the jail and I got directions for where to go to deal with the papers and the underwear. I walked around the back of the Riviera and a soldier poised on the corner smiled at me. Did he know? Could he tell by just looking at me what had happened to me last night?

I found a little café and had breakfast. My awareness now acute, I was able to see beauty in saturated color. The women beside me ordered a plate of *pan*, or sweet rolls, and egg sandwiches, then topped that off with thick French toast laden with syrup. Beer replaced coffee and they ate it all with vigor.

Taking my little map to find the underwear, I walked around the building to an area where I saw dozens of people standing in line. I tried to blend into the crowd, as much as a blonde in a big white dress could.

When the doors opened, people rushed to get a piece of what looked like a very sad pizza, plain dough with red sauce smeared and barely sprinkled with cheese. They all devoured it like they had not eaten in days. I moved in to examine the merchandise. There were no boxes of cereal or jars of mayonnaise, not even a bag of flour. It was shocking. People had few choices and no meat, bread, or candy. I found some shoes and boots, all plastic. They bore the Russian stamp and were poor quality. I thought about how much these beautiful people, denied by Castro's communist regime, could be helped by the bounty of America just ninety miles away.

There in a pile were bunches of yellow, green, blue, and pink underwear, worse than the granny panties mother sent. They were unisex, see-through mesh, and one size fits all. I laughed, imagining Bennett's reaction to these. I took out a few coins as a crowd gathered around me. They were all trying to give me stamps in exchange for the coins. They didn't have money, but instead a booklet of papers like food stamps. They wanted to trade the coupons needed to buy things for the actual money. I walked out with four pair of Cuban underwear and some stamps.

It was time to deal with my "special papers."

I taxied past the large buildings of the city and five miles out to a very remote area dotted with broken-down homes. When the cab stopped in front of a run down, two-story stucco house barricaded by a chain-link fence, I thought it had to be a mistake.

"*Perdóname, Señor, mira numeros, es la verdad?*" (Excuse me, sir, look numbers, is this true?) "*Sí, sí, sí,*" the cabbie said.

I got out and instructed him to wait. "*Uno momento, por favor.*" He took off. "*NO, NO ESPERO! AYÚDAME!*" Crap.

I looked at my destination, a dirty house with no sign of life except the chickens and goats that scurried in the dust blown up by the fleeing cab.

This wasn't looking good, but I thought I'd just have to give it a go. It's amazing what good sex can make you do. I opened the gate and walked up the large concrete staircase that wound

up to a massive wood door, where a tarnished brass doorknock-
er waited for me to do something. I climbed up and knocked. I
didn't feel very good about this, so I turned to leave, but then
the door opened.

The man was huge, his six-foot-three frame filling the doorway.
Bald, mustached, stinking of cigars, and garbed in green fatigues,
he towered over me. I had never felt so small. With all the medals, bars, stars, and stripes on his chest, he must have been a big
muckety-muck in Cuba. He stood there, looking me up and down
and then stopping for a menacing stare. I looked him straight in
the eye. He commanded me to come in: *"Entra ahora!"*

He stepped back as I walked in, and my bare shoulder
rubbed against his chest and scraped one of his medals. I could
feel his eyes all over me, and the hair on the back of my neck
rose, just like when I met Frank the boss.

He ordered me to sit down in a chair in front of his massive
desk. *"De dónde eres?"* he asked. (Where are you from?)

"Los estados unidos."

"DÓNDE?" he demanded.

"Milwaukee," I responded.

He laughed and said, *"La ciudad de la cerveza!"* (The city
of beer!)

I nodded quickly in agreement.

Then he waved his hand and said another long sentence
in Spanish that I did not understand, and I said, *"Pardóname,
Señor, pero me habla poco español."* (Excuse me, sir, but I only
speak a little Spanish.)

That set him off. He threw his hands around, pounded the
desk, grabbed a cigar, and just kept yelling and pointing at my
papers. My thoughts raced as I looked at the spinning ceiling
fans, the window blinds, and the maps on the wall. *People don't
leave this country—they go missing, end up in jail, or dead!*

Suddenly I heard the Voice: *SING!*

"*Mi trabajo es cantar!*" I said. (My job is to sing!)

And then it just flew out of my mouth: "Glitter and Be Gay" from Leonard Bernstein's musical *Candide*. Señor general, or whatever he was, seemed delighted, and when I picked up the tempo after the introductory section he grinned on either side of his cigar and clapped along. I swept through every verse of the coloratura song, pelting the humid air with flurries of high notes. As a finale, I threw my head down and tossed my hair back up as I sang the last flourish of musical laughter, "Ha ha ha ha ha haaaaaaaaaaaa!" Flushed and winded, I ended with a curtsy and a bow.

He was silent. I sat down and he looked to where my breasts were strapped down, now heaving as I tried to catch my breath. I had just sung for my life. And then I smiled. I smiled so hard I thought my face would stick that way. He smiled back, stamped my passport, signed the papers, and said in perfect English, "Miss Fries, if you ever come back to Cuba, make sure you can speak the language."

I nodded in agreement, "*Gracias, gracias!*" and scooted out of there. My dress was stinking wet from fear. I walked back the five miles to the hotel. Some children who liked the color of my hair followed me. I was happy to have the company.

Things had not gone well for Bennett at the jail. We went down to the saltwater pool and I took a swim. As Bennett sat and read, he brooded. Some Russian Olympic water polo players offered us Russian beers and we both loosened up. When we decided to get ready for dinner, I found it impossible to wash the saltwater out of my hair. Still feeling slimy from my afternoon, I tried to explain what had transpired at the "General's" office.

"I don't know how it happened, Bennett, but I just heard this voice tell me to sing, and I belted out this song I'd been rehearsing."

Bennett didn't seem interested in my unique experience. Instead, he asked, "Does that voice tell you you're wasting your life in Milwaukee, and if you had any talent, any skill, you'd be in New York, Chicago, or Los Angeles?"

Without a beat, I launched back, "Oh, and like you're the brightest bulb in the box. You, who got us into this situation—you, who promised me a weekend in Jamaica, not a holiday in Havana—give me a fucking break!"

I grabbed his new underwear and threw it at him, and he tackled me to the floor. He pinned me down and started to sing, "Feelings, nothing more than feelings."

"Oh, you can't sing your way out of this!" I yelled and struggled.

He continued, "Whoa, whoa, whoa, feelings . . ."

"Oh, my God, you really *can't* sing!" He just kept on until I said, "Okay, I give, I *give!* Just shut up!" We both laughed so hard, unable to catch our breath at the insanity of the situation we found ourselves in.

I went to bed with that bad singer. We stayed there all night, fearful of running into our friends, but happily working off our pent-up anxiety.

Our plane was scheduled to take us back to Jamaica the next day at one p.m. That morning, Bennett had one more chance to make headway on the young man's situation at the jail. We were both tired of the intrigue; we just wanted to get back to our Jamaican holiday.

Sporting a clean pair of pink Russian underwear, I put the venerable tube top and shorts back on. I left the dress behind in the hotel room—maybe someone else could enjoy it.

On the watch for any of our new "friends," I left through the back door of the hotel, grabbed a cab, and took off to the airport. I hoped Bennett was waiting for me there and had been successful at the jail. He caught up with me at twelve forty-five with minutes to spare, but there was no plane. We waited until one-thirty, and then Bennett looked at me and said, "I don't want you to be upset, but I think they got rid of our plane and are trying to keep us here. It's just a matter of time until they'll be coming for us, so our only recourse is to go the American Intersection." The relations between Cuba and the United States were not on good enough terms to have an Embassy in Cuba; it was called an Intersection.

"Oh, my God, Bennett, the men who stood at the door in the Rivera lounge just walked in over there!" Bennett looked over my shoulder and said, "Go into the ladies' bathroom and see if there is a window."

"Bennett, I saw a door out to the street from the luggage room."

"Good. I'll go through there and get us a cab while you go over to that vendor and use some of your acting skills to pretend you're going to buy an ice cream. You'll be able to come out the same door as I do. Now go!"

I casually walked over to the vendor and looked over the list of treats. Now I had a reason to use my intuition, which worked like a set of eyes in the back of my head. As soon as I felt that the men were not watching me, I darted around the corner. Bennett had grabbed a cab, and we were off.

I was now noticeably frightened. If they had the power to get rid of our plane, they had the power to do anything. I broke down in the cab. Bennett was upset—he didn't know what to do with my emotions or his.

We arrived at the U.S. Intersection where hundreds of people were waiting in line to get in. "What are all these people doing here?" I asked.

"They want visas. Castro makes it impossible for people to leave his country. Only after pursuing visas for years can they get in to other countries, and they must have relatives abroad to visit in order to leave." We walked to the front of the line with our American passports and were given immediate clearance.

The entrance led to an open office area with many desks where people were busily working and obviously surprised to see us. We were told to meet with Ed Beffel, an attractive man in a polo shirt with a tan and shaggy brown hair. He reviewed our passports and papers, and then looked at me and said, "You're from Milwaukee?"

"Yes."

"That's my hometown. I was just there two years ago working on the mayoral campaign for Dennis Conta."

"I know Dennis," I said. "I met him at the restaurant where I work. What a small world."

Ed got serious. "It's not a good idea to try and go back to Jamaica. They will follow you. It's best to get you out of the country as soon as possible. There's a plane leaving for Miami early tomorrow morning. It's full, so we'll have to remove two people for you to get on, but there's really no other choice."

We would be the reason two Cubans who had waited years for their freedom would not get it. I was heartsick until Ed said, "I'm not going to discuss the seriousness of the men you encountered, but let's just say you had somebody upstairs looking out for you." His hand pointing upward gestured to where I hoped my prayers had gone. "You will stay with me and my wife tonight, and we will get you out early."

Bennett was very happy, and so was I.

Ed's wife, Brenda, greeted me right away. "Ed says you haven't had a proper bath in days," she said. "Give me your clothes and I'll wash them for you. Oh, and here's some Prell shampoo."

I was thrilled. If anything could clean the salt out of my hair, it was that thick green magic. I was moved by her kindness in helping me. "Thank you so much," I said. "I'm sorry, but we don't have any other clothes. They kept our bags in Kingston."

She shook her head. "How did you get here from Milwaukee?" she asked.

"Long story."

"Well, don't worry. I have something for you to wear tonight, and I will have these clothes clean for you in the morning."

We could finally relax. The four of us sat around the kitchen table eating and laughing, a stark contrast to the guards with guns who paced in front of the barred windows of their home. Ed noticed me watching the guards and said, "Insurance."

Brenda served us a sumptuous Cuban stew and poured Russian white wine into coffee cups while Ed explained the good and bad of Castro. "The most dangerous man you met up with was the Secretary of the PLO."

Bennett let his guard down to say, "I have to say, as much as I have traveled to Third World countries, this time I was shaken up a bit." I was surprised at his frankness.

"The mistake was allowing you in the country in the first place," Ed said. It was a sobering reality check for all of us.

The next morning Brenda suggested we dress me down a bit. I pinned my Prell-clean hair up in a bun and Brenda gave me a top to cover my tube top. "This might keep their eyes off you until you are on the plane." I was so grateful for her help.

Ed and two guards took us to the airport. The plane was packed, and everyone except us were giddy with excitement. They had dreamed of the day they could leave Cuba. The sun was rising over the tops of the trees, time passed, and it was getting warm. My head ached from the previous night's wine. "Why are we not moving?" I asked.

Bennett was tense and agitated. To make it worse, we sat on the runway for hours. Babies were crying and I felt guilty for bumping two people off the plane. Bennett's failure of helping the young man at the jail had disappointed him. The seriousness of his thwarted plans left our romance in the bed of the Riviera. I was relieved to be going home.

Finally, the plane slowly taxied onto the runway, and then stopped. We could see both sides of the runway, dense with low brush. I felt like a sitting duck, and fear set in. I halfway hoped Bennett would break into another rendition of "Feelings," but he just sat there pale, gripping the arms of his seat.

After a flurry of Spanish voices, the plane began to move. Screams, then gunshots—we looked out the window. Three men were running to the plane from the fields. The passengers screamed as the guns fired. One of the young men outside, the one in a white t-shirt and closest to the plane, fell to the ground, and then we were off. Once in the air, we could no longer see what was happening down below. The passengers were quiet. We silently wondered about the young man as we flew through the clouds.

The ninety-mile flight was short, but so far away. As we landed there were screams of joy, laughter, clapping, singing, and crying, but none of it came from Bennett or me. He was sullen as he ushered me past all the Cuban passengers to one of the ticket counters.

"Okay, I have my ticket to Los Angeles, and here's yours to Chicago."

I looked at him. "Not Milwaukee?"

He tilted his head in irritation and said, "My credit is maxed out. You can get a bus to Milwaukee, and I'll reimburse you."

"Bennett, it's November and I'm in a tube top and shorts!"

"I'm sorry, Marla, but this is the best I can do. Your plane leaves in twenty minutes. I'll call you when I get back to Los Angeles."

He tried to hold on to me to create some kind of Casablanca good-bye, but I was disturbed. This was how we were going to leave each other after what we had just been through? I was too tired and disappointed to stand there and argue. Maybe these things happened to him all the time, but not to me. I was in awe of life, me, and the wild adventure he dragged me into.

Since Bennett would not take care of getting me home, I had to. Just like the word *SING* had popped into my head in the "General's" office, a family's name, *the Bonnards,* flashed through my mind. I pulled out of his grasp, ran to the phone, and placed a collect call to Sharon Bonnard, the mother of my college boyfriend Bill, who lived near the airport. She was my size, and I could use a coat.

"What are you doing in Miami?" she asked.

"Sharon, I'll tell you later. My luggage was lost and my flight is about to leave. Is there any way you can meet me with a coat?"

"Oh, Marla, we're leaving for Florida, but Bill is here. I'll pull together some clothes and he'll meet you." I was grateful. We didn't chat much, but she was intrigued about why I was stuck in Miami in a tube top and shorts.

The 747's door closed immediately after I walked inside. The flight was almost empty as I sat across from a couple nuzzling and cooing in Spanish. I moved to the middle of the plane in a row all by myself, wrapped myself up in three blankets, and broke into sobs. The flight attendants kept handing me small bottles of Rémy Martin, one after another, until the hysterical woman in seat C7 stopped crying.

The flight gave me the space to release the entire ordeal. I had held it together and listened to my gut, and now the whole experience washed through me. No matter what the goodbye was like, I had the romance, danger, and international politics graduate courses of a lifetime. I landed numb and quiet in cold, snow-spitting Chicago.

Very tan, blonde, and bombed, I got off the plane wrapped in a blue United blanket. Ex-boyfriend Bill ran to my gate and handed me a bag of his mother's clothes. I had nothing to say through my dried, drunken tears except, "Thank you."

Wearing his mother's turtleneck, brown-and-white checked pants, and my blue blanket, I was able to brave the cold November night and board a Greyhound back to Milwaukee. I arrived a different person than the one who had left. Two weeks later, my bags, which had been held hostage in Jamaica, arrived.

Bennett and I never de-briefed on our trip. I think he was just too embarrassed that our tryst had taken such a turn, but I was happy that he had given me the greatest gift. No amount of peril could take away my first orgasm that he helped me find in Havana.

Back in Milwaukee, as a thank you for all of his kindness (and also an avoidance of having to explain where I had been for the last two weeks), I gave Joe tickets to the opera's latest show, *The Beggar's Opera*. That happened to be the opera Kurt Weill adapted as *The Threepenny Opera* a couple of centuries later. The haunting signature song followed me home . . .

On my way back from the theatre, a tall, silver-haired man was waiting by the elevator in my building. I heard the Voice—*pay attention*. The man acknowledged me and held the doors open as I got in. I pressed the button for the seventh floor. I had not seen this man before. He was attractive in his navy blue cashmere coat and perfect features that complimented his very tanned skin. He neglected to press any buttons.

"How long have you known Joe?"

He took me by surprise. Had he seen me give Joe the tickets? Why was he asking me this, and where did he get that tan? I just looked at him and said, "Excuse me?"

His words were premeditated. "How long have you known Joe Balistrieri? Do you see him often? Do you know what he does?"

When the door slid open, I stepped out and turned around to see what he was going to do. He just stood in the elevator with his hands in his coat pockets, the top of his head glowing from the light. He didn't move. I told him a partial truth. "I worked at the restaurant, but I don't anymore." I watched until the elevator door closed to make sure he wasn't going to follow me, and then ran to my apartment. *Time to move,* I heard.

My Milwaukee mob could be just as dangerous as my international gangsters. Cuba had made me a woman, and I was learning to listen to and act on the messages I received from the Voice and the benevolent source that was watching over me.

9

Destiny

*"Human beings, vegetables, or cosmic dust, we all dance to a
mysterious tune, intoned in the distance
by an invisible piper."*
—*Albert Einstein*

I still had drive, ignorance, and intuition, the perfect combination to move to a new city where I knew no one. I took a train to Chicago and walked along Michigan Avenue, where Water Tower Place, the Drury Lane Theater, and John Hancock Center towered over patrons. I was pushed to turn down Delaware Street, where the apartment buildings looked posh and expensive. This area was not designed for the budget of a fledgling singing actress/waitress, but one building felt like it could be my home. Just as another tenant was giving notice, I showed up. I moved into that studio apartment with my few clothes, two chairs, and a non-sleeper sofa that I'd sleep on. I didn't know what compelled me, but I had no fear about looking for jobs, naively confident that I could do just about anything after surviving the mob and Cuba.

Cosmo man had inferred that if I had any talent I would be in New York, Chicago, or Los Angeles, so I traded the language of Milwaukee opera for ballsy cabaret singing at Chicago's Gaslight Club. The bar was a throwback to the original 1920s-era speakeasies that inspired the Playboy Clubs. We didn't have the signature tails and ears, but we had fringe that wiggled as we sang. It was also a step back for women's rights. I left after two months. I got a sales job at a clothing store in Water Tower Place and a waitressing job at the East Bank Sports Club. I started working trade shows, selling toaster ovens and rice cookers, and flying to Vegas to introduce new techno gadgets at the Consumer Electronics show. I now had money to begin professional training as an actress. I had found my destiny.

Joe Balistrieri came down to see me in Chicago. He picked me up in a cab and drove to a secluded place in Lincoln Park where we sat on a bench and talked.

"You've grown up," he said. He was pale, melancholy, and out of place away from his Milwaukee world. He had been playing a role all his life, and like me, he'd grown weary.

"Joe, do you ever think of leaving Milwaukee to work as an attorney someplace else?" I asked.

"It's a nice idea, Marla, but I don't think it's going to happen." He changed his tone and teased me. "We miss you at the Shorecrest. Even at the restaurant."

We hugged, and then parted. I didn't swoon as I had so many times before when smelling his cologne. I took that as a sign that I was moving on.

Many years later I learned that my friend Geno, the maître d' at Snug's who'd secured an audition for me at the Milwaukee Opera Company, was the brother of Dominic H. Frinzi, Frank Balistrieri's personal attorney. Known as the "opera-loving" attorney, Dominic was a great supporter of all the opera venues in town. I guess Geno had more up his sleeve than gold cufflinks to help me land my first job with the Milwaukee Opera Company.

It also came to light that while I was working at Snug's restaurant, the FBI had hidden a microphone at the table where creepy Frank had his red phone, and where I served him coffee. FBI special agent Joseph Pistone, who was working undercover in New York city as the real "Donnie Brasco," went to Milwaukee with another undercover agent to meet with Frank Balistrieri and create a partnership in a vending machine company.

Taped conversations provided the feds with enough evidence to indict Frank of skimming over two million dollars from the Vegas Fremont Hotel and Casino and the Stardust. Agent Pistone stated that when Frank Balistrieri had been caught, he laughingly admitted to Pistone and the other agent that he had been getting ready to murder them.

Frank got thirteen years in prison and he died soon after. Joe and younger brother John were convicted of extortion. Both got two years and had their licenses to practice law revoked.

Away from the drama of Mother, the hog farm, and mobsters, I had time to be with just me. What I found was a never-ending anxiety simmering inside. I couldn't calm my buzzing nervousness. I picked at my skin, bit my nails, and scratched my scalp. An irrational fear and terror haunted me even when things were going great. Although I knew I was being guided by a Voice that had saved my life more than once and helped me find where I needed to be, I didn't know how to handle this internal upset that came long before Cuba or Stan the man.

I decided to make sure Jesus found me by making Chicago's Fourth Presbyterian Church my second home. I sang with the Sunday night choir, taught art to kids from the Cabrini Green projects, and served turkey dinners to the homeless. But after going to Cuba, I was completely disillusioned with the notion of any religious group that believed it had special privileges over others. I believed in something greater. If Jesus was Jesus, he would not ignore unfortunate Cubans or Cabrini Green kids, or anyone else for that matter. He would save us all. I didn't believe that Jesus would demand that people become card-carrying club members for access to heaven over others. I knew he was busy with people who needed more help than I did, but if Jesus had time, I wouldn't mind some help with the anguish that plagued me.

Very early one morning the phone rang. "Marla . . ."

It was my father. He never called me.

"Daddy? Daddy, what's wrong?"

"Your mother had a heart attack. Come home."

My father and sister waited for news from the doctor in the waiting room. I sat on the only chair in the hall across from the brown door marked ICU. The fluorescent hospital light pulled from my eyes tears of a deep and frightened cry. Linoleum floors and green walls bounced laughter from the nurses down the hall. Didn't they know my mother was in that room? Didn't they care that she was dying?

Somehow, I knew she had to live for both of us. Cornered by the possibility of death and the hope that someday she might love me, I begged—*please, God, don't let my mother die. Please, Jesus, let her live.*

Mother, can you see me? I'm out here in the hall. Look! I'm wearing the dress you gave me, my hair is curled, my lipstick is on, I'm thin—I'm just the way you want me to be! Please, God, let her live, to live for herself and to live through me.

Mother had suffered a massive heart attack brought on by the news that my father owed seventeen thousand dollars to the IRS. Selling the farm had a price. So did the pain and suffering of their relationship. Her heart broke, but mother survived. Her blue-black toes and fingers reminded my father of his guilt and shame, and for many months to come he rubbed them back to life, slowly watching the stain of death disappear.

It was the first time I ever saw my father kiss my mother. Perhaps it was a restart for her heart on many levels. Her near-death experience gave me even more impetus to get myself into that TV box, become a successful actress, and give her more hope for some happiness.

I registered with some talent agencies, and within two years I'd done a few newspaper ads, modeled winter coats and boots, tasted pickles for a local *Shoppers Guide*, and landed a few commercials and my first acting job on TV co-starring in a cop show called *Lady Blue*. The story line for the episode was about two murderous brothers who had been abducting girls and killing them in a van. I played a nurse, their last victim who gets rescued by the cops, Jamie Rose and Danny Aiello. My co-star, who taunted me into the van, tied me up, and put duct tape over my mouth, was a young, unknown Johnny Depp. Lots of car chases had me rolling around in the back of that van for three days with Johnny. He was a funny, frustrated star in the making who argued with the director and was clearly cut out for something much bigger. He laughed at me because I was tied up and gagged, and I laughed and cried behind the duct tape at his antics. Who knew that my first dramatic role on television would be with a guy who years later would become a major star and eventually play the lead role of Donnie Brasco, the name for undercover FBI agent Joseph Pistone (who infiltrated my Milwaukee mob), opposite Al Pacino in a movie called *Donnie Brasco*?

I could not wait to share my great success with my mother. It had taken me eight years of hard work (and harder life lessons) from the time I left the heartland of small-town America to finally be on TV—in that little box she loved. I called home after the show aired to hear her excitement. I finally had done something I hoped would make her happy.

"Why the hell did they put tape over your face and make you roll around in that damn van?" Mother asked. "I told everyone to watch and you barely got to talk!"

Her anger and criticism activated terror with just a phone call. Even though I was far away and no longer subjected to her physical abuse, the pain still lingered. I decided to look for someone to help me.

But this was before self-help shows like *Oprah*, *Dr. Phil*, and *Intervention*, and way before the internet, which put everything conceivable at our fingertips. I had to go old school and let my fingers do the walking through the Yellow Pages.

My thumbs must have made my choice.

The waiting room was dark orange with strange wooden masks lining the walls. Black fertility statues of big-breasted females and visibly excited males peered at me from every table. Looks like Evanston, Illinois's version of Freud likes to talk about *sex*, I thought.

The door burst open. "Come in, Miss Fwees," he said.

Oh, no, he has an accent. His teeth clicked as he started to ask me questions. "So, tell me abaout yor akzietty. Vhat makes you so ankshous? Tell me about your muddar," click, click.

This wasn't really fair to him or me. He sounded like Elmer Fudd. I stood and said, "I'm sorry, this doesn't feel right. I'm not ready to do this now."

I walked back to the train, upset that I couldn't start the process of helping myself. I felt compelled to find answers. Another thought popped into my head: Maybe a "psychic" could help me.

The snow was just starting to melt when I hiked to the Andersonville brownstone of a woman I had heard was a talented psychic, Sonia Choquette. A handsome young man answered the door and ushered me into a softly lit room. "Have a seat. Sonia will be in in a moment."

I sat at the little round table covered with a lavender cloth where a deck of neatly stacked playing cards waited for Sonia as well. She came in, beautiful, lithe, and gentle, with a bright and graceful smile. She was in her mid-twenties, just like me.

I had never been to a psychic and didn't know what to do or expect, so I sat with my mouth shut and eyes wide.

Her sweet voice began to tell me things as she shuffled the cards, but then she laughed and snapped into a powerful, animated voice. "Your intuitions have been held back, but that'll soon be over. You, Marla, are moving to Cleveland, and your life will never be the same. *And*, you will be brought to great acclaim!"

Wow, Cleveland—how did she know that? I had just started dating Denny, whom I'd met in Vegas, where I'd been demonstrating a Sony doodad at a consumer electronics show. Denny was moving to Cleveland. Great acclaim? Are you kidding me?

It wasn't necessarily the impressive information Sonia delivered with her calm resolve that changed me forever; it was how she mirrored something that was so familiar right under the surface of my skin. It was as if a switch had flipped on and she could see my beautiful, naked intuition. After years of having my gifts doubted and buried, I was validated and empowered.

Sitting with Sonia that day released a lifetime of fears.

The next piece of Sonia's "brought to great acclaim" prediction was revealed a few months later on a hot and crowded Chicago train. I was with Denny, and we were confused about which stop to get off to go to a certain theatre. I turned to my left and watched an attractive, intense, and rather short Italian man, dressed all in black, get on the train. I immediately found myself pushing through the crowd like a heat-seeking missile to get next to him. I "knew" that this man would give me the right directions.

"Yes," he said, "get off at the next stop, Belmont." And then he cocked his head, smiled, and asked, "Hey, do you sing?"

I laughed and declared, "Do I!"

Jim Corti was an up-and-coming Chicago director and choreographer. He handed me his card and said, "I'm directing a musical in Cleveland and I'd like you to audition for me." Cleveland? Could this be the place of great acclaim?

I had heard about places in Hollywood where young starlets were discovered—maybe it could also happen on Chicago's L train. Within weeks I was cast in the Midwest premiere of the musical *A . . . My Name Is Alice* at one of the best repertory companies in the country, the Cleveland Play House, where I stayed as a company member for two years.

It wasn't just the acting career that got turned on—Sonia had flipped my intuitive switch, and I was burning bright. I just didn't know how to control the burn.

10

Words

*"Words have no power to impress the mind without
the exquisite horror of their reality."*
—Edgar Allan Poe

I walked into a hair salon and said, "Cut it all off." I was tired of trying to make my long, fine hair do something.

When I was a child, Mother had lightened my hair with Marchand's Golden Hair Wash and tightly wrapped my locks around pink foam curlers that I had to sleep in every night in an attempt to make me look acceptable in her eyes. Sometime between my freshman and sophomore years of high school she started taking me to the beauty parlor to have my hair "frosted." When I came back from my first semester in college she had hung Farrah Fawcett's famous red bathing suit poster on my bedroom door. I wasn't allowed to put posters of anything or anyone on any surface in my room, but she was. I didn't look like Farrah and never would. Yet I couldn't convince her that my follicles held no hope. I found freedom in cutting off all the trying.

I was ecstatic heading off to Cleveland with my new pixie "do." I felt beautiful, a word I never used to describe myself, a word I never felt until I cut off all my hair.

Jim, the director I'd met on the train, loved my new look. He crafted a wonderful show and kept me under his wing as his new protégé. We celebrated "great acclaim" together and knew we would be friends forever.

I started to explore Cleveland and found the best place for buffalo wings, miso soup, and shopping on Coventry Avenue. I was standing in a bookstore when a book flew off the shelf and landed at my feet. I bent down, turned it over, and laughed. Shirley MacLaine was smiling at me. Her book, *Out on a Limb*, was the perfect read to boost my new professional stage career and metaphysical life.

I wanted to learn more. I went to the Cleveland library, where I found Jane Robert's "Seth" books. I felt I had found a family heirloom, or the diaries of a grandmother I had never met. The idea that Jane went into a trance and took notes from an entity called Seth, who talked about consciousness and the nature of personal reality, was fascinating. Where did that entity come from, and how did Jane do that? What was it for? I hadn't come to Cleveland to study metaphysics ... or had I?

My first year at the Play House was driven by my delirious excitement of being in a professional rep company. What more can you add to great success? A torrid love affair.

Rodney had the emotional unavailability of my father along with curly brown hair, ruddy skin, deep brown eyes, a powerful hay-bailing farmer-boy body, and limited verbal skills. He was better when he kept his mouth shut. Our passionate frenzy needed no subtitles. When he finally did open his mouth, out flew the fact that he had been in a relationship for three years. Having no respect, at the time, for delicate boundaries with females and blind to karma, I proceeded, thinking I could handle being part of a triangle. I couldn't.

The next year, when Rodney was back with his girlfriend, I continued my dalliances. At the same time I found myself on a tear of intuition.

It happened when I was on stage in the middle of the musical, *The 1940's Radio Hour*. I stepped to the microphone to join two other actresses to sing "Boogie Woogie Bugle Boy." Right in the middle of the first line . . . there was a flash in my mind—an apartment filled with smoke. A sense of catastrophe began building up in my head. I finished the song, but could not shake the images. Did I leave ravioli on the stove? Forget to turn off the coffee pot? No, it had an automatic shut off. My head was filled with panic.

I had a big jitterbug number coming up. Holding on tight to my partners' hands was the only way to finish my favorite part of the dance with the cross-handed flip, but my hands were sweating. There was danger brewing. My mind was a blur for the last half hour of the show. I don't even remember flipping. I ran to the green room phone and called my building super. "Mr. Travers, it's Marla in Four B. I'm sorry to call so late, but have you had any calls from tenants smelling smoke?"

"Nope. Just made the rounds before I had to shovel off the steps. You know, I changed the bulb in the hall—"

"Thanks, Mr. Travers, I gotta go."

I sat on the floor of the green room wondering what the hell was going on. Alan, another actor friend, asked me to go have a drink before driving home. "Yes, a drink sounds right," I said. "My house or yours?"

"Well, mine is closer," he said.

We walked up the wooden steps to his kitchen door. The acrid scent of something burning startled us. Alan opened the door quickly. The burner on the stove was red hot. He'd left it on and the wooden handle to a saucepan had been singed off. A plate of butter was bubbling. We were amazed nothing else had caught fire and grateful we made the decision to go to his house.

was being guided by a force. I was beginning to see, feel, and hear other compromises. Things that needed to be fixed, situations in which someone or something could be harmed or in trouble—all sorts of crises became evident.

Alan was late for rehearsal one day, and no one knew where he was. I saw him in his tin can of a car sliding off the road in the snow. I felt the cold, but sensed no danger because he was safe. I seesawed all over the place with these comings and goings of images and feelings. I needed to feel grounded, and wished I had a foundation of love and a family.

I started rehearsals for Sam Shepard's 1979 Pulitzer Prize-winning play, *Buried Child*. I starred as Shelly, the girlfriend whom Vince, the other lead, brings home to meet his crazy, ranting, alcoholic family. Perfect casting.

I was smitten with my co-star, Jeffrey G., who played Vince. He was a powerhouse of sensual expression. Shorter than I, we were an unlikely couple, but I felt more free with him than I had with any other man. Behind closed doors, my sexuality unbound, I strutted around naked in high heels and argued with him for the sake of hearing myself talk. Much to the chagrin of the stage manager and techies, we used this chemistry before the curtain went up, while we were on stage, and after the curtain was down.

I had been having problems in a scene. Feelings must be organic, but I was stuck. I couldn't find the anger necessary for the action in the scene. Then the older actress, Evie McElroy, who was playing the mother, Halie (the hypocritical, promiscuous mother and grandmother to the strange Midwestern clan), walked passed me and made a crafty dig, "You can't act it, Marla. You have to be it."

My emotional life was hogtied. I didn't know my genuine emotions because I had not been allowed them. Emotions were too dangerous. There were too many painful consequences from the expression of authentic feelings, as Mother constantly reminded me.

So I hid behind the words of a story, the dialogue of a character crafted by someone else. "These aren't my feelings—these are the character's feelings." That way I didn't have to feel responsible for my truth. No wonder acting was so seductive. I could morph in and out of someone else's words, expressing all the craziness that I felt inside without being punished, but actually lauded and praised for "acting" the part. Some emotions were buried right under my skin, little land mines in my soul. The fear of being blown up could be triggered by just a phone call.

"Marla, we're coming see you in your show!" Mother was feeling feisty enough to travel outside her domain. I was feeling confident enough to entertain my parents as a successful actress.

The Play House had a celebrity club where Cleveland's finest would come to dine. I made reservations and invited Will Rhys, the artistic director of the company and director of *Buried Child*; Jeffrey G.; along with my understudy, Annie, an adorable actress who was not only after my role, but also Jeffrey.

My parents sat as strangers beside each other. My father was like a thought out of context, a foreigner who had just gotten off the boat. To others he seemed like a quiet, normal man.

"So, Mr. Fries, what did you think about the play?" Jeffrey asked.

I doubt if my father had ever been asked to comment on anything, let alone a piece of literature or theater. He was at a loss for words. "Well uh, it was uh, good. But what happened to the, uh . . . uh, the sister?" he asked.

There was no sister in the play, he was confused about the only other woman besides me in the play. Daddy's large hands fumbled with a glass of VO on the rocks. His pickled brain was searching for answers, but there were no hunting or fishing buddies to help him. He was an embarrassment for Mother as she pursed her lips and folded and refolded her napkin.

He was my daddy and before my heart broke my face into tears, I jumped in with some light humor. "Oh, you mean the crazy old mother Halie?" He smiled and chuckled.

I should have given my father books, a dictionary. He needed words.

My sister used words, crafting them to tell a cryptic story in poetry, artfully writing her way through the various modes of departure she took in her life. My mother used words as weapons and shields to defend or attack, her mouth a Gatling gun of text. But in public, Mother could craftily control her words. She was able to disguise her disgust of Daddy with a public invitation for me to come home for Christmas.

"Marla has not been home for Christmas in years," she said. "It would be so wonderful if she could just come and spend a few days with us. There are so many people who want to see her. We'd just love it." Everyone at the table nodded and Will, my director, said, "Of course, Marla, you should go!"

"Oh, my goodness, that would be wonderful," my father said as he smiled. Those rare and unfamiliar moments of Daddy using words to express love melted my heart. His words made me want to come home.

"Oh, Daddy, I'd like that," I said. But Shelly's dialogue from *Buried Child* burned in my head: *"This is really making me nervous, she doesn't want us here, she doesn't even like us. I don't believe in it, reuniting."*

The seven years of living far away from home in Milwaukee, Chicago, and now Cleveland perhaps gave me a false sense of security. I had reduced my communication with Mother to giving her what I thought would make her happy, photos and reviews of my successful and exciting life, a life that she could brag about. In this distancing I held out hope that if I changed and healed, so could she.

Her upsets seemed to go dormant for a brief time when the Christmas decorations came out: if you can't fix it, decorate it. Every year our house was a showpiece of holiday splendor. She tried to make a whole year of bad behavior disappear with showy gestures and piles of presents to blind everyone to what was really going on. But no piece of tinsel or gold could deflect the truth.

I had three days off for the holiday and took a six-hour bus ride that dropped me off in Bedford where the charm and beauty of the town I loved lulled me into a Currier and Ives fantasy. *I can handle a few days at home*, I thought. *Besides, I'm a rising star in Cleveland.*

There were calls from mother's friends. "When do we get to see you? We hear you are doing so well, a star of theatre, how exciting!" But I was exhausted from my eight shows a week schedule and just wanted to rest, so out came my comfy sweats as I flopped down on the sofa in the den.

"Dear God, you could at least fix your face, put on some makeup and look decent! I can't believe you chopped off all your hair, AND WHAT IN THE HELL ARE YOU WEARING?"

"Mother, you didn't have a problem with how I looked when you came to Cleveland. You told me in front of everyone how beautiful I was."

"Well, that was then. You're in my house now and I'm the one who has to look at you, so go change your clothes and put on some lipstick, for God's sake! I've got friends stopping by." The hourglass was flipped. She was the witch and I was Dorothy Gale—and my time was running out.

I had dreamed that if I were successful we would bond, that my accomplishments would bolster her self-esteem and she'd feel good, be kind, and not abuse me or anyone else. I believed that becoming a successful actress whom she and others could admire would solve everything. But Shelly's words were right. *"This is really making me nervous, she doesn't want us here, she doesn't even like us."* Was that the Voice warning me of the calm before the storm?

I started to shrink. "Who's coming by, Mother?"

"Bunny and Sherry are bringing a hat I ordered for you," she said.

Bunny Delany had the most successful dress shop in town. Sherry was the darling wife of Bunny's son, Page, who was my dentist. I loved them both and would be happy to see them, but I could not feel any joy. Something started to happen. I could not feel my feet, my hands, or my face. I became so very cold and started to tremble. The many years of my mother's incessant criticism, demanding I do things that might make me acceptable in her eyes, was closing in on me. My work wasn't enough and my hair, my clothes, the way I naturally looked without makeup, my feelings and thoughts were all unimportant. I hoped that maybe she would see me as an adult and not as the silent doll she had always dressed up. I rallied and made a plea. "Oh, Mother, can't we please just visit with them? I don't really need a hat or want one. Couldn't we just talk?" I begged.

She turned. "You're so ungrateful! I ordered it for you, and they're making a special trip to come up here and give it to you. I busted my ass making this Christmas nice for you, and I'll be dammed if you're going to ruin it!"

I had to get away from her; there was no being rational. I bolted upstairs to my father's office. Sitting in his swivel chair I looked at the photos of Daddy and me hunting in the woods, his pig trophies, and ribbons collecting dust. Where was he, and why couldn't he change this? My body shook with emotions that could not be expressed, and I collapsed into tears. This picture-perfect home was just a shiny sham, and I was tired of being a toy. My deep need for family and love had again blinded me.

I made a call to my friend, Tom, a chicken farmer from the neighboring town of Everett. I loved seeing him when I came home. Thoughts of being with Tom's loving family or snowmobiling through the woods gave me something to look forward to. No answer.

I had tried to contort myself to be a Marla that my mother would love and a Marla that I could live with—therein lay the rub. I felt I had no choice but to abdicate. I changed my clothes, fixed my face, and put on the mandatory lipstick.

Sherry and Bunny arrived. I could hear Mother swoop in to greet them with the flourish of a grand hostess as she orchestrated them into the divine living room. Bunny and Sherry gushed, "Oh, Reinette, this is just beautiful, and your tree is simply magnificent. I don't remember your home looking so grand." As I came down the stairs, I saw the glee that these words gave mother, and for a brief moment I thought all might be fine.

Mother gestured to me and said, "Well, here she is!" I hugged them both. I genuinely loved these women and was happy to see them.

"Marla, we are just so excited about your career. Are you having fun? What's it like?"

I looked at my mother. She was on the verge. Not of joy, love, or laughter but bitter, deep, poisonous resentment, the same look that would come across her face before she hit me with the yardstick. In that thin-sliced moment, I realized that my life plan to give her joy with my success had just the opposite effect. Dread started to consume me; I felt like I was dying. I could not bear to think that she hated me, so I diminished myself until all the joy of my life vanished. "Oh, well . . . you know, it's not New York or Broadway, it's just . . . Cleveland." I spiraled down a hole where at the bottom lie a beaten, dejected child.

It was a snowy, quiet Christmas morning. I was six years old and lying on my side, staring at the funny handles of my dresser drawers that looked like brass elephants. Did he come? Did Santa come and bring me any presents? Or was Mother right, that I had acted ugly all year and Santa skipped our house, like she predicted? I was terrified.

"Marla, are you going to get up?" Mother's cheery voice called from downstairs.

I put on my pink quilted robe and saw myself in the mirror. I still had the barrette in my hair, pulling back my bangs from the night before when I was vomiting. Christmas Eve panic, fearing Santa would be a no-show. I tentatively went down the stairs. What if there was coal in my stocking? Did I talk back too much? What could I have done to deserve being checked off Santa's list?

My father met me at the bottom of the stairs and said, "Oh, my goodness, you're shaking, let me warm you up." I wasn't cold, I was terrified. Christmas music was playing and I could hear wood popping in the fireplace. Then I saw the room. The tree was ablaze with what looked like hundreds of presents and dozens of unwrapped toys covered the floor and chairs like a department store display. My mother was wrong. Santa knew I had been good, and by God, there was the proof!

———✕———

Sherry handed me the box and I opened it and put on the hat. The mass of black fur with the knitted top smothered my head. I could not see out from under the dead animal. I took it off and said, "I'm sorry. Thank you so much for taking the time to drop this by, but it isn't the right size. I am so sorry you wasted your time." Mother was fuming. "Shit," she said, "put it back on and let me look at it!"

The ache welled behind my eyes as I was embarrassed that within seconds I would be reduced to tears of anguish that no one would understand. "No, Mother. Thank you, ladies. I'm so sorry, but I have to go." I felt like I could do nothing but run away. I flew up the stairs, threw off my clothes, and grabbed some jeans and a sweater. Would the hat have made me look so beautiful that she would finally love me, believe I was enough, and calm her nerves? No! I was going to go out into the country and find Tom and his family. My God, I would drive to the joy!

When I came down the stairs, Mother had just said goodbye to our guests and closed the front door. She turned, her face filled with a thousand grievances. "You're ungrateful and selfish! You acted so *ugly*—don't think you are keeping *any* of your presents!" And then she slapped me hard across my face.

I had no words. She needed the fight to feel her rage made physical, and then she could have a release. My entire childhood of little arms, legs, and buttocks welted to make her feel better flashed in my mind. I would not give her the satisfaction of what my pain and humiliation would yield for her.

I didn't go see Tom. I shut down. I methodically packed my bags, leaving behind the gifts I was not good enough for, and silently waited for my dad to come home and drive me to the bus station.

Neither Jesus nor my father had protected me. I had nothing to say to them on that drive out of town and past the holiday lights of other homes where good mothers lived. Acting was a means of emotional survival, a way for me to keep up a false front by hiding behind a character. Being myself was just too dangerous. I returned to Cleveland and resumed the *act*. I was beginning to see. My psychic awareness was slashing through, and yet I was trapped in the gauntlet of pain with my mother. I prayed for understanding. I prayed for insight.

Two weeks later I received a book in the mail from Mother, *You and the Law*. In the table of contents, the chapter "How to Disinherit Your Child" was highlighted and crookedly underlined twice by an arthritic, punishing, resentful hand.

I had found my anger. I had no problem using words to express it now, both on stage, and unfortunately, in my personal life. I coped with red wine and more drama as I shifted from Jeffrey G. to Alan, who was funny and emotionally arrested like Tom Hanks in the movie *Big*. We spent our days off in a little area called Chagrin Falls. As Alan fished in the lake, I read Whitley Strieber's *Communion*, a book that touched my soul. Words . . . important words that would alter my life twenty years later.

PART II

Insight

11

Unraveling the Act

"It will cost you sweat and tears, and perhaps . . .
a little blood."
—Nosferatu *(film, 1922)*

I moved back to Chicago and lived in a one-room apartment with a mini fridge, mattress, and microwave. The frustration of not being able to fix my family dynamic made me focus on work. *I'll just accomplish the pain away!* I told myself.

I'd been spoiled in the very best way from my two years of Repertory Theatre in Cleveland. With glowing reviews in hand, I tried to reacquaint myself with Chicago television and film casting directors. They weren't impressed.

I was fed up with selling toaster ovens and minivans at trade shows. I prayed for insight.

Within a few weeks I got a call from a friend living in L.A. who was looking for a roommate. Yes! In a fortuitous turn of events I received a small financial settlement from a lawsuit that made moving possible. Just thinking about the story behind that lawsuit still makes me break into a sweat. A month before I met Jim Corti on the Chicago train, I got all gussied up for a fun night on the town with my beautiful, leggy, tradeshow model friend, Julie. We started our evening with dinner at Maddie's Crab House restaurant. After just a few sips of my Chablis and three bites of my "seafood pan roast," I began to feel terrible. Within twenty minutes I was in a cab heading home. I got into the elevator with Mr. and Mrs. Steinberg, the sweet old couple who lived in the penthouse. As we stopped on my floor, the motion of the elevator settling brought on a wave of nausea. *Oh my God,* I thought, *I think I'm going to vomit right here, right now!* My mind quickly assessed that I was in trouble and needed to find a place. And there it was . . . I grabbed my purse, unzipped the top, and projectile vomited into it, right in front of the Steinbergs. When the doors opened, I didn't have time to apologize as I stuck my hand in my pants to keep from shitting on them and rushed out. I made it to my bathtub, where I lay purging uncontrollably from both ends.

There was a hospital right across the street from my apartment building, but 911 would not take me there because it was not considered a trauma hospital. I knew I was in serious shape when pain surged through my arms and legs and I heard the Voice: *Call the cops.* I had the presence of mind to retrieve my wallet from my purse that was also in the shower with me. The shiny finish on my leather wallet had been eaten off by whatever toxin my body was purging. Two Chicago cops came and carried me through the lobby and across the street to the hospital.

The doctors said that had I had a few more bites, or not arrived at the hospital as soon as I did, I might not have survived what they called paralytic shellfish poisoning. Julie, who only had one bite of my dinner, ended up on the shoulder of Lake Shore Drive, also having lost control of both ends in her brand new Pontiac. She ruined her Gucci purse and leather skirt and had to have the car towed.

Three days later, dressed in a hospital gown, I walked down the alley and back to my apartment building to recuperate. I called Maddie's Crab House to warn them about others getting sick, but instead of paying my hospital bill, the restaurant sent me coupons for free dinners. I sued them.

The judge ruled in my favor and with eleven thousand dollars I could now afford to move to Los Angeles. Strange how Spirit was working in my life. I packed up everything that would fit into my Mercury Lynx and drove across the country in the middle of January.

My new home was an apartment complex in North Hollywood where fifty-nine degrees was considered cold. I was in love with the palm trees, sunny days, and my new little home where all my neighbors were working or wannabe working actors.

I became a true student of the craft of acting with coaches Larry Moss and Edward Kaye Martin. Ed was the dynamic, passionate, opinionated, creative expression of every human emotion embodied in a bold, ruddy, strawberry blond, mustached man. I had briefly studied with him in Chicago, but he, too, loved the palm trees. I was so happy he accepted me as a student. For many of us, Ed's coaching represented an aspect missing in our war-hero fathers, emotional truth, which I had been craving all my life. My revelation in Cleveland of my need to "express dangerous emotions authentically" was now *demanded* by Ed. He was only interested in complete authenticity from his students. He could smell an "acted" moment a mile away. If we didn't "live" it and "be" it, it was shit. With every part I played, I found parts of me. I was unraveling my authentic voice.

Throughout my life, it had always been about the voice. Choked by an umbilical cord, numerous respiratory problems, and the fear of expressing myself, I ran to the safety of the basement and the record player, where I joined the voices of Motown, Carly Simon, and Carol King singing about love and heartache. I merged with the cast recordings of Broadway musicals and joy-filled choirs, singing the "O Come, All Ye Faithful" Christmas music and "Amazing Grace" hymns. These divine tones vibrating deep inside my bones along with breath, the prana of life, gave me life. Their harmonic resonances helped heal what my voice was trying to express. Ed's class was the new scary-as-shit-place for me to unravel more of the fear and work out the emotional mess of the little girl who had acted to survive. My heart was aching to speak the truth and my soul was demanding to tell it. We were all crushed when Ed was diagnosed with AIDS. He slipped away leaving behind a community forever changed by his love.

The AIDS pandemic was beginning to ravage its way across the country, devastating loved ones and even acquaintances. I met Marc Hirschfeld, a top L.A. casting director who was teaching an acting workshop. I had been fortunate to book my first guest-starring role in Hollywood on one of Marc's shows, 227. Marc invited me to join a group of actors and friends at a glitzy Hollywood club where he introduced his new talent find, The Blue Man Group. In this gathering was Alaina Reed, an actress I had just worked with on 227, and her husband, Kevin Peter Hall, a very tall, good-looking African-American from another Pennsylvania town, Pittsburgh. He had gained notoriety as Harry in the TV show *Harry and the Hendersons* and the creature in the hit movie *Predator*. Kevin was a gentle giant, the antithesis of the monster he played. I spent most of my evening with this loving couple and hoped I would see them again.

A few months later, Kevin died of AIDS, which he had contracted from a blood transfusion. Death was creeping in, and with the loss I felt the gaping void of family. In my desperation to find some connection, some love, I reached out to Mother. I had placated her with pictures and notes about my life over the last two years, and the sting of her slap had faded. Maybe she would be in a good mood, or maybe my daddy would answer and I could hear his voice for a brief time before he handed off the phone to Mother. Perhaps in the grief of death we might be able to bond and find compassion—together.

"Hello, Mother."

"Hello, Marla. Thanks a lot for the anniversary card."

I never sent my mother anniversary cards. I never felt they should have been married. But I still apologized. "I'm sorry, I guess it is your anniversary. Mother, remember that TV show I did a few months ago called *227*? I worked with that beautiful African-American woman, Alana Reed? Well, her husband just died of AIDS. He was a really sweet, gentle man. I went to dinner with them not too long ago and—"

She cut me off. "Well, he must have been gay. You don't die from that disease without being gay. And what are you doing hanging out with black people? I have to go—the girls are taking me to lunch for my anniversary." Click.

I lay on the bed immobilized by her hate. Why my mother behaved like she did would be a lifelong question. It was not so much about the why, but more about what to do in the face of her actions. I could not make her love me and was so tired of acting the role of the good daughter. It was time to stop the craziness and find help.

Judith Patterson, a warm, kind, compassionate woman, was my first therapist. Piece by piece, Judith helped me unravel the many layers of my trauma and drama. I felt safe enough to share the disturbing behavior that had no explanation and tell her what I could never tell anyone.

I could see myself as a six-year-old swimming around the bathtub with a bar of Ivory soap, practicing what I could remember from a TV commercial. *It's so pure it floats . . . you too can get so clean with Ivory.* Little did I know that I was destined to sell soap on television someday. Then Mother came in. It didn't matter if the door was locked or not, you could pop the button from the other side. There was no privacy in that house. "Okay, did you wash yourself?" she asked.

"Uh huh," I said, hunched over and fearful, not wanting to leave the safety of the tub.

"Get out and let me see." Mother stood over the sink, grabbed a coarse old washcloth and soaped it up with hot water. "Well, dry yourself off." I did as I was told. She thumped the toilet lid down and sat. "Come on." Mother was impatient.

This was the bath time routine for eleven years. She pulled me down on my back and laid me on top of her lap. I was too big to be on a lap. I held my breath as my mother spread my legs. The sting of the hot, rough cloth digging and scraping places that didn't need scrubbing didn't make sense. *I don't need this, I'm not dirty . . . I am already clean.*

"Oh, please stop!" I pleaded.

"I'm not finished." Mother seemed certain.

I stared at the ceiling and moved my mind up through the plaster into the attic and out into the night, flying to the amber-lit windows of families in the neighborhood, hoping they would see me and let me in. And for as long as it took, I was *gone.* I left my body behind, cold and numb. I could then reject my mother.

"Whatever your mother's intention was, Marla—shaming, hurting, cleaning, controlling—it didn't matter the reason," Judith said. "It was abuse."

Judith reflected back to me what a loving, normal mother could feel like. I learned words that described what was potentially wrong with Mother, psychological and pathological terms like "borderline" and "antisocial personality disorder," "narcissism," "Munchausen's by proxy," and "codependence" that helped give a context for her behavior. I read dozens of books about others who suffered from these mental afflictions and also, of course, about friends and family members of people so troubled. I was beginning to see how much I had survived, how I was destined to be intuitive, and that the benevolence of the Voice was becoming my greatest blessing. In *The Drama of the Gifted Child,* previously published as *Prisoners of Childhood,* Alice Miller helped explain my experiences:

There was a mother who at the core was emotionally insecure, and who depended for her narcissistic equilibrium on the child behaving or acting in a particular way. This mother was able to hide her insecurity from the child and from everyone else behind a hard, authoritarian, and even totalitarian façade. This child had an amazing ability to perceive and respond intuitively, that is, unconsciously, to the needs of the mother, for her to take on the role that had unconsciously been assigned to her.

I took a seminar with Dr. Peter Levine, an expert in healing trauma. Dr. Levine used a video of a gazelle being chased by a cheetah to illustrate the fight, flight, and freeze response. I was deeply anxious watching the gazelle try to escape the cheetah. The gazelle collapses, even before the cheetah sinks it teeth into its neck. It appears to be frozen in fear. When the cheetah walks away for a moment exhausted from the hunt, the gazelle bounces back to life and then runs away. I learned that the "freeze" response happens in humans too. Facing threats or traumatic circumstances victims become emotionally and physically immobilized, or even "leave their bodies" so they don't feel the attack. People like me. I realized there was much more to learn about fight, flight, and freeze.

I had stopped my mother's inappropriate bathroom behavior when I turned twelve, after the rape and murder of my classmate Kelly Jo Brallier. Now as an adult I cut the cord to the craziness, changed my phone number, and gave Mother a voicemail number that would never ring at my home. I stopped calling home, sent letters instead, and finally began to share what had happened to me. I had a lot to unravel. Yes, it would take time, but facing the abuse and talking about it instead of hiding, ignoring, or being paralyzed by the fear and shame was the only way to heal it.

After almost two years in L.A. I had appeared in a half a dozen national commercials selling toothpaste, cars, hamburgers, beer—you name it. I had guest starred as a bitchy stewardess on *Seinfeld* and on the only TV show a darling Sandra Bullock ever appeared in, *Working Girl*. The director of the show, Mathew Diamond, suggested I change my name from Fries to Frees. "If you want your name pronounced correctly and to shine in this town, then change the spelling," Matthew said. I contemplated severing myself from the family name altogether, but I heard, *Marla "frees" herself.* I liked the implication, so it stuck.

Even though I was in therapy and my career looked as if it was zippin' right along, I was itching for something. I wanted—no, I needed—the triumphs, heartaches, and connection of dysfunctional people bonding together for a common goal. I needed family, but for me that meant theatre. I was stuck in traffic on the 101 Freeway, frustrated and longing for the emotional connection and release the stage gave me. I gripped the steering wheel tight and yelled out loud, "Please, please, God, give me a show!"

Two days later Jim Corti called. He had discovered me five years before on the Chicago L train and took me to the Cleveland Play House. "Marla, I want you to come back to Chicago and play Lina Lamont in *Singin' in the Rain.*" Oh *yes*! This was what I wanted, a fabulous role in a terrific show. My little fit on the freeway had been heard. I'm not sure how these things work. This is a question I look at every day and it always fascinates me. Were my prayers being heard all the time, or did my pleas only hit the mark if they were made with heartfelt intention? Was everything already set up, and if so, how could I tap into it and feel it coming? I must have drawn in what my soul wanted, or really, what my soul needed. God heard me and delivered.

We had a terrific run of *Singin' in the Rain* at the Drury Lane Theatre in Oakbrook, Illinois. Lina Lamont was the dream role of a lifetime—the comic foil who couldn't sing, dance, or act, but who tried really hard. My sister drove down from Milwaukee and brought my mother, who uncharacteristically flew out to see my sister. I was delighted that they made the effort to come. They were gracious audience members, and perhaps my finally getting help indirectly helped them too.

Jim Corti directed and produced the show just like the movie, complete with silent movies and rain. All of us received rave reviews, a foreshadowing of my nomination the next year for Best Supporting Actress in a musical by Chicago's version of the Tony's, the Joseph Jefferson Awards.

My performance also caught the eye of the Nederlanders, big-time theatre producers who were interested in me reprising the roll of Lina at one of their theatres in Michigan. I was invited to New York City to meet with an agent to handle the contract. Lora Jeanne Marten, who played the role of Kathy Seldon in the show, lived in NYC and we decided we would make my trip a memorable one of dancing . . . and perhaps some romancing. Our first stop was The Waldorf Astoria. I was full of myself, as only someone in her twenties who senses herself a bright and shiny thing can feel.

I was dressed in a black, low-plunging body suit and fabulous white-and-black paneled skirt that was a dancer's dream. I could make that skirt move like a Japanese fan, and when I wore it I felt like a 1940s movie star. All I needed was some juicy, witty dialogue I could toss over my shoulder with aplomb and saunter off with a dashing leading man. I felt as if all the pieces of my scattered life had come together.

I stood outside the hotel waiting for Lora while she freshened up in the Waldorf's palatial restroom. It was getting dark, so I moved under the amber light of the street lamp where she would be sure to see me. The mid-July heat of New York was turning my sexy glow into full-on sweat, and I was getting that itchy psychic sensation that something exciting was about to happen. I was hot and my feet wanted to get moving. I heard a beat in my head that started the dance. I kicked up my leg with a long and high extension, spun around a couple of times, and let the skirt fall, creating enough breeze to cool me off. I didn't see him at first, as he slowly moved out of the shadows. His seductive voice reached out to me.

"That's quite a kick. Are you a dancer?"

His oversized aviator glasses and shaggy blond hair made him unrecognizable for a moment, but I knew the voice. I had admired this "A" list movie star's talent since I had been interested in becoming an actress. Let's call him—Homer.

"Who *are* you?" he asked. I was, of course, absolutely over the moon to meet him. I must have rattled on about what a fan I was even before I introduced myself. It was that weird kind of familiarity that fans think we have with stars because we have seen them up close on the big screen or in our living rooms, rented for the weekend. That doesn't mean we know them, and they certainly don't know us.

"I'm not really a dancer—well, I mean, I do dance, but—"

He smiled. "Are you staying here at the Waldorf?"

"No, I'm here visiting my friend who I just starred with on stage in Chicago—" *My God, I'm standing here with a man I've had a groupie crush on for years!* My heart was pounding out of my chest, my nipples were hard, and the hair on the back of my neck was standing on end. Lora bounced down the steps, took one look at him, beamed like a schoolgirl, and declared, "You're HOMER!" Lora and I were late for our dinner, but what a start to the evening. "So wonderful to meet you, Homer," I said, and he took my hand and held it tightly. "The pleasure is mine. Look, I'm in town doing publicity for a movie. Call me here at the Waldorf. They know me." Who didn't know him? He had quite a reputation between Hollywood and New York. There was no way I was going to call. On our last stop of the evening we bumped into him again near the Rainbow Room. Again he asked, "What was your name?" Lora and I repeated our names at the same time.

Lora had a darling place on the Upper West Side, and the next morning while we were sitting in her little red kitchen eating toasted English muffins, drinking coffee, and giggling about Homer lurking in the shadows of the Waldorf, he called. We must have given him enough information through the haze of a few martinis that we weren't completely surprised. Lora chatted with him for a moment and then handed me the phone. "He wants to talk to you!"

"Can you come to the Waldorf?" he asked, oozing confidence and charm.

"Well, no, I'm spending time with my friend. We're going to Cape Cod for the weekend—join us."

"I'd love to join you, but I have to stay to promote the movie. When will you be back in Los Angeles? Give me your number." He was persistent and demanding.

I was more than a little flattered. One of the Hollywood bad boys wanted to see me. Thoughts of Cuba and the mob were good reminders that there was more to learn about powerful men and why I was attracted to them. This was long before the Cosby and Weinstein scandals alerted all of us about what some young women may encounter in the business, so at first I felt more flattered than guarded.

But that first phone call was just the beginning. Back in L.A. a few days later I was spending my day with other wild stallions at the Burbank Equestrian Center when I got a page. Homer had tracked me down, and communications started. Throughout the rest of July and into August, he called every day. Sometimes brief, sometimes long conversations, like we had been dating for months. But we weren't dating.

I was back to working. That meant my days were filled with creating the best roles of secretary, lawyer, mom, teacher, wife, best friend or hooker by pulling together wardrobe, hair and makeup, working with acting coaches, memorizing dialogue for TV shows, commercials, and stage auditions. Then driving all over town reading for the casting directors, producers, and writers who held the power to give me a job. I spent my nights in acting classes or watching the shows I wanted to be on.

One late afternoon at the end of August, when Homer was particularly pushy and I had no more audition excuses, he caught me. "Come up to my house. I want to get to know you."

The Voice said, *Go face what you have set in motion.* I couldn't see it yet, but there was a reason I needed to heed that directive.

I wondered if he would still be interested if he saw me the way I really was. Jacky, my roommate, was far more excited than I was. "What are you going to wear? You look so great in that short skirt and tight white top. Wear that." He had already seen the dolled-up, overly confident woman with legs flying in the air. That was not who I really was, just an occasional act I could pull off coming off the rush of a great show, or if I had the best wardrobe in the world, or if I was in another city under a lamp post with a movie star in the shadows. It had been fun in New

York, all dressed up and puffed up, but the reality was I wasn't a stunning beauty and I wasn't famous. I was far less than perfect.

"Okay, Homer, I can be there by seven."

I liked how I felt in my cut-off shorts, high-top white sneakers with white socks, and oversized, faded blue jean shirt. I decided not to change, thinking he might not even recognize me and would just send me home. The critical voice of my mother crept inside my head: *"You look like shit—go put on some lipstick, for God's sake."*

Homer's house was tucked away up in the Hollywood Hills. The gate swung open for my little blue, two-toned Mercury Lynx. I was driving into unknown territory and more frightened than excited. There was a hint of light left in the haze of the sky, and the bright white house glowed majestically against the falling darkness. I leapt up the front steps and didn't have time to ring the bell as he opened the door. Oh my God, he's dressed in a pair of "Hugh Heffner" maroon silk pajamas—how creepy. As he moved to embrace me, his hands went under my shirt and in a stealth molester move skillfully slid all over second base. I didn't react but my body did. It was August, and I was getting cold.

He escorted me into the kitchen and asked what I'd like to drink. He opened the huge refrigerator and I spotted Perrier, which was fine for me, and he pushed a plate of brownies across the counter with a smile.

My legs dangled under the high chair at the kitchen counter. "Come on," he said. "Let's go into the living room and talk." He took my hand and led me back through the foyer again.

Now I could really see the house. It was a showplace of windows. We moved into the dimly lit living room to a long white couch. Ah, that venerable Hollywood tradition—the casting couch. The place where the casting agents, producers, and directors who were not as attractive as the movie stars they hired could use their power to push aside their imperfections. The trading of needs so common on the Hollywood market.

Here I was with one of the most powerful film icons whose prowess, talent, sexuality, and creativity were a mesmerizing combination. What part was I going to be auditioning for in this drama? As I sat down, I realized we were on the edge. Only the glass separated us from a fall into the jungle below. I was soon seduced by his openness and charm. He made me feel like I was the only person in his world. It was as if he had known me forever, or was it that I felt I had known him my whole life because of that weird fan familiarity?

We talked about growing up with the sprawling green back yards of our home states. As we talked he gently pulled me across his lap. I looked up at his handsome face and gazed deeply into those hazel green eyes. My chill began to warm. Homer's next question snapped me out of my fantasy and back to the reality of what was really going on. "You like pussy?" he asked. "I have a female trainer you might really like . . . I could call her right now. What about your roommate? Is she hot? Is she home?"

My laughter bounced me off his lap. In fact, I was so rattled that I couldn't think of anything, least of all a threesome with my roommate or some pussy trainer. But this is where the evening was moving and I was naive to think anything else. So I changed the subject and asked about one of other women I knew he'd been spending time with. He started to tell me something about her being sick during an out of town gig, when he stopped midsentence, leaned back on the couch, and said, "Well, you're either going to have to suck my cock or get outta here." So much for brownies with Homer.

I could feel myself getting cold again. The blood drained from my face and the fight-or-flight response was activated in my body. Would I freeze like the gazelle caught by the cheetah as it sinks its teeth into its neck, or run like hell?

I nodded like actors do when a director tells them they're not right for the part. I stood and said, "Well, I guess I'm outta here." It was awkward, but as I silently walked toward the door I realized I was comfortably uncomfortable not being right for the "part." Then he grabbed me and pressed me up against the wall. My purse dropped to the floor, his tongue pushed my mouth open and slid its way down my throat, and his hand reached down deep into my shorts. I gasped, not out of pleasure, but because I was wearing a tampon. It didn't faze him. He pressed up against my body and whispered in my ear, "You're not gonna need that, because I'm going to drain you dry." I was speechless. I pushed him away, tripped over my purse, grabbed what was left of my dignity, jumped in my car, and didn't look back to see if he was waving.

When I pulled my car into the refuge of my little apartment building, I was laughing at the insanity of the fantasy. *What a dumbass I've been. Drain me dry? Jesus. What was I thinking?* This wasn't something I could even brag about. I threw off my clothes, climbed into the shower, and tried to shampoo him out of my hair.

Within days I came down with the worst case of strep throat and laryngitis I had ever had. I had just been cast in a great guest-starring role on *Married . . . with Children* and was now sick as a dog and had completely lost my voice. I worried I would not be able to shoot the show. Fortunately, they had a set design problem that delayed shooting and I had two weeks to get well.

Even after his failed conquest, Homer continued to call. I couldn't talk and didn't bother to answer. His messages were nice at first, but then he became incensed that I didn't call back.

He blew raspberries on my answering machine. Late one night the answering machine clicked on. He was leaving a rather snarky message when I picked up the phone and croaked out the words, "Homer, I've been sick."

"Why haven't you answered the phone?" he demanded.

"I've been really sick!" Hearing his lack of concern and irrationality I felt the resolve that sickness can foster. I was pissed. I knew right then that I would never sleep with a man for a job, put up with the games of the business, or feel frightened for not putting out. I summoned back enough of my voice to say, "Look, Homer, this is never going to happen. I will never be with you—not now, not *ever*."

He topped my level of upset and shouted, "You are *no one* and you are *nothing!*"

Dialogue is cheap in Hollywood, but we could have done better than that. We were both wounded, our puffed up fake versions of ourselves calling the shots until our souls demanded something better. I was a new girl in town, and standing up to a Hollywood icon might have consequences, but I didn't care. I had to trust that this incredible lesson of saying *NO* to a powerful, gorgeous narcissist was better.

The recklessness and abandon that unaware girls offer to gain the attention of powerful men is a dangerous dance.

Dangerous to all girls like me, hunched over mirrors working makeup into our skin to hide the shadows of our acne scars, self-conscious about every hair out of place, but not a thought given to the fact that in our quest for love—because our daddies were not available—we might be making the biggest mistake of our lives as we bare the fresh necks of our youth to the vampires who have lost theirs.

Dr. Levine taught that along with the fight-or-flight response that is wired into us for survival, there is also the "freeze" response that gets activated when there seems to be no hope or help out of the situation. But I had rescued myself, bouncing off Homer's lap, claiming my voice, and running out the door. I was unraveling more of the fear that had been instilled in me.

Years later as a psychic medium I would hunt for the bodies of girls buried in the desert and the perpetrators who had drained them dry. It became my job to hear the voices of those girls who had surrendered themselves to the darkest part of male desire and paid the price with their lives. It would be my responsibility as a wiser woman to warn them.

When we have the courage to face all the shadows that lurk in the corners of our lives, God responds with more gifts than we can ever imagine.

12

The Gift of Fear

"Intuition is always right in at least two important ways:
It is always in response to something.
It always has your best interest at heart."
—Gavin de Becker, The Gift of Fear

I could see the merit of working on myself. I was gaining strength through therapy, pulling apart the curious life I was in. I began to examine the possibility that I chose all of this. Perhaps all of this crazy shit with my family and the timing of all these uncomfortable lessons were actually for me. Even though I believed that God was assisting me and that I heard the Voice intermittently guide me, I felt that there was a bigger picture to all of this.

I heard stories through the acting grapevine about a guy who could get you to face your issues in a way that would transform your life. That was exactly what I wanted and needed, so I began life coaching classes with Breck Costin and his BCC & Associates.

Breck had been married three times, worked through his challenging childhood, and was now able to assist others in crafting out careers and relationships from a place of freedom. At one point he had been a Landmark Educational leader until he merged his whole life experience to develop a program in which he advised Fortune 500 companies, famous actors, sports teams, and thousands of individuals. His work is about emotional freedom, and he believes that tackling one's life issues and deficiencies is best done by separating the image/ego from the authentic self. His training attracted large groups of people from all walks of life who wanted to transform their difficulties into "freedom" and success. We gathered excitedly every week. Clearly my life lessons were coming in rapid succession. I'd just gone up against the horniness of Homer—what's my next insight going to be?

I landed one of the most coveted commercial campaigns for Duracell batteries, directed by Barry Sonnenfeld, the famous film director. Barry hired me to play Flo, the mom in the robotic, doll-like family called the Puttermans. I was making gobs of money as an actress, an incredible blessing because I needed it to pay for all the therapy, life coaching classes, and things I didn't yet know I needed—like having all my wisdom teeth removed. I would learn there's a reason people call them "wisdom" teeth.

I was still on Percocet when I met Nick, who worked at the local hot-spot coffee house. He looked like a cross between Antonio Banderas and Leonardo DiCaprio. He was charming, younger, adorable, and made a terrific double decaf, no foam latte. I became one of his regular customers.

At about this time I was invited to a dinner party where I met Jerry Rubin, the 1960s-era social activist, leader of the Yippees, and cohort of Abby Hoffman. He was now an entrepreneur and marketing expert. Jerry was smart, sharp, and synergized with an energy that was captivating. He and his girlfriend, Tiffany, invited me to join them at a Whole Life Expo convention. We walked the aisles of the first "green" movement and purveyors of transformational health. We enjoyed each other's company and planned a Thanksgiving dinner the next week to talk about all the possibilities in the fields of transformation and health. Two days later, while walking across Wilshire Boulevard, Jerry was hit by a car.

I walked into the ICU to see Jerry's head bolted to a traction device. He had been dissected from his groin to his throat and sewn back together. No one is ever prepared to see a friend or loved one like that. Somehow, I knew he was not in his body. But where was he? I felt helpless.

I went into the waiting room, closed my eyes, and prayed. Oh God, what do I do? How can I help Jerry? I heard a man's voice say, *"I'm done ... I'm not coming back."* Jerry died the next day. At that time I did not believe that people could talk to the dead, so I decided I had made up that brief conversation in my head. I didn't know Jerry that well, and if he was going to talk to anybody I doubted it would have been me.

While ordering my morning latte at the cafe, Nick commented on my sadness. "Hey, I have something that will cheer you up. Can you wait a few minutes for me to take my break?"

I sat outside at a table. It was a beautiful southern California fall day, the sun felt wonderful, and I thought, *I will embrace my life because it can be whisked away at any moment. I will trust the lessons Spirit wants to send me.*

Nick joined me and handed me a rectangular flat box. "What's this?" I asked.

"You look like you need a present," he said. I felt it was an odd gesture. I opened the box and found a pair of vintage, dark navy blue cloth gloves in perfect condition.

"Oh, they're beautiful," I said. I put them on and they were a perfect fit, but I didn't feel comfortable accepting them. Then my gut flipped. Figuring it was a reaction to the oral surgery or meds, I tried to pass off the feeling, but I was unsettled until I took off the gloves.

"Thank you, Nick. They're lovely, but I can't accept them."

Nick kindly said, "Well, maybe you'll need them soon. I'll keep them for you."

Something was wrong, the same kind of wrong I feel when I think I have left the coffeepot on, that psychic electric buzzing of something coming. But this time it was oddly dulled by the Percocet. I was second-guessing my intuition.

"I'm trying to buy a place up on Eureka Street," said Nick, "but I can't move in until the house is fixed in about a month. Can I store some things in your apartment? In return I can build you some shelves or bookcases and we can hang out."

Hmm. He was younger. Cute. But I was told, *Pay attention.* I told him he could store some of his things in my second bedroom and "hanging" out with me for a month might be fun. He was a talented carpenter and handyman, and yes, he was handy in other ways too.

I was trying to heal a dry socket from the wisdom teeth extraction and was in quite a bit of pain when another present popped out of Nick's seemingly generous heart. He offered me a soft, golden leather jacket. Like the gloves, it was vintage. "Here, this will go perfect with your eyes" Nick said. As I put it on I heard, *"It's not yours to wear!"* Now, this was not the Voice I had learned to listen to. It was a different feeling entirely, like the person who owned the jacket at one time was basically still connected to it and talking to me.

"Nick, thank you, but I can't accept this."

He shrugged his shoulders and as he sauntered down the street to work I heard a woman's voice, *"Hey! Go check out the house he says he wants to buy."* What the heck is going on? This communication had a different personality than the divine Voice. It was as though someone that I could not see, but hear and feel, was trying to talk to me. Curious about this, I did what I was instructed to do.

Nick's mention of the house he wanted to buy led me to Eureka Street and straight to the door of the only house a carpenter/barista-boy could possibly buy, an unkempt empty property. I was pushed to the mailbox next to the door on the porch. It was full of old junk mail addressed to the Greenbergs, Carl and Evie. My gut flipped in the same way the gloves made me feel. I knocked on the door. There was no sign of life, so I went home and searched the white pages for Carl and E. Greenberg. I dialed and got a referral number, which I called, and a woman answered. "Hello, could I please speak to Carl or Evie Greenberg?" I asked.

"Who's calling?"

"My name is Marla, and I was at their house today on Eureka."

"I'm sorry, Marla, they were my parents. They died last year. I'm Susan, their daughter."

Surprised, I said, "Oh, I'm so sorry, Susan. I spoke to a man who said he was living at the house and trying to buy it, and that there are repairs that need to be made first."

"Oh, no, it's not for sale. No one is living there, but there was a young guy who broke in, squatted in the house, and stole things that were left in the closets. The only way we found out was that he tried to have the gas put in his name." My mind raced.

"Oh . . . I'm so sorry to bother you, Susan, and I'm sorry for your loss. Thank you."

The strange combination of fear and fury over Nick's lies made me shake. I went to the closet and pulled out Nick's suitcase and opened it. Inside was a folder with old magazines and photos. There captured in various Polaroids were pictures of a wooden table covered with an array of treasures, like how Santa displays his gifts at Christmas. The photos showed *Life* magazines, records, jewelry, and there in their box, the blue gloves. Next to the table, the leather jacket that *wasn't mine to wear* hung on the back of a chair. As I looked at the photos of all these items left behind by the dead Greenbergs, images flashed through my mind of Nick breaking in, living in the house, collecting their belongings, and giving them to strangers to ingratiate himself to them—including me.

I put the folder back in the case, but not before a gleam of silver caught my eye. He had a switchblade. I couldn't stay blind to this. I sobered up fast from the Percocet knowing that the first thing I had to do was get him out of my home.

I went to the cafe. After he handed me my morning latte I casually said, "Hey, Nick, I think it's best that you take all your things and stay with your friend for the rest of the holiday."

I could see his wheels turning. "Sure. I'll come over after work."

My little North Hollywood apartment complex was shaped like a big U. Everyone kept an eye out for one another. Leslie and Lisa lived across from me, and I gave them the news. "Nick is not who we think he is. He's conning people, and we can't trust him."

I kept wondering if Evie Greenberg was telling me those things were hers. Was I talking to the dead? Was she warning me? Dear God, please help me to be clear.

Nick came over. I was nervous and pretended to straighten up the living room when he went into the spare bedroom to collect his bag. "Did you look in my bags?" he yelled. He stormed into the living room. "What the fuck! Did you look in my bags?"

He caught me. He must have been obsessed with the order of his items.

"Yes," I said, "and I know about the house on Eureka." He grabbed me and pushed me up against the wall, holding my arms tight and yelling, "YOU FUCKING BITCH!"

I was calm and had the presence of mind to say, "Look, we can do this the nice way, or I can start screaming and someone will call the police. Just get your things and go." He stormed out.

Lisa and Leslie ran over. "Are you okay? We heard him yelling!" I was shaken but felt I had handled it as best I could so he could move on and grift someplace else.

A few months went by and I started to feel edgy and prickly. Cryptic notes would be left on my car and flowers ripped out of the ground on my doorstep. My safety and home were being compromised. My intuition was fully engaged and I could feel when these violations were coming. Then he left a voice message on my machine: "Marla, you can't stop me. I will do whatever I want."

I hoped he would move on, but the strange, intermittent harassment continued off and on for a year. I thought that if I ignored him he would go away, but that was the denial I knew so well from wanting things to be better in my home, wanting danger to disappear. It was just a matter of time before I would have to face this.

I kept every creepy message, note, and dead flower in a box. I switched my morning coffee shop from the cafe to Pricilla's, and he knew it. Within days he sent a message that he always knew where I was. A freshly carved FREEZE was cut in four-inch-tall letters out of the bark of a ficus tree in front of Pricilla's. Images of him using that switchblade to carve chunks of the tree disturbed me more than anything. I prayed for protection. When I heard the Voice say, *Move your car,* I did. Fear forced open more of my awareness as my psychic antenna busted out of me. I was on fire and then something shifted in me. I was done with this victim conversation.

The dance of victim and perpetrator, the unconscious dance I had done from the time I was born, was taking another form. This wasn't an ill mother from whom I could not protect myself, a successful narcissistic Hollywood heartthrob, or a couple of mobsters—this was an unstable, volatile young man. I now had to protect others as well as myself.

I called Cindy, the owner of a local book store. She had hired Nick to help her. Nick had also built her husband a beautiful bookcase in their home.

"Cindy, this is Marla, Nick's friend. Do you have a few minutes?"

"Sure."

"Cindy, I'm sorry I've not told you about this. I guess I was too embarrassed to talk about it. But Nick is not who he is claiming to be, and I think we have a problem." I proceeded to tell her about the Greenbergs and all the other behavior.

"This is incredibly disturbing," she said. "This can't be Nick." She didn't believe me.

"It's very upsetting, I know, but I assure you it's all true. We've all been conned. I'm going to the North Hollywood police to tell them what's going on, but I wanted to call you first to warn you."

I grabbed the box with all the creepy evidence and went to the police station.

Detective Uriebe was a short, sweaty detective who looked like he slept in his clothes. He listened as I explained the series of events.

"Well, this doesn't seem to be so threatening and we don't have a report on the Eureka property, so there is not much I can do," Uriebe concluded.

I noticed a photo on his desk and picked it up. It was a shot of a mattress with an unrecognizably burnt corpse on it. Aggressive sexual images flooded my head. Before he could ask me not to touch it I said, "This guy was picked up and taken back to his house like a trick."

"What?" he asked.

"This photo is of a murder victim, right? This is a homosexual rage murder."

He was flabbergasted. "Look, I don't know what you're doing, but I can't talk about the photo. When you get more evidence about Nick, come back."

As I walked out of the station I was dumbfounded by what had just happened, seeing and feeling things just by picking up a photo. My fear was morphing into psychic clarity.

It didn't take long to collect more evidence. Cindy had fired Nick and he was on a rampage, leaving another message on my answering machine that chilled me to my core: "Marla, I'm coming to your house and I am going to take you down!"

I stayed at friends' homes. Ed, my apartment manager, said he had seen Nick come to the building enraged, pound on my door, and yell at every window. "I told that boy I was going to call the police if he came back," Ed said.

This was not going well. Nick continued to leave messages like, "It is a painful thing to live in fear. Well, I guess you're going to have to live with it."

He didn't know me. Fear was how I had lived most of my life and elements of fear created my sensitivities. The anxiety was part of the warning, my nervous system telling me something was not right *in my body* even before my mind could grasp the message. Trauma had forced me to listen to the Voice that wanted to help me. And guidance from the Voice came at all hours.

It was a warm night. I had left my side bedroom window open and was asleep when I heard what I thought was a bell chime right beside my head, and then a loud whisper from the Voice, *"WAKE UP!"* I sat up. I then heard footsteps on the gravel path behind my bedroom wall inching their way to the window beside my bed. It was Nick. I screamed and screamed. The building managers sleeping above me called the police.

The next day detectives Gary Van Esch, Sam McCauley, and Doug Raymond showed up at my door.

"Marla, we're from the Los Angeles Threat Management Unit. Our team of detectives was assembled after the tragic murder of actress Rebecca Schaeffer by a stalker. We handle harassment and stalking cases and take these situations very seriously."

I shared all the documentation I had with these detectives, including the recent voice machine recordings of Nick threatening to "take me down."

"We strongly encourage you to file a restraining order," said Detective Van Esch. I had to trust that the Threat Management Unit would help me with Nick, who was now considered a stalker.

13

School for Skeptics

"Skepticism is the beginning of faith."
—*Oscar Wilde*

I was cast as Teri Hatcher's assistant, Diane, on *Lois and Clark: The Adventures of Superman*. My character was a small recurring role that under most situations I would have been happy to have, but when I found out that Nick had tried to get a job directly across the street from the Warner Brothers Studio lot where we filmed the show, I was concerned. Barry Sonnenfeld, the director of all of my Duracell commercials, had written me a role as a stewardess in the film *Get Shorty*. But when Barry called me at home, with his distinguishable Bostonian accent, to tell me he was saarrry to say that they had to cut my scene out of the mooovie, I didn't care. None of these accomplishments or being edited out of a soon-to-be successful movie mattered. Nick's behavior had derailed and incapacitated me. I had no interest in my acting career, and there were days when I did nothing but close my blinds, lie on the sofa, and watch TV.

One morning I flipped the remote to a little program on NBC called *The Other Side*. It was about all things paranormal, way ahead of its time, and featured someone I'd never heard of, James Van Praagh. As soon as he came on, I heard the Voice encourage me, *Watch this*, so I did.

The set of the show was a modest light-blue backdrop with a chair where James sat and tuned into the deceased relatives of audience members. I was highly skeptical about people talking to the dead, but nothing about the set, format of the show, James, or the audience smacked of pretense or cliché "séance" theatrics. These people were obviously deeply moved as they listened to details that no one could possibly know about their dead relatives, unless, of course, they were planted in the audience. I decided that I needed to see Van Praagh's work up close. As legitimate as the show appeared, I was still doubtful about his ability to talk to the dead, or anybody's ability, for that matter. I certainly wasn't convinced that Jerry Rubin or Evie Greenberg were actually talking to me.

Shortly after watching the show, I got a call from Kim, my partner in life coaching class. "Hey, girl, we have to reschedule our weekly chat because I'm going on a trip to Sedona with James Van Praagh."

The striking coincidence was odd, even for me. "Do you mean the guy with the blue eyes and mustache?"

"Yes!" Kim said.

"Kim, I was just watching him on TV!"

She laughed and said, "I'm best friends with Cammy Farone, James's personal assistant. If you want to see him in person he'll be at the Beverly Garland Hotel in Studio City next week."

"This is really amazing," I said. "That hotel is just around the corner from me." I was going to have my opportunity to watch up close.

A few days later, I was surprised to see dozens of people standing in line outside the hotel. How gullible and desperate are these people, hoping someone would prove that their relatives are still alive? Why are they paying thirty bucks a pop to watch someone "seem" to talk to their dead daddies? I felt suckered, but also began to wonder if any of my relatives would show up. I hadn't known any of my grandparents, so I thought it would be all the more strange to hear from someone I had never met. I threw out all expectations, tried to forget my judgments, and took my seat with the attitude of a neutral investigator who was happy simply to observe.

James took the stage and began with a meditation. He talked a little bit about his work and then started to connect to a deceased man who was trying to get through to apologize. James went on and on about the man, and I thought, *This is a load of crap and now he's going to make something up to explain why this doesn't match anyone in the audience.*

Then he said, "If this does not fit with anyone, I am going to have to move on." He turned, stepped to another part of the stage, and said, "I'm sorry folks, but this man won't leave me alone. He says his name is Glen and that his wife is here and he has to talk to her."

A woman in her fifties two rows away slowly stood up, looking nervous and frightened. Her apprehensions melted into tears of relief during her amazing conversation with her husband.

The two hours flew by. Each episode of communication had moved me so deeply. I was humbled. My soul had just experienced the truth that love never dies and that our loved ones are still able to see, hear and feel us! When I arrived home that evening, I got down on my knees and prayed.

"Dear God, I have no idea what is happening to me. Please continue to protect me from Nick. What do I do with my psychic gifts? Can you please help me understand what this talking to the dead business is all about? And thank you. I am most grateful—love me."

That night I had a dream. A four-hour dream consisting of two words, *"the Center,"* repeated over and over . . . *the Center, the Center, the Center.* I finally sat up and blurted, "Okay, I get it!" Could those words be the answer to my prayer?

The next day Kim called to ask how I liked James's demonstration and I told her about my fitful dream. Two hours later, Cammy, James's assistant, called.

"Marla, Kim just told me about your dream. Could you please come to James's office?"

"Seriously? Of course I'll come, but what's this all about?"

She was happy and laughed as she said, "I'll let James tell you when you get here."

I headed off to West Hollywood without a clue about what all this could mean, but excited that Spirit had orchestrated this in a matter of twenty-four hours.

Cammy was warm and bubbly as she escorted me into the comfortable, shabby-chic living room. James walked in, smiling and laughing. His television and stage personality, though charming, was calm and controlled, but in the comfort of his own home he was exuberant, excited, and mischievous. He was solidly built and vibrated with energy. When I stood to meet him I was a good four inches taller. We laughed and immediately connected through joy.

In anticipation, he asked, "You had a dream about the Center. Do you know what the Center is?"

"I have no idea."

"The Center is a healing temple in Brazil, and I'm working with its leaders and some entrepreneurs to develop the same sort of facility in Los Angeles. I've been dreaming of it too." Then he announced, "I guess you're going to Brazil with me."

What started out as a quick meeting turned out to be a three-year association. I was making enough money as an actress to afford to freely volunteer for James and travel. The volunteer work was a relief and a distraction from thinking about Nick.

I had just finished my lunch at the CBS commissary before going back to rehearsals for a guest-star role on *Cybil*, a TV show starring Cybil Sheppard and Christine Baransky, when I got a call from Pat, my parent's housekeeper.

"Marla, your father had a fender-bender at the post office and your mother took the car keys away. You know what that means—he couldn't get to the bars. He started going into withdrawals. He got violent and your mother had to get him into the VA home."

"What do you mean, violent, Pat?"

"Your mother had to call the police. They got the ambulance to come take him away, and now he's in the VA home."

"Oh, my God."

"I know you haven't been in contact with your mother, but she's really upset and needs you."

"Pat, I'm leaving for Brazil in two weeks. I'll come out this weekend."

I had not spoken to Mother in months, but my father was in trouble and it was easy to put aside grievances. I called home. Mother answered and sounded weary.

"Mother, what is going on?"

"I had to put your father in the veteran's home. His sundowners were getting bad and he could not sleep through the night. He started to argue with me and I had to keep him out of the bedroom. He was yelling, 'There is going to be bloodshed in this house!'"

This was all so hard to comprehend, but she had been through an ordeal and I asked, "Do you want me to come home?"

"Oh, what on earth could you do here anyway?"

"Mother, I'm going to Brazil in two weeks, so I'll come out now."

"Well, God knows what kind of shape your father is going to be in if you come back, and why the hell are you going to Brazil?"

I drove Pat and Mother to the VA hospital. I followed Mother as her five-foot-three frame with her newly coiffed hair powered though the lobby. She knew where to go; I didn't. Dozens of men who had bravely served our country, proudly stood at attention, and were decorated with honors and medals now lined the corridors and TV rooms with wheelchairs, walkers, oxygen tanks, baseball caps, and bib-framed faces that stared like deer caught in headlights. I watched Mother fill out forms, demand assistance, and basically run the show. "Now Marla, get prepared. You have never seen your father like this."

She had purpose, authority, and had stepped up big time to fight for Daddy. I was proud of her. I kept wondering, what happened to my daddy? Maybe it was more than not being able to have a drink. He had had a long history of trauma to his head from boxing, football, farm accidents, diving into a pond and hitting his head on a rock, as well as the landmine that ended his military career. This was before Chronic Traumatic Encephalopathy, or CTE (a degenerative disease from numerous blows to the head) had come to light in the medical community. I braced myself.

"Pat, don't forget that bag of clothes, and I think we are going to have to trim his damn mustache." All good preparatory words before we got to Daddy's room. Mother was right—I was not prepared for this.

"Look, Fries,"—Mother still called him Fries—"Marla is here."

His eyes darted at the three of us while Mother made her grand entrance. He was happy to see Mother, but wasn't sure about me. He was wearing his beautiful light blue cashmere sweater he wore for special occasions. It was now smeared with food, in spite of the bib tied beneath his neck. He was hunched over, tethered to a wheelchair, and wearing a diaper. Tears spit out of my eyes as I kneeled down and tried to hug him.

"Oh, Daddy, I'm so happy to see you."

He pulled at my arm and pointed to the corner of the room. "Look over there, do you see 'em ... the fuzzy ones in the corner?"

I looked at Pat. "What's he talking about?" Mother was folding a piece of clothing and shaking her head.

Pat said, "He sees furry animals in the corners."

"It's part of the Parkinson's," said Mother. "He has dementia."

I was heartbroken. "How are you feeling, Daddy?"

His sky blue eyes flashed wild as he motioned for me to come closer to hear his whisper, a veiled attempt to keep our conversation hidden from Mother and Pat. "Do me a favor; go down town and get me a beer. Will you do that for me? I'll give you a dollar."

I looked at Pat and Mother. "My God, he's still craving alcohol."

"Yes, he'll do anything for a goddamn beer," Mother huffed.

He was not happy that I wasn't doing what he wanted. "Do you know who this is, Mr. Fries?" said Pat. She always called my father Mr. Fries. He looked at her like a toddler who is trying to understand what he's hearing.

"Uh huh, Marla," he said.

Mother grabbed a washcloth and rubbed his face like he was a messy kid. "Fries, that mustache of yours has to be trimmed." She had purpose. I sat there with tears streaming down my face. It was the most care I had ever seen Mother give my father. Her rubbing was not gentle, but she was loving him the best she could. He seemed to enjoy it.

I left the VA that day with a respect for Mother that I had never had. My father and mother had some karma to work out between them, and I was not so important. Ghosts of war, trauma, sickness, and probable death put things in perspective. Life with my parents was real and mature for the first time. Along with the deep pain of my father's demise, I also felt the strange relief that my mother was not focusing on me.

I had been working as a volunteer for James for about four months by the time we traveled to Brazil to visit the Center. Making the trip, which would involve four cities and various tour destinations in ten days, was a leap of faith. I had no idea why I was going. I surrendered to the process. The Threat Management Unit detectives had gone with me to court to file a restraining order against Nick. If he came anywhere near me or my home, he could now be arrested. The manager of my apartment building said he would keep an eye on things.

I was part of a group of twenty from different parts of the country who came to experience the unique spiritual culture of Brazil and hang with James. We flew to Salvador, danced with locals, sailed to rustic islands, dug for crystals, and witnessed psychic artists who channeled the masters, creating paintings in the style of the artist they were channeling within minutes, right before our eyes.

We made our pilgrimage to what James called "The Center," the Temple of Good Will in Brasilia. But James did not have an opportunity to meet with the Brazilians about the Center. That was strange, because meeting the people who were in charge of the Center was the reason James had made the trip to Brazil in the first place. It was my dream about "The Center" that seemingly brought he and I together and why he invited me. Or that's what we thought.

Back on the bus, James announced, "Okay, now we will be flying to Rio de Janeiro to have psychic surgery, a procedure to remove physical manifestations of emotional problems in our bodies. The surgeon uses his bare hands with no anesthesia," he explained. "Oohs" and "aahs" sprang out from the group.

"We can't have any beef, alcohol, or cigarettes or engage in any sexual contact for forty-two hours before our visit," he added, "so that means starting now!" James delighted in saying provocative things to the group. It kept all of us spiritual seekers in check.

John of God is the most well known of the Brazilian psychic surgeons who induces a trancelike state in his patients and is able to cut, pull, and yank out all sorts of things from their bodies to promote healing. We, however, were scheduled to meet a psychic surgeon who channeled the spirit of a German World War I surgeon, Dr. Adolf Fritz. I questioned James about being operated on by the spirit of a dead German, and quipped something about hoping he wasn't a budding Nazi.

"Marla, don't worry, he's operated on me a number of times." That was no comfort.

Our destination was an orphanage hospice called Lar de Frei Luiz, about an hour outside of Rio. The drive outside the city was a culture shock as we passed miles of shanty towns butting up against palatial estates. The huge discrepancy between classes living side by side was saddening and bizarre. Luiz himself had come to Brazil in 1894 as a Franciscan priest. The Center became a portal through which divine aid could flow with love and charity.

Dressed in white, we were all led into an open playground area where children gathered to welcome us. They were beautiful, well cared for, and loving. They took our hands and led us to the Center that was a home for the teachings of Spiritualism, the belief that the dead can communicate and influence the living through a medium. Perhaps this was the "Center" I had heard over and over in my dream and the reason I was on this trip.

The robin's-egg-blue walls of the assembly hall were covered with paintings of ascended masters and spiritual teachers. The room had a calming effect on everyone. We were told to pray and prepare for the experience. None of us was asked about any of our health conditions. We were told Dr. Fritz would "know."

It was getting hot and the ceiling fans only shifted the warm air around. I followed James as we were led up, eight at a time, to a room lit with red light. It was dramatically colder upstairs, but I could not see or hear any air conditioning unit.

"There is a substance that is produced by physical mediums when in a trance state," our host Pedro explained. "It is called ectoplasm. The red light you see stimulates the ectoplasm, and that is what produces the cold. Ectoplasm will aid our psychic surgeon in channeling Dr. Fritz and performing the surgeries."

Wow, the only time I'd ever heard of this ectoplasm was in the movie *Ghostbusters*. I didn't want to think about the gooey, slimy, flying muckball of a ghost called Slimer, but my God, what *do* you think about when you are getting ready to have psychic surgery?

We sat in prayer and were then led to the "operating room," a long, dimly lit space with white linen-draped gurneys that lined each side of the room. It looked like a hospital recovery room in a Third World country. James and I were the first of our group to go in. He walked ahead of me down the middle aisle and took the last gurney on the left. I took the one beside him. The only light came from one corner of the ceiling where a strange strobe light filtered through a cluster of crystals. The "doctor" started with James. I tried to see, but the large-headed, stocky doctor stood with his back to me, blocking James.

Then the doctor turned to me. He touched my left shoulder and I heard, "Heart and thymus." His lips did not move, but I heard him clearly. Even though I was a willing participant, I looked for some sleight of hand. Would he draw blood by squeezing the chicken livers hidden in the folds of his hand? Part of me wanted to catch him in one of the tricks by which so much psychic surgery has been debunked.

I watched his hands as closely as I could. The other part of me was intrigued and anxious to experience what was going to happen next. He put his hands over my stomach, on top of my white t-shirt, and then lifted my shirt. It felt like he was just drawing a line five inches from my belly button up toward my heart. Then I perceived the strangest sensation, like a deep pinch. I stopped looking. It felt like his hand was inside my stomach. Not more than a minute passed from the time I heard him communicating to me telepathically to when my surgery culminated with a sound like a slurp and a vacuum seal. The doctor turned, dropped something in his assistant's pan, and moved on.

I started to feel coolness on my stomach. Then it ached, and I was anxious to find out why. When we were all finished and escorted out I saw three rows of people in white sitting like a choir at church, arms resting on their legs with palms open. They were praying and sending energy to the doctor. These were the mediums helping to facilitate the channeling.

Back in the big blue room, everyone looked shell-shocked. Some cried, and most were pale. I discovered the source of the coolness on my tummy. All of us had wet, slightly bloody stains on our tops. My first thought was that he *had* used a handful of squeezed chicken gizzards that had stained us all! My spot was directly in front of where I felt his hand inside me. I raised my top to look at my stomach and found a red mark the width of a pencil and five inches long stretching upward from my belly button. It was very red and looked like a scar from a previous surgery. How in the hell did that mark get there?

A Portuguese man came out after all the surgeries were completed and explained through a translator what had happened. His translator said, "You have all been operated on. The doctor took negative charges off your etheric bodies to remove the possibility of more disease. Disease comes from negativity in your etheric field. Negativity of thought, word, or action. Either your own or someone else's energy. We were all overwhelmed, not understanding what had actually happened but knowing that something definitely had. Dr. Fritz would not accept any donations for his services, but the orphanage did.

For several days afterward I had a terrible problem with my stomach area, the region of the third chakra. The fresh scar was still there and I felt like I had actually had some kind of operation.

Whatever "surgery" happened to me opened my third energy center. I felt like I had an invisible, six-foot-long pole sticking out from my stomach, and whenever someone crossed in front of me, the pole moved. It was excruciating. But I had also developed an acute awareness of other people's medical issues. Two of our travelers, Mary and Marilyn, were having health problems. Mary had been on blood thinners, and as I took hold of her hand, I could see the walls of her heart weakening. I could feel that whatever drug she had been taking was compromising her physical system. I saw the internal organs, the blood supply, pressure, and pain, and this frightened me. I had not experienced anything like it, and it reminded me of the movie *The Dead Zone*. Christopher Walken's character had the ability to see future events when holding a hand, but there was a place, a "dead zone," where the future could be changed if a different action was taken. From that moment forward, this new awareness would affect the way I understood any psychic piece of information that came my way. Life wasn't set in stone. We had CHOICE! If Mary's medications were *not* changed, there would be serious consequences.

"Marla, if you are seeing things through your hands, then you are developing your gift of psychometry," James said. "Holding another person's hands or objects can give you a link to the information about the object itself or who or whatever is connected to the object." It was clear that I needed to pay more attention to whatever I touched.

I sensed that there were even deeper levels of transformation happening to me on the Brazil trip that were not as obvious as my ability to feel and see a person's physical condition. My empathic sensitivity was exhausting. I felt overwrought from receiving too much information at one time. I was ready to go home.

We left Rio and flew to the final destination of the trip, Iguassu Falls. I have never seen such beauty and raw power— the falls are truly one of the greatest natural wonders on Earth. Wider than Victoria Falls and taller than Niagara, Iguassu is a mighty force. I was excited and frightened by the power of that natural wonder and found even more beauty in the thousands of butterflies that followed us everywhere.

I felt a sore throat coming on as the sun went down. Clearly, something was changing in my body. I passed out in my room and never even heard the knocking on my door. The next morning at breakfast I was greeted with, "There were UFOs, Marla! We knocked on your door but you missed quite a show." Apparently my whole group had watched colored lights hover over the falls, split, and fly all around. I was still skeptical of flying saucers.

When I returned from Brazil, Detectives Doug Raymond, Gary Van Esch, and Jeff Dunn from the L.A. Police Department's Threat Management Unit met me at my apartment building. "Nick came to your apartment looking for you," Van Esch said, "which means he violated the restraining order. We picked him up and he's now in jail for a couple months; however, we strongly advise you to move."

Detective Van Esch continued. "Marla, we have an interesting situation. The BBC came over from London and started to film our Threat Management Unit while we were conducting arrests and interrogations. Their intent is to do a documentary to help others understand the dangers of stalking and help victims get past their experience. They want you to participate in telling your story."

That was last thing I wanted to do, and yet I heard, *teach what you have learned.* I said, "Let me think about it."

In hindsight, it was all incredibly perfect. The grief of Jerry Rubin's death, having my wisdom teeth removed, being doped up on Percocet and inviting the dark angel of a con artist into my world who activated my deepest fears, my psychic antenna exploding out of my head, Threat Management coming to assist me, a deceased Evie Greenberg urging me not to wear her clothes, the Voice telling me to watch James Van Praagh on TV, my girlfriend Kim calling, the amazing night of mediumship with James, my prayer, my dream of "the Center," my meeting James and working for him, going home to grow up with my parents, the trip to Brazil and back to find Nick now in jail—all lined up in seamless order in the most incredible, seemingly designed, daunting experience of my life. I was no longer a skeptic.

14

The Apprentice

"My brain is only the receiver. In the Universe there is a core
from which we obtain knowledge, strength, inspiration.
I have not penetrated into the secrets of this core,
but I know that it exists."
—Nikola Tesla

On the urging of the Threat Management Unit, I begrudgingly moved to the other side of the hill. My daily job of volunteering for Van Praagh was fun and a relief from my ordeal with my stalker and perhaps a brief departure from the pain of my father living in the VA home.

Cammy was the stabilizing and organizing force behind James. She ran his website, did all of the paperwork and bookings, and basically kept him on track, or at least tried. We had great fun working together. She felt confident giving me office tasks and anything of a psychic nature with which she needed help.

Late one afternoon, after most of the volunteers had gone home, I was sitting on the floor organizing papers when Cammy handed me a letter and said, "Do something with this." She'd often slip me a correspondence because James was just too busy to handle all of them. She trusted me and knew I wanted to help.

Curious yet apprehensive, I opened the letter, which was postmarked Savannah, Georgia, and pulled out a picture of a man wearing a blue T-shirt and white cap. The name "Billy" was written on the back. At that moment I went blind to my present circumstances. A screen showed up in my mind and began to play what looked like an old home movie from the 1950s. The grainy images of two men appeared. One guy was tall and skinny with black hair. He wore a white T-shirt and stood in front of a white van. The other was a shorter, older man with grey hair and a mustache, sitting behind the wheel of a silver Cadillac. While looking at him I heard, *This man is Stanley*. Then the screen scrolled up, revealing the exterior door of a bar. Over the doorway were two large, red neon letters: "CC." The place was inviting, so I merged with the movie. I was now *in* the bar!

I saw Billy, the man in the photo. He was sitting at the bar drinking beer and laughing with friends. Somehow I knew they were all connected through softball. The two came up behind him. They all left the bar and I began to feel anxious. The scene shifted and they were outside a white house. The two men became aggressive, one behind Billy and the other in front, goading and pushing him. Then I saw a series of fragmented, explosive, and violent images of one of the men bludgeoning Billy to death with something that looked like a hammer. When they finished, they dumped him in the dirt.

Then I saw the skinny black-haired man slumped against a white van, dead, with a bottle of tequila beside him. Next, a woman with shoulder-length hair appeared in a police station. She was smoking, and the screen said, *She turns state's evidence against the man named Stan.*

As quickly as the movie started, it ended.

I was astonished. Grasping for words, I tried to explain to Cammy what had just happened, but she had to leave, so I just ran out and drove home. I was beside myself and felt pushed like never before to do something with what I had seen, so I called the woman who had sent the letter.

I learned that the sweet Southern voice on the other end of the phone was that of Billy's sister, Suzanne Charnock McIntosh. As soon as I mentioned Billy, she was unable to control her emotion. The Voice said, *Ask for the name of the district attorney on the case.* I did as instructed, and she gave me the information.

I had been dealing quite a bit with law officials in the capacity of victim, so I had no problem talking to them now as an advocate of other victims. I had no idea if my information was correct, but I immediately called the DA and was relieved that he would listen to me.

The DA confirmed my psychic movie by stating that Stan, who was now incarcerated, had murdered Billy and was awaiting sentencing because a woman had come forward and turned state's evidence against him. The other skinny, dark-haired boy who was involved, drank himself to death. They all knew one another from softball and met at the bar, Coaches Corner, after every game. The police were still looking for the murder weapon, a hammer. Had holding onto the letter unleashed this psychometry and linked me to this information?

A few months later I shot a Budweiser commercial. I played a socialite at a fancy restaurant for dinner with my husband, and instead of Bordeaux I ordered a "Bud." When I got home from the shoot, I started to clean out the snack bags, wrappers, empty water bottles, and other junk from my bag. At the bottom I found a cap from one of the Budweiser bottles on the shoot. I sat down at my desk and for some reason decided to call Billy's sister to see how she was doing. She was deeply grateful for the call. Even though I had not done much to assist the DA, she said I had brought closure to the family.

While we chatted I played with that bottle cap and "saw" Billy sitting at the bar again. He was smiling and cracking open a beer to toast me. I said to his sister, "You know, I think I have Billy with us. He's toasting us and I can see his ball cap. It's like the white one I saw before with red writing on it."

"Yes," she said, "That was his Budweiser cap! It was his favorite cap and Bud was his favorite beer." I told her about the beer cap and the commercial.

"I'd like to think Billy had something to do with that," she said, and we both laughed. Was it Billy sharing information about his murder? Could I be really talking to the dead? And did Billy have anything to do with me getting that Budweiser commercial?

Things seemed pretty odd in this unique realm in which I now found myself. I realized that the fear I'd experienced because of my situation with Nick and the trip to Brazil had opened me in ways that I was still trying to understand. I wanted to learn more in order to be able to help people and at the same time feel—normal.

Rick Kuhlman, the actor who played Mack The Knife opposite me in the Miami University of Ohio production of *The Threepenny Opera*, called me out of the blue and asked for help.

"Marla, I hear you have become some sort of psychic or something. Can you help me with a thirty-year-old murder case from my hometown? I'm compelled to try to find out what happened to this girl."

"I don't know what you've heard, Rick, but I'm not sure I can do anything."

"Can you just try? I'll come by and show you a crime scene photo, and maybe we could just see if you get anything."

"Okay, sure. I'll try."

I wanted to understand these gifts, and seeing my old friend from college was about as close to normal as I could get.

Rick explained that he had become obsessed with an unsolved murder case in his home town. He handed me a black-and-white crime scene photo of a blonde girl, dead in a field. As soon as I held the photo I immediately went blind to my present circumstances and my mind shifted to another place and time. I was standing in a field in between sets of houses. It was nighttime, and I had the feeling that I was the young girl, Carol, crossing the field to get home. I was shocked by what came next—I was hit in the head with something. I turned to see, in a plaid shirt, Mike, my (Carol's) friend, standing there with a large piece of wood. I couldn't understand why he hit me. I lay in the grass.

I told Rick about the impressions, drew maps, and provided other details about what I thought happened. Rick wrote notes furiously.

"Marla, I don't know what to say. You've not only corroborated things we knew but given me information that could move this case forward."

"How do you think they'll react to a psychic giving you this information?" I asked.

"Good point. I'll see if the investigative reporter can get this info introduced."

Months later I heard that they did in fact collect enough evidence to reopen this small-town Ohio cold case. The perpetrator was brought before the court. Law enforcement had found the piece of wood used as the murder weapon with Carol's DNA on it. However, the court ruled it inadmissible due to a flood in the basement of the courthouse where evidence was stored. I'm sure Carol was still happy that we all fought for her.

I had judged, shamed, and beaten myself up enough over allowing someone like Nick into my life. Spirit's request, *Teach what you have learned,* was the catalyst to transform my victimization into being part of a documentary that might help others. I agreed to talk to the BBC about my ordeal. The country had just gone through the murder trial and acquittal of OJ Simpson for the murders of Nicole Brown Simpson and Ron Goldman. This conversation was front page news. If my story could help one person, it was worth it to share.

I became an advocate for the Domestic Violence hotline, where I flew to Austin, Texas, to talk to law enforcement officers and film a public service announcement (PSA). I was invited to attend the American Threat Assessment Professionals (ATAP) conference where cops and psychologists discuss developments around the issues of stalking, domestic abuse, and the murders that too often are the result. I spoke about my ordeal and talked to dozens of law enforcement professionals. Dr. Chris Hatcher, a clinical psychologist at the University of California, San Francisco, who became known as a chief hostage negotiator; Dr. Kris Mohandie, a police and forensic psychologist; and forensic psychologist Dr. Reid Meloy all gave me support. Even though they were somewhat skeptical of my new gifts that seem to have been "activated" after my life was threatened by a stalker, they felt that this could very well be a place I could use my newfound abilities.

The "Stockholm Syndrome" that these and other assessment professionals discussed helped me understand my family trauma. The syndrome was originally developed to explain the phenomenon of hostages bonding with their captors. But subsequent research found that it occurs in battered women, incest survivors, and physically and emotionally abused children. I learned how trauma can affect the body and brain. The health of the brain depends on the health of the body, and vice versa. To be healthy, you have to fix both. I had pretended to be whatever my mother needed me to be so she wouldn't hurt me with her emotional or physical rage. I would do or tell her anything to survive. I buried the shame of having to be so inauthentic along with the dangerous feelings of hate, fear, and anger toward my mother and myself. The blessings of acting, therapy, and the American Threat Assessment professionals had given me healthy ways to process the trauma. The unusual gift of my stalker, and in turn meeting James and the miraculous life that was unfolding, could not have happened if I had not had my challenging mother. I was now fascinated about this unique path I had been thrust upon. I became a voracious student of more mindful thinking, seeing, feeling, and healing.

Working for James was like getting a graduate education in the world of mediumship. It was exciting to help set up James's public demonstrations and a real treat when James invited two up-and-coming mediums, Robert Brown from the UK and John Edward, the East Coast favorite, to join him on stage. John would become one of the most beloved of psychic mediums and launch a very successful TV show, *Crossing Over*. This was twenty some years before Teresa Caputo, of *Long Island Medium*, and Tyler Henry, of the *Hollywood Medium*, would come to light. James forged the way for everyone when fear and ignorance first demonized these unique abilities. I had been vehemently skeptical myself, so I knew how challenging it was for the public to accept the nature of this work.

I assisted Cammy in setting up the demonstrations, making sure the lighting and sound systems were working, and managing the attending press and VIPs. James's first book, *Talking to Heaven*, was almost finished. That book would propel him to fame, lead to numerous other books, and notoriety on TV with his own show, *Beyond*, and as an executive producer on *Ghost Whisperer*. But before that happened, Spirit had a few more lessons in store for me.

In gratitude for the volunteer work I was doing, James invited me to take one of his mediumship classes. Sensing that Jerry Rubin, in his untimely death; Evie Greenberg, who didn't want me to wear her stolen clothes; and Billy, who showed me his abusers, might really have been talking to me, I resolved that it was time to personally explore this side of the paranormal.

Sixteen of us were in the class with James. He began by blindfolding us to block out visual distractions. "A big part of the process is allowing you to make mistakes and not try too hard to do it right," he said during the first class.

When it was my turn, James said, "Allow any image, sound, or feeling to come to you, and then talk about what you see or hear."

When I put the blindfold on, all of a sudden *I could see!* I allowed the images to reveal themselves, and then I started talking...

"I see a slender woman with shoulder-length brown hair who's wearing an apron," I said. "She's pulling out ties, dozens of ties from a closet and laughing about it. She is presenting one to me in a wrapped box, and in her other hand is a birthday cake. Now she's smiling and showing me two silver rings. I like her and I can feel her humor and love." As I took off my blindfold, I declared, "Oh, my God, this is so exciting!"

"Does this information make any sense to anyone?" James asked.

An older man seated just a few feet from me raised his hand. "My wife, who was skinny with brown hair, used to give me a tie each birthday as kind of a joke. I turned seventy last week. We had our silver rings made from a single piece of silver." He paused for a moment, twirling the ring on his wedding finger. "I was hoping she'd show up. I'm happy we're still so connected, but I must tell ya, she wasn't much of a cook. I didn't like her birthday cakes. But I loved her." We all laughed.

I was stunned to have this validation that I was actually hearing, seeing, and feeling the dead. James's response was to assist my growth by inviting me to sit in a development circle with him. Several of his other medium/psychic friends and I met once a month to practice our skills.

I had attended various churches in L.A., but none had specifically become my home base. I had developed a different relationship with Jesus, not just finding Him when I needed Him, but finding Him in everything. I wanted answers from clergy and the medical/psychology community in response to what I was now experiencing. I was cautious of religious ideology because of the way religion can divide people. I never wanted my mind to be crippled by a polarizing or divisive belief system that excluded others. This work of uniting the living and the dead was all about connecting love. I went to the local Church of Christ, the Agape Church of Los Angeles, and even to the Catholic Church across the street from where I lived to ask anyone what they thought about my receiving divine information and communication with the other side. None of them whipped out the Old Testament fire and brimstone stories, but instead each lovingly explained in their own way that the Holy Spirit speaks to all of us if we are willing to listen. That the Bible is filled with teachings, vision, prophecy, dreams, and divine guidance. They assured me that God hadn't stopped talking to people after the Bible was written. I concluded, *God works in mysterious ways.*

I also sought the help of a new therapist, Dr. Drue Bogdonoff, who had started her career with an A.B. in bio-psychology from Vassar, an M.B.A from UCLA, and C.F.A. from the University of Virginia. Then, after three bouts of spinal meningitis she was catapulted out of finance and into a life of healing with an M.A. and Ph.D. in Clinical Psychology and an S.E.P. as a Somatic Experiencing Practitioner. She became my rock, helping me navigate the new life I had been thrust into.

I was an apprentice on a mission. I didn't think that this phenomenon should be sequestered to the old clichéd ideas of backroom séances. This needed to be shared out in the open, in the light, and I decided to research this new kind of *sight*.

People are skeptical; I'd been skeptical. The only way to change one's perception is to have your own experience. What we need to learn we often have to learn experientially. I had to let my own personal growth speak for me. I knew without a doubt that life exists after death, that people do talk to the dead, and that the dead talk back.

15

A Quantum Leap of Faith

"People like us, who believe in physics,
know that the distinction between past, present, and future
is only a stubbornly persistent illusion."
—Albert Einstein

I heard laughter as I ran up the steps to James's loft. Cammy was at the computer and my regular fellow volunteers, Ron and Phyllis, were excitedly ranting about something they called "military psychic spies." Phyllis jumped in with her rendition of show and tell. "Look at this flyer, Marla." She held it up for me to read:

Learn the Declassified U.S. Top Secret Psychic Technique
"Controlled Remote Viewing"
with Retired U.S. Army Intelligence
Sergeant Lyn Buchanan.
This is a scientifically validated, trained skill which teaches minds to communicate, expand awareness, access inaccessible information and data, locate missing persons,
predict outcomes to +85% accuracy.
Anyone can be trained!

"Oh, Marla," Phyllis said, "let's go take his class. Buchanan is a real-life psychic spy!" Then she cut to the chase by asking, "You do want to help find dead people and perpetrators, don't you?" I didn't need to give it a second thought.

"I'm in," I said.

We flew to Tempe, Arizona, and stayed at a worn-down little Travelodge with a faded Southwestern motif and tired cacti. In the training room, twenty of us sat at long tables like we were back in a high school cafeteria. Lyn Buchanan was a big, gentle bear of a man. With his soft-spoken voice and genuine care for his students, he guided us through the introduction to Controlled Remote Viewing, or CRV. It was mind-blowing to learn that the subconscious mind knows so much that it can identify a blind target thousands of miles away. We were taught to put pencil to paper and allow, with one involuntary motion, our subconscious to draw a strange scribble (an ideogram). Lyn taught us to identify each part of that ideogram and ultimately describe a target we knew nothing about.

Lyn entertained us with amazing stories, like one of his psychokinetic (PK, the ability to move or affect inanimate and remote objects, purportedly by using psychic abilities) episodes that he performed while in the military: crashing an entire computer network. Normally that act would be a terrible, time-consuming, costly event, but General Albert Stubblebine was so impressed by Lyn's odd ability that he invited him into the new top-secret government program. Lyn also shared that Stubblebine felt the best psychics had suffered head trauma and Post Traumatic Stress Disorder (PTSD) sometime in their lives. My horse accident and childhood with Mother was part of my badge of honor in this group.

Lyn taught us about the "father" of CRV, the gifted psychic Ingo Swan. Due to his heightened sensitivities, Swan ended up at the Stanford Research Institute where he became a guinea pig for scientific researchers to try to understand his psychic functioning. Swan developed the CRV protocol. The Defense Intelligence Agency took Swan's work seriously and funded the top-secret unit. These military men and women were now able to access their innate psychic abilities and use their minds to explore military and political espionage, as well use the more practical applications of CRV in law enforcement, medicine, and business. Being a new student of this scientific exploration was thrilling. Just practicing the remote viewing exercises expanded and focused my senses in ways I had never experienced.

At dinner we students sat enraptured as Lyn stunned us with numerous remote viewing adventures and an incredible story of his encounter with a UFO and subsequent abduction. "To recover my memories, I made sure I went to a hypnotherapist who didn't believe in UFOs," he said.

But the story took on a different tone when Lyn shared that after word got out about his close encounter, he was visited by two men dressed in black who ushered him into a room at the Defense Intelligence Agency for a "debriefing." That encounter with those men not only convinced Lyn that the government knew a lot more than they were saying about UFOs and the abduction experience, but through their interrogation, Lyn realized that they were corroborating his own experience. I was fascinated, even though I was still skeptical of flying saucers.

Lyn also talked about his training at The Monroe Institute outside Charlottesville, Virginia, where program attendees experience altered states of consciousness, accessing intuition and gaining a greater understanding about life—without the use of drugs. Robert A. "Bob" Monroe, the founder of the institute, was a successful radio and TV broadcasting executive and author of *Journeys Out of the Body* and two other books. Along with the help of physicist Tom Campbell and electronic engineer Dennis Mennerich, Bob had developed a technique for affecting brain-wave frequencies through sound that Bob called "Hemi-sync" that often resulted in expanded awareness on many levels. Wow, physicists and engineers all focused on helping the brain produce more awareness! As Lyn talked about the Monroe Institute, I received a mental image of the rolling hills of Virginia, and then the Voice corroborated what I felt: *you will go one day.*

Lyn's vast experience and tutelage opened my mind. His support of my talents warmed my heart and completely turned my fears into confidence.

Over the next year I continued to train with Lyn in CRV, technical map dowsing, and a unique way of "natural" remote viewing. Lyn simply placed a paper with a name in my hand, and I would go to where I thought that person was and describe what I saw and felt. At the same time, I started drawing maps related to the trajectory of a perpetrator or victim's location from one point to another. It was as if what I had learned as a young girl, to split/leave my body and fly in my mind to other destinations when my mother was abusing me, had prepared me for this unique way to "see" things. However, controlled remote viewing presented unique challenges for me in the intermediate level training when I was out of the classroom and left to my own devices.

It was quite a process to find a *good* Los Angeles "monitor," a guide who assists the viewer during the session to move through parts of the protocol and help the viewer when he or she gets off track or into some kind of difficulty. I was so sensitive that when I got to the part of the CRV protocol when we are supposed to feel the emotions around the target, I found myself in trouble.

We students received targets (usually photos) through the mail in sealed envelopes. When we got together to practice, we took turns acting as monitor or viewer. We did not open the sealed envelopes, keeping both the monitor and the viewer blind to the target until after the session. Sitting with another student who was acting as my monitor, I found myself putting my pencil in the column of the emotions at the site of the target. This meant my subconscious was tuning in to the target's emotions or emotions in his or her surroundings. Regarding the first target I was working, I became anxious, fearful, and upset. This was just part of the process for some seasoned viewers, but I had heightened emotional wiring, and not knowing why I was feeling these emotions was more than discombobulating. I continued to push through the protocol and finally heard a loud POP, followed by the odd smell of hot dogs. My anxiety then ceased. I could not for the life of me continue to try to identify the target, so we opened the envelope. It was a picture of a cow. Its nostrils were flared and ears perked up against the blue sky. The caption read, "Cow going to slaughter." I realized I was picking up just from the photo in the envelope, the cow's emotion—going to slaughter! Feeling that cow's fear was shocking. I could not bear to think about that animal or any other suffering creature. I tried to focus on the CRV process without getting overwhelmed, but it was difficult.

My next target stopped me in my tracks when I put my pencil in the emotions column. I immediately became freezing cold to the point of shaking and was on the verge of passing out. I felt like I was in a yellow tin can, like a sardine inside a refrigerator. It was deeply disturbing, and my monitor was no help in getting me out of that predicament. I collapsed on the floor. I had the presence of mind to pick myself up and get into a hot bath. After I thawed, my monitor told me my target was Denise Huber who had disappeared in 1991 and was found three years later, dead, nude, and handcuffed in the bottom of a freezer that had been stored inside a yellow Ryder moving truck.

This training was incredible. I was on the ride of my life, leaping in and out of targets; moving between the past, present, and future; and learning everything I could about consciousness, awareness, and psychic connection. And I sensed that Spirit was about to deliver something even bigger in my life.

James surprised me with an invitation to participate in a seminar on a cruise down the coast to Ensenada, Mexico. I am not a fan of tall hotels on the water with copious amounts of food, gambling, and black-tie ballroom dancing. But the trip started to sound more like fun when I heard that Catherine Ray, a psychic detective, was one of the speakers, along with Dr. Brian Weiss, who had become the nation's foremost expert in past life regression. Since that was a subject I knew nothing about, I chose to be skeptical. Homicide work was at the top of my list, and hearing what a psychic detective might have to say, pushed me to take another leap.

Catherine was a funny, spunky redhead. Her talk was interesting, but I wanted to get to the nitty-gritty about her homicide work. I had been on the ship for two days and for some reason didn't get a chance to speak to her. There had to be another reason I was out there floating to Ensenada.

Dr. Weiss graduated from the Yale University School of Medicine in 1970, completed an internship in internal medicine at New York University Medical Center, went back to Yale for a two-year residency in psychiatry, and then went on to become head of psychiatry at Mount Sinai Medical Center in Miami. Brian's work stunned the world of psychiatry with the stories of past-life regression therapy detailed in his first book, *Many Lives, Many Masters*. Brian would write many more books on this fascinating topic. The night before his talk, I was invited to join Brian and his lovely wife, Carol, for dinner. Brian's voice was so mellifluous that I was drawn to whatever he talked about, which most of the time happened to be past lives. After a few glasses of wine, I shared my thoughts. "I'm skeptical," I said, "because most of the regression stories I've heard involved people who were told they had been famous figures from history like Marie Antoinette, Joan of Arc, or Cleopatra."

Brian laughed and said, "I've heard lots of skepticism, Marla."

"So you're convinced we've all lived before? Like reincarnation?" I asked.

"Yes, many times. And I have my research to document hundreds of experiences."

As the evening progressed over prime rib, king crab, tiramisu, and Pinot Noir, my misgivings turned to fascination.

The next morning, seventeen of us traveled down, down, down into the belly of the boat. It was hard to ignore the thought of the weight above and around us in the catacombs of that cramped conference room. I gave myself more room by staying in the back near the open door to the hall where the breeze of moving air helped me relax.

Brian exuded comfort at every turn, from the tone of his voice to his casual clothes. He started out by explaining his work and then began the group hypnosis designed to help us connect with a past life. Soon I fell deeply into a vision:

I was in a long white robe, being led by a red-haired, bearded man wearing a shorter white robe with a dark red sash. He escorted me up a curved staircase, lit by moonlight diffused through an oval, geometric window above us. I stood on a round, marble precipice that jutted out into space. Stars sparkled in the blue-black darkness. I was in a structure that seemed suspended in space. I looked down and saw the bare feet of a woman. They were mine.

The Earth came into focus and zoomed in closer. I was shown postcard flashes of Greece. I said, "Been there, done that." Then North America appeared. I saw beams of light that seemed to be pointing and connecting to places on the East Coast. Other beams shot across the country to the west, back and forth and multiplied. I was told, "You must go back again to pole light." What? What does that mean? I could feel that I had been to Earth before and I *didn't* want to go back. I remember saying, "Oh, shit."

I was then transported to a square room with enormously tall wooden walls where I was surrounded by a structure like the grand benches of a high court. On that high bench sat a council or court of "beings" that was in agreement about my assignment. They gave me my papers, I signed them, and I was gone.

I woke to find myself sprawled out on the floor. I was stunned to be back in the room because my experience had seemed so real. To be sure I wouldn't forget any details, I jumped up and blurted out the entire story. I remember Brian smiling, but I didn't care what anyone else thought. It felt real. There was no denying it.

Nothing was the same after that afternoon with Brian Weiss. Catching a glimpse of where I may have been before and how that impacted why I might be here again gave my life a whole new meaning. This regression was the culmination of some fragment of an unconscious past meeting up with the present. I was certain that the story was true, even if I didn't completely understand what it meant to "pole light." My vision in the regression was daunting, but to have it validated later on by a stranger's dream on the set of a sit-com was beyond imagining.

Guest starring on a hit TV show is always exciting, and the process of getting there is a miracle in itself. You have to be invited by a casting director to audition, and if you don't know that casting director, you have to trust your agent to get you in the door of the casting office to read. So it's up to the agent to push for you and then casting to give you the opportunity to read for a role. Then, after you read for the casting director and he or she thinks you are what they want for the show, you "go to producers" and audition again in front of the casting director, writers, and director. That group makes the final choice. Getting a role on a show like *Everybody Loves Raymond* is like winning the lottery, and that week, I won.

I stepped onto the set to start rehearsals for the episode called "Super Bowl." I was playing Mary Jo, one of Deborah's friends. Patricia Heaton (Deborah) was very gracious and we connected immediately. Ray Romano was funny and professional. Peter Boyle was sweet and welcoming, and Doris Roberts was the warm, grand matriarch. Everybody loved Raymond and it was easy to see why.

I was looking for the assistant director while the crew was camera blocking a scene, and one of the stand-ins ran over to me excitedly. "I had a dream about you last night!" she said, clutching a script to her chest. "They showed me a map of where you are supposed to go." She was a slender, attractive blonde woman in her fifties, and she didn't look crazy.

My head was swimming. "I'm sorry," I said. "Do we know each other?"

"No. But I dreamed of you—they said you were sent here to do your work!"

Confused, I said, "They? Who's they?"

"I don't know. It's what they told me."

She grabbed a piece of paper and diagramed a map on the table where I was sitting. I watched as she drew lines on the East Coast of the United States like beams of light, and then did the same on the West Coast. Then she connected them, like she was plotting an airplane's route. "You must go through this physical life and attempt to remember who you are. When you make that connection, you will go through a transformational process to become whole, centered, and connected with your higher self. Once you realize this, you can anchor light and information to Earth."

Time slowed way down. She looked completely sane as she drew what I had seen in my regression with Brian Weiss. But a higher self? Oh, please, I was trying to get to know the only self I knew. But this woman had no agenda other than her excitement in relaying her dream. "I'm sorry, I must sound crazy, but I really did have a dream about you last night," she said kindly. "They want you to know."

I tried to compose myself about this past life reflection. I had to get present and go to work, but she was adamant.

"You must do your work!" she said sternly, like a teacher telling a student to sit down.

There was no more time for talk; my work for the time being was on this TV show. It wasn't the time or place for more chatting, but clearly Spirit set this up. I wanted to assure the woman that I didn't think she was crazy, so I quickly explained that I too had had a similar "dream."

It was difficult for me that first day on the set to analyze the significance of what she was confirming. This woman working as a stand-in on the week I was cast, her dream, my past life regression—my mind was spinning! The idea of what this woman validated was more interesting than my guest star dialogue, which included nuggets like:

"Oh, my goodness, Deborah, you wouldn't believe it—arts and crafts from fifty different countries!"

I believed that this woman reconnected me to the past life experience I had with Brian Weiss to confirm that it was absolutely real. Reflecting on the part of the past-life regression that showed me "poling light," I read in the dictionary that "pole" is defined as a stabilizing object for something to attach itself to, or a "fixed point of reference" for light waves of energy at a certain frequency. It started to make sense that I was holding a frequency level for another form of energy. Was my purpose this time around to act as an anchoring point for Spirit, for information, for the dead? I was being guided into arenas that were so "out there" and beyond my knowledge and experience that I simply had to trust that Spirit had my back.

Years before, when I left Chicago and drove across the country to L.A., I made a stop in Sedona, Arizona. I loved it so much that I stayed an extra day to hike up Cathedral Rock vortex, a stunningly beautiful vista of powerful feminine energies. Going with James for a spiritual retreat in Sedona would be our last adventure together before he became famous and I had to learn things on my own.

Both James and I were highly sensitive to any change of energy. Sedona has energy up the wazoo, and we started to feel it before the plane landed. James and I always had fun together, but by the time we got off the plane we were high on frequency and bantering with each other about everything like a well-tuned comedy act. We didn't expect the events of that cold November night.

Ten of us were stuffed into a van and driven to a remote ranch outside of town. If that didn't make us crazy, the conversation did. Our guide, Rob, had been taking people into the desert on UFO tours for years. "Tonight we are going to communicate with extraterrestrials that appear in the skies over Sedona," he said.

I shook my head in disbelief, rolled my eyes at James, and then challenged Rob. "How will we communicate, Rob—tin cans and a string?" I was simply not going to buy into this communicating with ETs nonsense.

One of the other women in the van piped up and asked, "Why do most people think that someone who says they've seen a UFO is crazy or a liar, but when someone claims to have been visited by Jesus or angels, that person is sane and blessed?" She had a point.

"And what if Jesus was an extraterrestrial?" she asked.

James turned to me and said, "Marla, you thought talking to dead people was nuts until you started doing it."

He had a point too. But I just couldn't stop questioning the whole thing. "Look, I had to go buy all this cold weather gear to hunt for UFOs and the critters that drive them, so I better see some!" I grumbled back.

Thank God I'd bought those clothes; it was freezing. Rob was equipped with state-of-the-art gadgets. He handed out binoculars, set up a telescope, and gave me a Russian level 2 night-vision telescope. This was my first experience with such gear, and I was amazed at how I was able to see everything in the dark of the desert. Anything that moved on the ground or in the sky was illuminated in striking detail. If there were "critters" out there, I'd see 'em.

Rob directed us to pay attention to the sky. It was a clear night with the exception of a few small clouds that looked like wads of cotton. The moonlight illuminated more detail as they moved and were then joined by other clouds to make the shape of a triangle: the back row was made of five small clouds, then four, three, two, and one at the front. They rolled over us like a cluster of bowling pins. Then the clouds split up and circled us.

We were all silent, watching this strange cloud orchestration, and then I held up my night-vision scope.

I had never really been interested in UFOs. Remote viewing expert Lyn Buchanan's experience had alerted me to the notion that perhaps there were unexplained events involving extraterrestrials, but I had never felt inclined to look into it. Reading Whitley Strieber's book *Communion* back in 1987 was as close as I got. That year I was in my second season at the Cleveland Play House and I had been switched on by Sonia Coquette's psychic reading. I was undergoing my full-blown psychic awakening. I saw Strieber's book in the window of a store and was immediately attracted to the strange but familiar alien face on the cover.

Alan, another actor from the Play House, and I spent our day-off Monday afternoons out at Chagrin Falls. He fished in the lake and I sat in a little rowboat and read *Communion*. I was moved by the courage it took to share the story of what Whitley Strieber called the "Visitors." If Whitley Strieber's experiences were in fact real—if he was an alien abductee and he and his family had contact with extraterrestrials—I wanted to meet them. *Communion* gave me a glimpse of life and its challenges that made me think way outside the box, but the whole UFO thing still demanded a giant leap of faith.

Out in the cold desert of Sedona I was beginning to feel really stupid. Dragged out there to watch little clouds moving around and communicating with UFOs sounded ridiculous, but nothing could have prepared me for what I saw when I lifted that scope.

Behind the puff of a cloud, the object sat motionless. It appeared to be a dome top with a saucer-like bottom. It looked exactly like objects I had heard so many people describe. There it was, and I was witness to it.

"Oh, my God! There's this saucer thing out there!" I said.

"Oh, yes, that's a gull wing," Rob responded calmly.

"It's a frickin' flying *saucer*, Rob!" I said, not so calmly. I noticed that it was still not moving. I even checked the telescope lens and scraped it with my fingernail, just in case there was a little picture stuck to it. I looked away, and when I looked back it had apparently flipped on its side, giving me a completely different view of the craft, the underbelly. The "saucer" was now a perfectly round shape with a hole in the middle. Illuminated green in my night-vision lens, it looked like a neon-green Lifesaver. "Oh, my God, it's flipped now and it's mooning me!" I gasped.

This experience shifted my perception of reality. It was as simple as that.

After seeing that craft, I have no recall of what happened in the desert that night. All I know is that we all had a difficult time with the energy of the evening and James and I ended up in a bar. Twenty years later, James and I discussed this night. He also had no recollection of what happened after we engaged with the UFO.

"Marla, I don't think your father is going to last much longer. You need to make plans to come home." That was Mother's message waiting on my answering machine when I got back from my trip.

My dad was three thousand miles away in Pennsylvania. I didn't know if he would hear me, but I decided I would talk to him the best way I knew how.

I sat with a photo of him and remotely told him things he needed to know. I talked to him as if he were right there in the room, listening and understanding. I told him how much I had always loved him, how much it meant to me to spend time at the farm together, and how grateful I was for the joyful times we had shared. And I thanked him for giving me the most wonderful gift, my horse.

I also allowed myself to finally be angry that my dad did not protect me from Mother. I shed tears of frustration about his drinking and how, with youthful ignorance, I tried to change him. I spent an entire weekend crying, yelling, and laughing at him and with him. I told him that I'd pray he would get help on the other side.

I put on my hiking boots and went up into the woods where I knew he would love to be. I felt a surge of energy move through me like a warm, vibrating gust of wind pushing straight through my chest and out the other side. Was that my dad? I ran to the apartment and on the machine was my mother's stoic voice, "Marla, your father died about twenty minutes ago. It's time to come home."

I took a red-eye to Pittsburgh and then the first flight out to Martinsburg, the closest airport to Bedford. The flight on the small Beechcraft was short and bumpy, but I had the perfect view of home to help my aching heart.

It was the week before Thanksgiving. The vibrant fall colors of Pennsylvania's heartland had almost faded, leaving only a hint of rust on the Allegheny Mountains. I was so close I could see white-tail deer running the golden fields. This is where my daddy would normally be on a beautiful November day, hunting grouse, pheasant, quail, or squirrel. The scene brought back memories of the last time I'd been home for Thanksgiving.

I'd left behind my bucolic childhood for city life. Seven years had passed—it was 1983. Mother was recovering from her heart attack and Daddy's memory was beginning to fade. Daddy and I had always run to the farm to get away from Mother, but now the farm had been sold. So when he suggested we go squirrel hunting down in the Cumberland Valley, I said, "Sure."

The relationship between fathers and daughters is a twisted road map, always needing direction. I realized early in my childhood that to bond with Daddy I had to do something he loved. That meant either becoming a football player or a hunter. I chose the gun. I was a better shot than most, and often better than him.

I scrounged up some baggy old hunting gear and dragged myself along with a rifle, camera, and picnic basket into the woods to be with my father.

"Let's eat!" I said as soon as we got to a clearing beneath the sparse canopy of trees. I handed him a Lebanon bologna sandwich and he pulled a flask of Frangelico, the hazelnut-flavored liqueur, out of his hunting jacket. I set up the camera, programmed the timer, and took pictures of us. I had him pose with his gun.

"Is this gonna be a photo shoot or are we gonna shoot some squirrels?" Daddy asked.

I was out there to get something, but it wasn't a squirrel dinner. I wanted to connect with him. I wanted him to love me. I wanted to make him proud. So I raised my gun. A crisp breeze blew. Leaves dropped and I pulled the trigger. There was a tiny yelp. I'd wounded a squirrel—not killed it, but hurt it. It kept crying, and from that point on I was completely inconsolable. The stillness of the woods erupted with the wails of a child/adult who never wanted to kill, but did it anyway to be loved. Daddy tried his best to convince me that squirrel probably died soon after that. I wailed even more.

Years later I worked out my squirrel karma from the urban balconies of every home I lived in. I became a champion for my furry friends. Fruit, nuts, water, and love would always be available to them when I was home. They in turn trusted me with their babies, gently held my fingers, greeted me in the morning and hung out . . . just because.

The things we do for love are the rich memories that continue to give us joy.

As I stepped into the funeral home, I realized that I was nervous to see my father. I had been praying that he was relieved to be out of that broken body.

The room was empty as I walked to the casket. The dark blue-suited corpse looked like a homeless man dressed up. This has to be a mistake. My dad used to be a strapping 220 pounds, a cross between John Wayne and Gene Hackman. I tried to process the nightmare of what had happened to my father since I had last seen him in the VA home.

His mustache, once glistening silver, was now strawlike and stained yellow. Hands that wrestled bulls and fumbled hugs were paper-maché-covered bones. I still wasn't convinced it was him, so I moved to the left of the casket to look for the familiar scar indented on his big, bald head from diving into a pond as a child and cracking his head on a rock.

I saw the scar. This was my daddy.

He would never discuss his pain. His needs and wants were never shared. He wore a Freemason ring instead of a wedding band. He hid behind the intoxication of an altered reality. What was his reality? What happens to make a man hold himself inside a prison? He was the son of Pennsylvania farmers, put in the fields to work, sent to war unprepared for the horrors of what he saw or did. A terrified young soldier frozen by the trauma of being blown up by a landmine with no tools to help him cope as he recovered and his friends lay dying. Was this why he could never talk of feelings? Was liquor the only way he could find his voice, in a bar with other men castrated by life and their wives, huddled behind cigarettes and stories? It seemed medicating was the only way to handle the trauma.

As I stared at him in that coffin I had the oddest sensation that he was watching me from the upper corner of the room. I heard him laugh, and in that moment of death I was shown a memory, one of our favorite moments in life together: We were climbing in deep snow to try to find the perfect white pine tree that would cast waves of scent through the house announcing Christmas. I was hard to please. Not one too fat or too thin; I wanted one full and dense with life. A foot of fresh snow blanketed Beegle's tree farm. We had hiked with a chainsaw up one hill and down the other, plodding through the open fields of trees.

I was ahead of him prattling along as I always did, filling the silence with my chatter. I did not hear his footsteps crunching snow behind me. I turned around to see him fall into in a hole as deep as his legs, a hole that had been dug to get a tree out, a hole covered with snow. His body smacked forward. He slowly lifted himself, his face and body wrapped with that cold, frosted meringue. He was a comedy. He resisted the smile, as he always did when he found himself in an uncomfortable place, a dumb place where a smile would admit he had been caught. Now it had him, had him in the place I had always wanted. We both laughed hard and fell into the humor, and I peed my long johns. My one-piece snowsuit, now soaked by the force of joy, was getting cold and I settled for any tree he chose.

It was the best moment he could have shown me as I smiled through tears. Touching his withered body, I said, "Oh, Daddy, we did find some joy."

That afternoon, before the military gun salute fired and they lowered my father in the ground, I reached for my mother's hand. She would not hold mine. She was in a new chapter of her life and I hoped that she also might find joy.

Back in L.A. I was leveled. My father was the first significant loss of my life. I was learning to move between worlds and leap into other timeframes, lives, and feelings, and yet my father's death unearthed the despair of his inability to protect me in life. It was a deep bruise I wanted to heal. I had forgiven him, accepted his limitations, but his death just made it clear there was more work to do. I knew he could see me and I trusted he was getting help on the other side.

The holidays came, then a new year and part of a bright new spring. I was invited to lunch with Tarrin and Lisa, casting directors who had hired me for a few guest-star roles at CBS. We started our lunch talking about the weird guy who had been looking in Lisa's apartment windows when Tarrin, in between bites of a Caesar salad, suddenly stopped talking. She wiped her lips with her napkin and said, "Oh, my, I'm sorry guys, but I have a man here named Harold who wants to talk to you, Marla."

Tarrin was a student of mediumship too, but knew nothing about my family, let alone that my father Harold had died five months earlier. She then said, "He wants you to know that he got everything you told him before he died."

This was amazing. What I had said to my father miles away as he lay unconscious in a hospital bed was now being confirmed by my dearly departed Daddy . . . through another medium.

Tarrin had more to say. "Marla, he says you recognized him by the top of his head." He was confirming what I had done at his funeral to identify him! "Marla, he's saying something about hanging up the phone. She voiced his words as they came to her: *"I want you to hang up the phone with your mother. Build a wall around yourself to protect yourself from her."* Tarrin said he was crying and so sorry that he didn't know about the terrible things that happened as I was growing up. Then we were all crying.

No one could have imagined receiving such heartrending information at lunch over a Caesar salad. He then topped it with, *"I am getting help, and Fred is with me."* Tarrin asked if Fred was black and I said, "Oh, yes, jet black." I started to laugh, knowing Fred as I did.

Fred was my cat that had been run over by our next-door neighbor. He loved my dad and I was so happy they were together. It was no surprise that Daddy chose Tarrin to talk to. She was someone he would have really liked in life, down to earth, sweet and sensitive. "Oh, one more thing, Marla, he says, *"I like Brett."*

I laughed and said, "You've got to be kidding me."

I had had one pretty great date with a former New York Jets football player a few months before. My father commenting on my romantic life was more than funny. I said, very sternly, knowing my father would remember my bronchial sensitivities, "No, Daddy, my God, he smokes! My deceased father trying to give me dating advice? Dead people humor, for sure.

16

Visitations

"When the flower blooms, the bees come uninvited."
—Ramakrishna

Getting to my home was a circuitous route up into the Hollywood Hills that required very specific directions. I was not easy to find. I was fixing my hair in the bathroom one morning, getting ready for a dog food commercial audition, when I heard some commotion in the street. There was a woman who seemed in distress as she was talking to a neighbor, so I poked my head out the door and said, "Morning, how are you?"

"Not very good. My husband died."

"Oh . . . I'm so sorry."

I didn't want to intrude, and I certainly didn't want to assume that I could or should help her, but as soon as I shut the door I heard—the way I hear things—*Please tell her that I am so glad that Robert has been with the boys.*

"Oh, no!" I yelled out loud. And then a definitive statement popped out of my mouth: "If you want me to talk to her you had better find a way to make that happen, because I am NOT going out there and intruding in her life." The next thing I knew I'd opened the door and escorted this woman through my front door.

Kathy Graf lived a few miles away in Sherman Oaks. She was praying and asking for help to be led someplace where she could talk to her husband. She felt pushed up the hill.

Spirit found a way to get her here and now I had to listen.

I asked if she knew who Robert was. "Yes," she said, "he's the minister from our church."

"Kathy, do you have a son named Daniel?"

"Yes," she said.

Things were moving fast inside my head and heart, images of people, places, events, feelings, and a predominant feeling of love that needed to be expressed, so I just started with what I was hearing and seeing to make sense of what was going on.

"Well, I think your husband is here and he wants to talk about Daniel, Memaw, his mother . . . the ring with the blue stone . . . Oh, heck, I think your husband wants to talk to YOU."

Kathy gasped and was clearly shaken. David was a bigger-than-life personality. She shared that Memaw was the name of his mother, with whom Kathy was having some issues. David had left behind a ring with a blue stone in it that he wanted Daniel to have, but he had so much more important things to say.

David visited us for over an hour, infusing Kathy, the whole house, and me with his big personality and presence. He urged Kathy to get behind her own talent and come out of his shadow. I found out that her husband, David Graf, was a well-known TV and film actor. He wanted to work with her to continue to parent their two boys, and he was sorry, so sorry for leaving, but very happy that against Kathy's will he did not cancel his life insurance policy.

Kathy and I continued this communication in a number of sessions with David, but what Kathy did in her healing process, with David's help, was most remarkable. She took that day of being pushed up the hill to talk to David as the impetus for a one-woman theatre piece called *Surviving David*. She premiered it in Los Angeles to packed houses and it was picked for a prestigious New York City theatre festival the following year.

Loss had become an incredible impetus for Kathy's growth as she played every character in the daunting experience, including the death of her husband on the dance floor at her brother's wedding and her divine meeting with me. She seamlessly guided her audience, showing how her life was rocked by her husband's death and how he still showed up afterwards to help her with the boys. David inspired Kathy to write.

I was amazed that Spirit had set up this divine intervention. I was blind to how and when these events would come, and yet I accepted and embraced each new introduction to the dead.

David continued to parent from the other side. I sat with his son Daniel when he was twelve, and David told him that he saw him not only in surfing class, but that he knew his math teacher was challenging! David also suggested Daniel take an acting class, which Kathy shared was incredibly helpful in Daniel's healing. David insisted that Daniel be helpful to his younger brother, Sean, despite sibling rivalry. David said that Sean should draw and build things. This too helped Sean heal, and years later Sean is an excellent artist.

David inspired Kathy to find her voice and express her talent and heart. Kathy has become a successful playwright, author, and friend. David was a powerful force of love in life and in death.

Robert Bock, whom David spoke of when I first met Kathy, was the pastor of the First Christian Church of North Hollywood where I had been singing carols every Christmas Eve for years. I finally got to talk to Robert about my experience with David, and we all shared a new bond. Instead of the usual courteous handshake after the service, Bob began to hug me.

I started rehearsals for a new musical called *Falling in Love Again* at the Santa Monica Playhouse where I took on the starring role of Marlene Dietrich.

Playing the iconic femme fatale Dietrich was an opportunity to embody the essence of a complicated, beguiling, beautiful star of stage and screen. It was Dietrich's strength and conviction to stand up to the Nazis in WWII, privately fund ways for Germans and Jews to escape, and renounce her German citizenship to become an American citizen that intrigued me. Entertaining the troops both on stage and off was a compelling expression of Dietrich's talent, insecurities, and sensuality. The kind of character that I understood. Every night as I sang "Lili Marlene" or her signature song "Falling in Love Again," I felt the love she had not just for the people of her homeland Germany, but also for her new home America.

I received the best reviews of my entire stage career. It was the last stage show I did.

The profound, palpable love I felt when making the connection between the living and the dead became more important than my day job as an actress. Though I loved the camaraderie of working with a talented team of creative visionaries in the entertainment world, Spirit was guiding me to work with the entertainment business in a different way.

I was delighted when I got a call from a casting director, Susan Peck, who three years earlier cast me in a little B movie shot in Estonia called *Out of the Cold*. I had the sheer joy of singing in a movie, playing a cheesy cabaret singer who gets booed off-stage in the first ten minutes of the film. The great cast included Mercedes Ruehl, Keith Carradine, Judd Hirsch, Bronson Pinchot, Mia Kirshner, Kim Hunter, Brian Dennehy, and me. Susan wasn't calling to bring me in to read for a role; instead, she said I had to meet her friend Fred Fontana, a film and TV writer/producer who apparently had "a life-altering" paranormal experience in Washington, D.C., and wrote a script about it.

We all agreed to meet for dinner. Fred was excited and animated as he began to explain his adventure with a ghost in a DC hotel. All of a sudden I could no longer hear Fred, the laughter, or the chatter of our dinner table. All I could hear was *BOB! BOB! Talk about Bob!* I stopped the conversation to blurt out, "Fred, there is a man behind you drinking bourbon and saying something like 'Bob, Bob, who's Bob, where's Bob?'"

Fred's face lit up with recognition. "Bourbon was my father's drink and *Where's Bob* was the name of a racehorse that my father bet on! My father died at the racetrack with winning tickets in hand."

We were all stunned. "Okay, your father is so excited and he's laughing because he has been trying to get your attention for a long time! He's showing me a little black dog with a white collar, and now he's blowing smoke at me. Does this mean anything to you?"

Fred smiled. "When I was little, our family dog was a black Chihuahua with a white collar and his name was Smokey." Fred then started to say, "The only time that I ever—" and I jumped in with what his father was saying to me, "The only time you ever saw your father cry was when you and he went to put the dog to sleep."

"Yes!" Fred said.

That divine intervention and completely impromptu communication began an exciting new chapter of my work. Fred graciously opened up his house to invite his family and friends to meet me and experience love from the other side and messages from Spirit.

In one of those group sessions at Fred's I was trying to give a young African-American woman wedding advice from her deceased grandmother. This spunky grandma showed me, in the way I can see things, her waddling into a den carrying a TV tray, sitting down on a sofa, and grabbing the remote control. As she punched the buttons she told me she had seen me on her 'Heavenly Channel' in a commercial for "How to talk to your living relatives." Who knew they had television, complete with commercials, in the hereafter? We were all so stunned that this grandma was so vibrant and helpful both to her granddaughter and me. However, another deceased woman, Rebecca, demanded I turn to the opposite side of the room where a cute, young woman with wild, colorful streaks in her hair anxiously waited. I looked at her and said, "I think a woman named Rebecca wants to talk to *you* about Randy," This darling girl, named Mindy, could not have looked more shocked. "Randy," she croaked, "was my dad."

"Rebecca says she wants to talk *for* your father and that he needs prayers from the family. She says your father is in a place where he cannot move forward yet." Rebecca's emotions flooded through me as those of the deceased who need to have their feelings known had begun to do. I was overwhelmed with Rebecca's love, grief, and sorrow, and then just as those emotions had taken over me, something shifted. Gone were the overwhelming feelings that had made my body burst into tears when Rebecca talked about Randy. Now I felt bright, clear, and filled with joy.

Rebecca had shifted as though she had the strength of God behind her and said, "Mindy, go home, get a white candle, and light it every night and talk to your father. Please tell your mother that Randy is so sorry, and please pray for him." Through a handful of tissues and tears Mindy agreed. But as I turned to work with someone else, Rebecca spoke up with a parting question. "Do you remember the little stuffed lamb your dad gave you?"

Mindy nodded and said through her tears, "Yes! He gave it to me when I was four."

"Mindy," Rebecca said, "Your dad wants you to know that he knows you still have it."

Five months later Mindy came back for another session. Randy came in right away to thank his daughter and the family for praying for him, forgiving him for the mistakes he had made, and loving him. He was out of his self-imposed prison and said, "I'm back on the water." Mindy nodded with relief and explained that he and Rebecca had had a houseboat that made him very happy. Mindy was now ready to tell us what had actually happened. Rebecca was Randy's fiancée. In a drunken upset he had gotten into a fight with Rebecca, resulting in her falling, hitting her head, and dying. He was convicted of involuntary manslaughter and was in prison for five years. When he got out he could never forgive himself for having killed his beloved, and he died of a broken heart.

Rebecca was someone Mindy and her family loved, and this tragic loss both of Randy and Rebecca had ravaged the family for twenty-plus years until Rebecca punched through the veil to ask for help for her beloved Randy, who could never forgive himself for her death. WOW! I had no idea until this experience that hell is perhaps a mental construct. Not the place a wrathful God flings you, but a self-imposed mental prison created out of deep grief, regret, anger, and shame that the dead take with them to the other side. But love, prayers, and forgiveness can help heal our loved ones, can break them free of their own pain. In turn, we heal too.

What a huge revelation. My experience with this family was a game changer. Forgiveness had seemed so slippery in my own family, but now Spirit in its divine wisdom had lovingly delivered the awareness that forgiveness can change not just us, but also our loved ones on the other side.

As my new life was unfolding, I felt a longing, a kind of homesickness for the beauty of Bedford's rolling hills. I pulled out scenic snapshots of my hometown, fun moments of me smiling with various Bedfordites, and farm animals. A photo of Mother caught my attention.

We were having dinner at one of Bedford's favorites, Ed's Steak House. Mother, in a rare good mood, was being charming and kind to the waitress as she ordered fried shrimp. She giggled that she had ordered something she wasn't supposed to eat. I loved her in those rare moments of humor and kindness because it never lasted long. Her profile had collapsed along with her life. I burst into tears. She should have married her distant cousin Sonny Davenport or someone like one of her soap opera stars, dashing, fun, sexy and attentive. Perhaps she would never have become so angry, beaten her daughter, or lay on that sofa.

I looked out my living room window into the beautiful blue sky. As my heart broke I prayed, "Dear God, please help my mother. She is so miserable. And please don't let me look like her, be like her, or have that same hook at the end of my nose—she looks like such a witch. PLEASE," I pleaded. "Oh, and while you're at it, could you please send me a new teacher to study with?"

Such a strange prayer, but I meant it from the bottom of my soul.

That evening I went to an entertainment party. Actors all hungry to fill their plates settled instead for the free shots of tequila and really great guacamole.

I came home to find my dog, Sonny, curled up on his blanket in the kitchen. Sonny was a well-trained buddy and companion without a mean bone in his body. I squatted down behind him and rubbed his back, a gesture that always made him happy. "Oh, you are such a good boy," I said. "What a good boy . . . I wuv you!" He was in ecstasy.

All of a sudden I saw blood all over my arms and white top.

My God, what's wrong with Sonny? I thought as I scanned his body. There was no blood. Was I bleeding? I jumped up and ran to the bathroom mirror to see in horror a nickel-sized bloody hole on my face. Somehow the end of my nose had been sheared right off!

I never felt anything. I never saw anything. Then I heard in the way I hear things, *Call Schwartz.*

Dr. Joel Schwartz, my dermatologist, was an orthodox Jew. It was just before midnight on a Friday night and to my amazement he answered the emergency call.

"Go to St. Joseph's emergency," he said. "They handle dog bites really well."

This wasn't a bite—this was a mistake. It didn't matter. I grabbed a bag of frozen peas and raced to the hospital.

Holding on to the steering wheel and pressing the peas against my face, I realized what I had done earlier that day, and then I heard the Voice: *You asked for this, Marla, and now every time you look in the mirror you will know you are a part of us, and we are a part of you. Do not worry, you will be fine.* WHAT? I could not believe that just twelve hours earlier I had prayed for my nose to not look like my mother's, and now it never would.

I kept silently praying as I lay behind a curtain in the emergency room trying to make deals with God, Spirit, Jesus, the angels, and the Voice. Okay, look, I know I must have asked for this, but let's consider what this could mean. My acting career could be over, I'd have no income, no way to take care of myself. Will I ever be able to look at myself? Oh, and if you are part of me and I am apart of you, do you SEE THIS HOLE ON OUR FACE? Dear God, please help me!

A male nurse came to check on me. I had been pretty calm up to that point. He pulled back the cotton swab that had been put on my nose to stop the bleeding and took a peek at it. He grimaced like he had just sucked on a lemon and made no attempt to hide his disgust. I burst into tears and from that point I was inconsolable. That is until a strapping, six-foot-four, white-haired Nordic god so bright he almost looked albino walked in. Doctor Steven McNeese had come to my rescue.

We recognized each other right away. "You look familiar," he said.

"Yes! Oh, my God, Dr. McNeese, you operated on my arm when I had stage three melanoma, look." I pulled up my arm to show him the two long but very faint scars where he had crafted his handiwork six years before.

"Oh, yes," he said in recognition. I was so relieved. "If there was anyone who could help me, it is you, Dr. McNeese." I sounded like one of my mother's soap stars.

"You know, Marla, I don't take these calls from the hospital to come in and do emergency surgery anymore. I didn't know who it was or what had happened, but something told me to come for this." I was crying again. "Nurse, give her a shot of Diazepam just to take the edge off. This will help you calm down, Marla."

"I'm okay. I'm just so grateful that Spirit sent you to help me," I sobbed.

"Yes, God works in mysterious ways," he said.

Everything was still. Dr. McNeese sat behind my head and started to examine the damage. Minutes passed in silence and then he said, "Marla, the only thing we can do here is graft a piece of skin from behind your ear to the end of your nose and pray the graft takes."

It was a five-hour surgery. McNeese sent me home and my life started over again.

Sonny was pure love. This was the most freakish accident ever. I never saw it happen, I never felt it, and it never hurt. The slice was so precise it was as though it had been carefully measured to be a certain width at a certain angle. The next day I found the slice stuck to the bottom of his blanket. Was Sonny an instrument of God in answering my prayer? I had no choice but to trust that the message the Voice had given me meant something.

Even after the surgery it never hurt. I went home and for two days I simply prayed. And then it started. I heard things inside my head, voices that wanted me to listen. I was scared because I thought the trauma was making me go mad. Then I got a call from Dr. Drue Bogdonoff, who said she was coming to visit me. That was a blessing. She had been my stabilizing force, the strength that had helped me heal my life.

I lay on the sofa in the living room and told her about the voices I was hearing and she asked me to close my eyes.

"Keep calm" she said. "You are experiencing an initiation."

"What did you say? A hallucination, a visitation?"

The room suddenly filled with light and I heard, *You have been called for a higher purpose, and do not question what takes place. Take notes and listen.* Drue and I continued to talk about this amazing experience until it was time to go back to see Dr. McNeese.

I was prepared for anything, to be marred for life, give up my acting career, or watch mothers shield their children and grimace at me in the grocery line. He removed the bandage and I held up the mirror. To my amazement, I still looked like me. McNeese's work was so perfect that I said, "Wow, that's good. I'm fine. I like it! It's just me with a shorter nose." I cried in relief. The collective "us" behind the Voice was right—I was fine, better than fine.

I started to take notes as I had been asked, spending days sitting on the sofa while I healed and jotting down what I heard. At the same time I was given a most wonderful little gift—a young orange-and-white cat that belonged to our neighbors started coming into my home and loving me. He would not leave my side. The neighbors thought he was out hunting every night, but in fact, he was sleeping with me. Then one morning I heard, in an East Indian accent only Hank Azaria from *The Simpson's* could do, "Hello, my name is Baba. I live in India. I want you to go to Macy's and get yourself some brightly colored tops, orange, green, pink. You wear too much black. And I want you to eat the ash." Who was this guy, a dead fashion designer? Eat the ash? I must have misunderstood, but I did what I was told. I made a trip to Macy's and found a whole rack of beautiful colored tops, and on sale to boot. I had darkened my hair to a russet red brown and this Baba guy was right: I did look better in those brighter colors.

I started to go back to work auditioning, sharing with my actor friends and colleagues my very odd accident and the miraculous intervention of Dr. McNeese. The skin graft just required a bit more makeup to hide the redness. A month later I booked a commercial.

"Yes, now I am going to give you some teachings," this Baba voice began. I was sitting every morning and taking notes. Again he said, "I want you to eat the ash."

Okay, now it was time to find out who this was. I went to see Drue for the first time since she was in my living room walking me through my experience. I told her about this Indian guy who sent me to Macy's on a shopping spree for new clothes and she sat up straight and said, "He told you to eat the *ash*?"

"Yes. What's the ash? Is that a bad thing?"

"No, no, it's incredible. This sounds like Sai Baba."

"Is he a dead fashion designer?"

"No, Marla, he's an avatar in India, a guru, a teacher. The ash is the sacred vibhuti (vuh-BOO-tee) that grows on his photos and that he manifests out of his hands as a blessing."

"What?" I was shocked. "You mean to tell me that this person is real? You mean he's not dead?"

"No, very much alive, and my brother is a devotee of his. I actually have some of the ash in my purse." Drue picked up her purse and started to dig around.

"Look, Drue, this is just too weird. It's one thing to talk to dead folks but now I'm taking notes from a person alive on the other side of the world who makes ash out of his hands? And you have some in your *purse*?"

With that, Drue handed me a piece of foil that looked like a stick of gum. "Here it is."

"Don't you think this is weird? And what the heck do you do with it?" I was simply flabbergasted.

"Well, I eat it," Drue replied.

I opened up the piece of foil. It was a grey powder with a gritty consistency. I moved it around with my finger. "It smells divine," I said. "Catholics wear ash on their foreheads, so I guess I can eat some." I dabbed my finger in the ash and put it in my mouth. It felt crunchy, as though I had swallowed the earth. Relieved, I said, "It feels like I am connected to this. It feels great!"

"Baba is like the Christ consciousness in India," Drue said. "His teachings are all about benevolence, nonviolence, right conduct, truth, and love. I believe there is an ashram north of Sacramento that holds the essence of Baba. I will get you the details."

I was interested in understanding God in any way I could. Faith is expressed all over the world in different ways. God's blessings and the Christ consciousness are a part of all loving religions, described in different ways. Finding a teacher from India and losing the potential of my nose looking like my mother's was my answered prayer. I had also prayed for God to help my mother. I looked forward to how that might unfold, but for now I'd have to be more conscious of what I asked for.

I was setting out on a great adventure, and I started my six-hour trip up north to the ashram for Sai Baba in Colusa. It would be an adventure all right.

What am I doing here? I sat across the street of the home where the supposed essence of Sai Baba had manifested. I watched Indian men and women arrive with bags of fruit or flowers for offerings, take their shoes off, and enter the little stucco house.

It was a very modest place, probably built in the 1960s for a farmer or perhaps a truck driver who drove Interstate 5. I took off my shoes and walked in. Smiling faces greeted me. I handed a woman a bag of oranges and bananas and said, "I came up from Los Angeles. I'm the one who called and spoke to Ami's wife."

"I'm his wife. Oh, yes, please come in." She pointed into the main room. "You see the women are on the left side and the men on the right. Go sit down, but don't step on the white cloth. We will sing bhajans and then have a blessing."

I reverently walked into the room. It was a rectangle of dark red carpet split down the middle with a long, white cloth path sprinkled with flowers. At the end of the room was a burst of color: a large photo of Baba in an orange-red robe framed by twinkling lights. My eyes focused on the many photos, art pieces, and flowers that adorned a long altar. Grey patches of ash that looked exactly like the sacred vibhuti Dr. Drue had in her purse covered the walls and every object on the altar, including pictures of Jesus and Mary Magdalene, statues of Ganesh, candles, flowers, and incense.

Singing bhajans is like trying to sing a song you sort of know but in a different language. By the time you start to get the hang of it, it's over and you're on to the next. A trancelike, peaceful quality came over the room and a palpable electricity bristled in the air. Then things became clearer and I could see that one photo was of just Baba's feet. Something on it covered his toes and was dripping like honey into a square plastic Tupperware container. Now that's odd—what is that stuff?

One of the women sitting next to me said, "That is the holy nectar called 'amrita.'" The more the music was sung, the more the golden amrita oozed. Then, as I looked again at the altar, I also noticed the crusty golden amrita on a statue of Jesus, dripping from the heart and collecting into a smaller plastic container. I was mesmerized and wanted to get closer, but there were more prayers and blessings.

It was probably my natural skepticism, but I thought if this was all real and Baba had actually been talking to me, I would ask for a confirmation. I thought it would be nice to receive a blessing, so I said a silent prayer. "Baba, if you would like to give me a blessing, will you please drop a flower out of the ceiling and into my hand as a confirmation?" I was shocked that I had had such a thought. Where in the world did that come from? After two hours of these songs, I was woozy. Just as they finished and I was getting up, a beautiful Indian woman who had been sitting to my right looked at me, lovingly took my hand and placed a flower onto my palm. "You are blessed," she said.

I went to a motel and fell asleep. The next morning I drove back to L.A., quietly wondering how to integrate this experience.

Ever since the accident with my nose, Sonny was not doing well. He had hip dysplasia and was increasingly in pain. The tabby cat who was cheating on his owners with me would not leave his side.

One of the connections I made at the Sai Baba Ashram was with Sarah, a hospice worker who had made a trip down from San Francisco for the weekend. One of Sarah's many gifts was helping people cross over to the other side. I was intrigued with the strength and compassion it took to be able to do that. She was a Sai Baba devotee, and I invited her to come and talk to a group of women I pulled together at the house.

I had a lot to do to prepare, but I went to the computer that morning as I always did. Waiting for me was an email sent by Barb, a classmate from Bedford with whom I had not communicated since I graduated from high school some twenty years earlier. Her email shared a story of how a woman who went rock climbing lost her contact lens.

Brenda was almost halfway to the top of a tremendous granite cliff. As she rested, the safety rope snapped against her eye and knocked out her contact lens. She looked and looked, hoping that somehow it had landed on the ledge. She felt the panic rising in her, thinking of the danger of having blurry vision on the climb, so she began praying that she might find her contact lens. She had to move on. When she got to the top, she was saddened because she could not clearly see across the range of mountains. She thought of the Bible verse, "The eyes of the Lord run to and fro throughout the whole earth." She thought, "Lord, you can see all these mountains. You know every stone and leaf, and you know exactly where my contact lens is. Please help me." She carefully hiked down the trail to the bottom of the cliff and her group met another party of climbers just starting up the face of the cliff. One of them shouted out, "Hey, you guys! Anybody lose a contact lens? There's an ant moving slowly across a twig on the face of the rock, carrying it!"

That was a wonderful little story, but I could not understand why after twenty years of no communication Barb decided to send it to me.

Sarah arrived, and as she walked in the door, Sonny did something very strange. He went straight up to Sarah and started talking to her. These were sounds that I had never heard come out of him before. Sonny looked up at this lovely woman who helped people cross over to the other side and what I felt him communicate made my heart sink: *Oh, I'm so glad you are here, I've been waiting for you. It's time to go and I want you to help me.*

I made a psychic snapshot of that moment, but shook that thought out of my head and greeted my friends who had come to hear Sarah talk about her amazing life with Sai Baba.

Sarah started the evening off with telling us about the first time she went to see Baba in India.

"I was getting divorced," she said. "I did not have a spiritual life and I longed to be part of something. When I heard about Sai Baba's teachings, I felt that I had to go see him in India. When I got to the ashram I was anxious; all I wanted to know was if God loved us, and me, in a personal way. I wrote Baba letters and held them for his assistants to take. Mine were not taken."

"Then I lost my contact lens the first week I was there and I couldn't see well at all. I had to move to different places to stay in the ashram, and on my last day I sat down and cried. I was telling God, 'All I want to know, Lord, is if you care about us individually, and if you think I am special.' And then something directed me to look down at the cot I was sitting on. There on the blanket was my contact lens."

I immediately told everyone about the contact lens email I had received that morning. We were all astounded. Both women shared similar stories from different sides of the world, feeling blind, praying for help, wanting a special connection to God, and both were given sight through the lenses of different belief systems. It didn't matter . . . God/Spirit/Jesus/the Larger Consciousness System shared the same optics of the heart for healing.

Sarah left the next morning to drive back north. Sonny became deathly ill with seizures and vomiting. He had suffered a heart attack and died. I was inconsolable.

Sarah called us that night to say, "You know, I had the oddest thing happen. When driving home I felt Sonny in the car with me."

Sonny knew it was time to leave, but we are never prepared to lose anything that connected us so deeply to our hearts. He was an instrument of unconditional love, fulfilling a prayer and opening a door to more wisdom and learning. Sarah's visit was perfectly timed.

Teachers come in many forms. How they show up in our lives is an exercise in trust and tolerance.

17

Awe-thentic

"Until we have seen someone's darkness,
we don't really know who they are.
Until we have forgiven someone's darkness,
we really don't know what love is."
—Marianne Williamson

My twenty-fifth high school class reunion was coming up. I had not intended to make the trip back until I heard, the way I hear things, *Go home, Marla.*

I often dreamed of driving along country roads with the windows rolled down and Bedford's WBFD 1310 on my radio dial, singing at the top of my lungs the popular songs of the 1970s like "Band on the Run" and "Sister Golden Hair." Then I would reach my neighborhood, Meadowbrook, with the oh-so-familiar feel of crossing the one-lane bridge over the creek called Shober's Run, then making the turn and going up the hill to my home at the top of the street where the beautiful house that my father, in tribute to my mother's Southern heritage, built with the town contractor Dale Arnold, when the craft of building homes was an art. That red-bricked, white-pillared colonial manse loved me when it was hard to find love between the walls. But going home meant—Mother.

I had not been home since my father's funeral, yet I continued to share with Mother photos and Hollywood stories that would give her some joy and bragging rights at the beauty parlor. At the same time, she had absolutely no interest in my new life of helping others in communicating with Spirit. When that subject came up, her brain seemed to drop into some sensory deprivation tank and she had nothing to say. Perhaps that was a good thing.

Within minutes of the six-hour red-eye flight and three-hour drive through the sultry summer thunderstorms in the mountains of Pennsylvania, I was home. Mother met me at the kitchen back door, the portal of possibility where she waited in excitement for infrequent visitors. Her face broke into a smile. I tried to hug her but she didn't hug like normal people. She pushed me back to take a look at me.

She was a good four inches shorter than I am, but always adjusted herself to stand up straight. Her frosted angel-fine hair was freshly coiffed from a visit to Judy's Beauty Parlor. She looked crisp in her small-town-trying-to-be-upper-middle-class tailored white shirt tucked in a pair of navy blue polyester pants. Her little belly, held back for years by girdles, pushed against the sink. Her hands were now busy in the dishwater, like she was trying to scrub away some stubborn pain or the overwhelming emotions that my visit brought. I had only been there ten minutes and she was already agitated.

"You look tired," Mother quipped.

"I am tired," I said.

"Well, what are you doing or not doing to make you look like that?" she smirked, slapping the dish towel on the counter and standing with her hands on her hips like I'd done something scathing to raise her scorn. With no idea what she was concocting, I chose to think she was recreating what she had just watched on one of her soap operas, pretending *she* was the actress on set, and in this scene she had just found out her daughter was sleeping with the low-life nephew of her dreaded rival. The camera closed in on her indignant smirk and the cheesy music swelled before cutting to a commercial.

She needed connection. A need she would not admit. Instead, she projected her fears onto others, pushing them away and punishing them for not being what she needed, for not reflecting what she wanted. With that, she created the opposite of what she really wanted—love—and had the satisfaction of being right, that no one loved her.

The last time I'd seen her was when I tried to hold her hand at my father's funeral. I hoped that with his death she would have no more reason to be so angry. I knew she was capable of being normal because she had shown me from time to time . . . the most memorable episode was when I was ten years old and just the two of us drove to Nags Head, North Carolina, to spend a week at the Cavalier Motel. Mother was a completely different person as soon as we crossed the state line into her home state. The scent of pine trees and ocean spray softened her heart and the frown in her face disappeared. With the warmth of the sun and the rhythm of the surf, she grew young again and was happy.

She delighted in making me cheese eggs with chopped green peppers before I'd hit the beach for a full day of swimming, moving between the ocean and the pool. This was the only place where being Marla's mother was easy and being a wife to Fries was forgotten. Under the North Carolina sun and summer rainstorms, she never uttered a mean word. No pain came to any part of me when we were there. Maybe the sand and Boone's Farm wine pumiced away her callousness.

"Where do you want to eat tonight?" she'd ask. "Wanna go get Kentucky Fried Chicken or run across the street for cheeseburgers, or dress up with our fresh sunburns and go to the Port o'Call restaurant for shrimp?" It was a rare adventure to escape our lives, falling asleep to the magic vibrating beds. In those fleeting moments I felt she loved me, and I got a glimpse of what "normal" might feel like. But we had to come home eventually, and the dream scabbed over. This was the mother I tried to remember.

Spirit had guided me home and therapy helped me, so I was prepared. I faced her as she stood by the sink with her bad-tempered smirk. "If you can't be nice to me, Mother, I'll stay in one of the seedy motels out by the turnpike that's known for trysts and one-night stands." And with that calm resolve I left the room and roamed around the house to still my nerves.

Every room was picture perfect like no one lived in it. In the little den off the kitchen, a bookcase filled with volumes for show and a set of Encyclopedia Britannica gave the impression that someone in the house knew something. My father's La-Z-Boy rocker was empty, but not of the memories . . . *I love you, Daddy*. I could always get a feeling for how Mother felt about me when I walked in that room. She loved to display moments of my life for others to see—photos from a TV show, backstage antics with stars I'd worked with, or one of the handsome men I'd dated. If she wanted to punish me for some unknown reason, those photos would be removed and in their place would be pictures of some relative she didn't speak to or my sister or niece. That day, a photo of me with Cindy Crawford stood on the coffee table.

I went upstairs. My pink bathroom seemed so small. I had to bend down to see my face in the mirror. There on the little shelf was the pink-and-white plastic cup that sat there since I was eight. "Virgo," it said. Yellowed with age, the list of astrological traits was still legible: *loyal, kind, compassionate, and intuitive.* I let the water run in the pink sink until it was really cold, the way I liked it. This was the bathroom where I had practiced soap commercials, where Mother had hurt me, and where I learned to leave my body. I was grateful I had overcome and healed so much. I felt that there was a deeper reason I'd come home and hoped Sprit would help me figure that out.

I would have been glad to go to town for lunch and bring food home, but mother was happily fussing around where she felt most successful, the kitchen.

Mother was a great cook and always made delicious, well-balanced Southern meals. Her famous fried chicken, various vegetable concoctions from our garden, meats raised on our farm, delectable pies, and even all of Daddy's hunting trophies were prepared to perfection. Mother pointed and announced, "We're going to eat lunch in the dining room!"

My father's hard work and Mother's decorating tips made our dining room like the highlight of a historic Southern plantation, and today I was part of the tour. A far cry from the little tobacco farm where Mother was raised.

The Duncan Phyfe dining table was appointed with silver candelabras and a pink crocheted tablecloth that matched the drapes and the blossoms of the wallpaper. Grand baroque silver and bone china edged with gold rested in locked cabinets, waiting for visitors worthy enough for them to be used. The only thing missing was the velvet rope for us to stand behind.

This was a place of bygone days, where fantasies of happy dinners still lingered in the phantom aroma of roasted turkey.

"I hope you'll eat cornbread and cod," Mother said as she plopped a dime-store plastic dinner plate in from of me. I never ate cornbread or cod, and she knew it. I ate a banana, and just as I did as a child after every meal, I wanted to get the hell out of there. But instead of my childhood routine of jumping on my bike and riding all over the place, I said, "I think I'll drive around town."

With windows down and the radio on, I sang at the top of my lungs along the hilly, narrow country roads past dairy farms and Egolf Park all the way over the mountain to the Cumberland Valley and our farm. I made my way back into town past the Bedford Springs Resort and Spa. This National Historic Landmark was the town jewel and Allegheny getaway treasure between Pittsburgh and Philadelphia. I had lifeguarded here at the pool, dressed up for proms, celebrated friends' weddings, flown on the rope swing into cold deep water of Red Oaks Lake, and made out with boys in the parking lot. I fell in love with every little downtown shop and business again as I walked the square for hours, hunting down friends who worked at the bank, post office, dress shops, and the hotspots for vintage tchotchkes and arts and crafts by local artists. Finally, I made a last stop at the Golden Eagle Inn and Pub, owned and run by friends, where the food was as delicious as the hospitality. As I sat looking at the familiar street scene out the window, I realized how much I loved every part of this town and the land around it.

I knew Mother would be on the sofa while I was gone, the place she chose to recline her life. When I returned she'd either be happy to see me or angry that she had been abandoned for so long, so I came home with a sweet gesture of contrition, caramel corn from Gardner's Candies, her favorite.

As soon as I handed Mother her treat, neighbor Joyce called on the phone. "Hey there, Marla, how do you feel about coming to my house and maybe talking to some dead people?"

Joyce was the beautiful blonde neighbor who was as sweet as she was kind. She did her best to be a good friend to Mother, deflecting Reinette's occasional comment of, "Joyce, your ass is getting big." If it was a really bad comment, Mother might feel guilty, make Joyce a pie, and sashay it over to her back door. Never actually hearing an apology, Joyce would always forgive her anyway.

I sledded Joyce's hill, trick-or-treated at her door, endured her son Jack using my right arm as a punching bag in the fifth grade, shared each other's joys and maladies in phone marathons, and stayed best friends for life. Her son, Bobbie, had been tragically killed in a drug deal gone bad. Joyce knew that I was beginning a new vocation with the dearly departed, and I was more than delighted that she had called. "Joyce, whatever you would like to do would be fine with me," I told her. "Actually, if you have any other friends who would like to come, I will work with as many as ten, and maybe we will connect with Bobbie."

"That would be great," Joyce said. "I'll set the whole evening up." Mother, who wanted no part of my event, stayed on the sofa.

Joyce's gold and velvety blue living room was set up with chairs and people. I was so excited to see what might happen. A cute, spunky redhead caught my attention, and I immediately started with her. I don't usually ask people their names because I don't remember them while I am working, but I looked at this woman and said, "Hi, what's your name?"

"It's Betsy."

Without a beat I heard, *That's not her real name.*

"But that's not your real name," I said.

Everyone in the room murmured, "Oh, yes, that's her name. Yep, she's Betsy, uh huh."

"Nope, you were named something different."

"Well, I was adopted."

The room shifted and I felt this love and deep compassion and realized I had a group of loved ones on the other side that had been watching her from afar for a long time.

"Well, that makes sense. Some of your birth family want you to know that they still love and watch over you. I'm not going to tell you things that cannot be corroborated about them, but they want you to know they know all about your son, his red car, and the accident near Dutch Corner."

"Yes, my son has a red car and had an accident out in Beldon not too far from Dutch Corner."

"They just want you to know they still care and they want the best for you and your family." Her boyfriend, Gary, was smiling.

Gary was the pharmacist at the popular family-owned Ickes Drug Store where many years ago I sat at the ice-cream counter relishing the monthly reward that our Trinity Lutheran Church choir director, Gertrude Shaffer, would treat us to after a good rehearsal. As I looked at Gary I laughed out loud and said, "You may have heard people who pretend to be psychic say, 'Oh, you have an American Indian guide with you,' a trick of the trade to tell you something that you can't really prove but sounds exotic and special. But Gary, you *do* have this huge Indian with a massive headdress standing behind you! He's saying that he is from the Dakotas, assigned to you because he promised never to leave your family!"

Gary was calm as he told his story. "Years ago there was a serious car accident on the Turnpike. It was a family of Lakota Indians. The chief was hurt and had to stay in the hospital. When he was better, my grandparents, Ma and Pa Ickes, took the chief and his wife by train back to the Dakotas. In thanks, the chief said he would always protect them." We were all amazed; clearly, the chief had made good on his promise.

It was an extraordinary evening, even though Bobbie didn't come through. But Joyce's husband, Don, had a busy night with his deceased brothers entertaining us with "down at the river" fishing stories.

That night was such a gift. A divine confirmation of my new work.

I was ready for the reunion. I wore a little green and purple dress that set off my eyes. I felt comfortable to face my classmates after twenty-five years, at least as comfortable as a born-again-former-high-school-majorette-turned-Hollywood actress who just had the bottom of her nose sheared off and was giving up her acting career to be a psychic and communicate with dead people could feel.

Mother had been very quiet since my evening at Joyce's. I was cautious of what was coming next.

Before I walked out the door Mother took my hand and looked at my nails. "Oh, you have such pretty hands. Your nails look nice. Let me see your teeth." I went through some version of this inspection routine every time I came home. She needed me to be perfect for her equilibrium, but I never was. She was so disconnected—I understood that I was not really a daughter, but a prop. I still smiled. She didn't notice my nose, and I wasn't about to tell her. Learning to be authentic with my mother still needed some work. I was wary of how she could turn, since she could easily be triggered by anything. For years when Daddy and I left for the farm, Mother would sit on that sofa and stew, feeling abandoned and plotting how to make us pay. So before I left for the reunion, I suggested she set up a lunch the next day for us with Joyce and Pat. Perhaps we could have some fun!

We high-school reuniters looked past the extra pounds and fewer hairs to see each other through sixteen-year-old eyes, which was strange but comforting. The personas we had created to survive hormone high left us all scarred by acne, lost loves, and dreams that died and morphed us into unique realities. Our class science nerd became a decorated admiral, our star basketball player a hospital nurse, the quiet mousy girl in home room a gorgeous business executive. Tara, our class president, whom I adored, was missing, and Harvey, the boy I loved, would be the elusive one who never came back to Bedford except for the funerals of his family members. We all came together to remember who we were, let go of what we thought we knew about one another, and share who we had become.

The evening was great fun, full of laughter at ourselves and each other as we reminisced. The truth was I loved my hometown and the people in it. I was happy and grateful that Spirit had suggested I come back.

As I drove home, Mother flashed in my mind's eye. I could see her the way I was trained by the U.S. military psychic spies/ remote viewers to blindly see a target and identify parts of it. She was in the den, stuffing the photos of me into the cabinet behind my father's rocker. Something had set her off while I was gone. I hoped I was wrong.

When I got home she was lying on the sofa in wait. I walked to the edge of the den and confirmed what I had psychically seen: all traces of me and the life I tried to share with her were gone. She pointed to the wall where my majorette photo used to hang, now replaced with a photo of the house. Before she could say anything, I jumped in.

"Oh, Mother, that is a lovely photo of the house. I'm tired and I'm going to bed."

Our lunch date was still set. Joyce and Pat were welcome allies in lightening things up. Mother wouldn't dare misbehave in front of her support team, and if she did, I had the girls to protect me.

We all arrived at the restaurant at the same time and waited by the front counter to be seated. Joyce, with perfectly coiffed blonde hair, was beautifully dressed in one of Bedford's finest dress shop outfits and gracious as always. Pat commented on how much she liked the big pink flowers of my Ann Taylor sundress, and Joyce said, "Oh, Marla, don't you look darling in that dress? It shows off all of your terrific curves."

Mother turned to me and said, "Yes, doesn't she look nice?" And with that, she took her right hand and fondled my left breast and right breast and back again.

Time stopped as my body tried to register the shock of what just happened—and then I hit her.

I knocked her arm down so hard my sunglasses flew out of my hand and smashed to the floor. "How *dare* you touch me!"

I screamed. "You have no right to touch my breasts! What the *fuck* do you think you're doing? Don't *EVER* touch me again!"

There was no way I could have prepared for that.

She had slipped, exposing a hint of the physically inappropriate abuse I had suffered for years.

I finally stopped the perpetrator. For years I had prayed for someone to stand up to my mother and protect me—Daddy, various boyfriends, even Mother's friends—but I could finally take care of myself. I walked to our table feeling very different. Pat, and Joyce, the other patrons of Hoss's Restaurant, and the heavens were my witnesses.

Things were very quiet during that lunch, but I rallied and told story after story. Mother was silent.

I had never fought back until that moment. I guess I believed in a humanity where she would face her problems and get help. I didn't like that I had used force to stop her 'touching,' but standing up for myself in the face of an unpleasant truth was another layer of being authentic as I continued to forgive her and struggled to forgive myself.

I wanted to make sure the righteous anger I had demonstrated was in check. I went back to L.A., debriefed with Dr. Bogdonoff, and started Taekwondo, punching and kicking out any darkness left inside me.

I was different. Spirit's guidance to *go home, Marla,* and knowing that there was more to the trip than my reunion, was surprising and unsettling. As an actress I'd always played characters who were aspects of my mother. From the crazy, angry, nasty parts to the quirky good friend, wacky mother, sublime, or seductive dangerous roles, oozing Southern charm with deadly intent. Moving those emotions and expressing them on stage prevented them from getting stuck inside my body. Emotions that could make me sick and debilitate me. God gave me the opportunity to integrate the light and the darkness, heal the brokenness, and find compassion for the humanity of the wounds. I was so grateful I had an outlet for those elements.

The life of an actress was grand, fun, and rewarding in so many ways, but Spirit's healing grace extended far beyond what I could see for myself.

I booked a guest starring role on *Strong Medicine* playing a cunning diet pill sales woman peddling Ephedra, and another guest spot on *The Drew Carey Show* playing Sylvia, the glamorous, well-coiffed business executive that opened the show with Wanda Sykes and Drew. It was great fun, and then it was over.

I had just packed up all my belongings and was stepping out of my honey wagon (the little dressing room trailer) outside the Warner Brothers sound stage where the *The Drew Carey Show* was filmed, when I saw the director of my show, Gerry Cohn. Gerry had also directed me eleven years earlier in my *Married . . . with Children* episode called "We'll Follow the Sun" (an internet favorite) when Gerry said, "Marla, nice job. Good working with you again."

"Thanks Gerry." And then I felt it. I had come full circle. I'd shot my first show with Gerry in 1990, it was now 2001, and I was happy to have had some pretty great success for a Pennsylvania pig farmer's daughter. As an actress, you play yourself in a role with as much authenticity as you have found in yourself. God's grace had given me a lifetime to find Marla. I was developing my own character and helping others, making something good of my trauma and drama. I no longer needed to be someone else for someone else. I no longer wanted to play anyone else but me. I was done. I had a new job and I surrendered to it.

It was now September 11, 2001. Just after dawn the phone rang. I couldn't imagine who would call so early unless it was bad news. My heart skipped a beat as a familiar voice said, "Marla, turn on the TV. We're being attacked!"

My dear friend Barbara was hysterical as she continued to describe what was happening in New York. I sat up, clicked on the TV and watched the World Trade Center billow with the fires and smoke of hell and then collapse. We were both in tears, immediately thinking of our New York friends and family. Then reports came in that a plane had gone down in Shanksville, Pennsylvania, only twenty some miles west of Bedford. I started making calls to Mother and everyone I could think of back home, but the phone lines were jammed. All of America was in shock. The war we had raged in other countries had come home. Darkness was made visible in America. Everything and everyone mattered. From that day on we spent all our time with people we loved and doing what we were compelled to do. Grief gripped life for months.

Fred Fontana called and asked if I would be willing to do a group at his house. People were looking for understanding. Everyone was trying to make sense of all the death and destruction. They wanted guidance from the divine and deceased loved ones, and if I could help them, I would.

One of the guests who came to Fred's home was an angelic man with long blond-white hair dressed in a beautiful suit and tie. His name was Chris Dane Owens. When I looked at him, I immediately saw a deceased thin, dark-haired woman who had passed from some problems around her kidneys. Chris had tears running down his cheeks. His wife had died from adrenal cancer.

Chris's deceased wife, Nancy, came in from the other side to love Chris. She had so much respect and appreciation for him that the whole group was moved to tears. When Nancy started to laugh, I realized she was a bit of a prankster. I tried to catch what she was saying, but it wasn't until she showed me a mailbox that I began to understand what she wanted Chris to know. She had a happy, funny surprise for Chris, and it was coming in the mail.

"Did anything come in the mail that was funny or odd?" I asked Chris.

Chris didn't know what I was talking about; nevertheless, we ended the session feeling deeply moved about Nancy.

Just a few days later, Chris got a past-due notice in the mail from Blockbuster. It was a postcard stating that Nancy had checked out a video called *Rock Chris: The Best of the Chris* on November 24 and kept it out beyond the due date, which was November 29. Chris was confused by this, of course, and called Blockbuster.

"Mr. Owens, it looks like Nancy checked out a video called *The Best of Chris Rock* on November 24."

"That would be impossible," Chris told him, "because she died this past January."

We were shocked. How could a video be checked out in Nancy's name with such a significant title ten months after she died? Chris clearly got that Nancy was communicating that the *Rock Chris: The Best of the Chris* was what she had tried to share in our session.

Chris understood that the postcard message was Nancy's way to nudge him back to a talent he had left behind, singing and songwriting. He and Nancy had been in a band together and recorded several rock videos. Chris had not written a song or picked up his guitar in ten years. He knew that Nancy's surprise was encouraging him to get back to his passion, something that fed his soul and brought him so much pleasure. The idea that Spirit could manipulate electronics to make this happen was such a surprise.

After the *Rock Chris: The Best of the Chris* card came in the mail from Blockbuster, Chris slowly set a course to get back into music. He rebuilt his music studio, started working with a talented producer, and recorded song after song in the hopes of doing a full-length album.

After Chris posted his *Shine on Me* video on YouTube, *The New Yorker* named the video "Best Music Video of the Year." Later that year, Chris appeared in *Rolling Stone* magazine—his dream come true.

"Marla," Chris told me, "my work with you and the messages from Spirit and Nancy were the force of inspiration in the creation of my art and changed my life forever." Love had pushed through the veil and all of us were in awe.

18

The Loving

"If you want to become fearless, choose love."
—Rune Lazuli

"Sure, I will be happy to see them!" I told Laura. Laura was one of my longest-known and dearest clients, a successful player in the television and film business. Laura trusted my gifts and wanted to share them with friends who were visiting from out of town. I could feel the group even before they came to the house. It was going to be one of those nights in which both the living and the dead needed some help.

Charlie was a powerhouse, well compacted in her hip-hugging jeans, long jet black hair, and shimmery pink lips. She walked into my living room with a personality that could drive the evening, but unprepared for what the dead had in store.

While I was engaged in communicating information to another woman in the group, Charlie kept interrupting, giving her interpretation of my interpretation of what I was hearing from the woman's deceased loved one. She wouldn't be quiet. This is indicative of the nervousness that sometimes happens in groups, but she was disrupting the session.

"Ok, Charlie," I said, "I need you to be quiet until I can get the information out for other people. But I can tell you that I have your mother here, who is very sorry for how she treated you."

Charlie launched back, "Oh, *now* she wants to talk! Of course she treated me badly, and *now* she wants to talk to me. Jesus!" She threw her hands up in the air in defiance. I am always surprised when Spirit sets up these wonderful opportunities for healing. I decided to stay with Charlie's mom for the moment and return to the other woman's relative as soon as this was finished.

"Charlie, it was your choice to come here tonight," I said. "I have no idea who your mother was when she was alive, but I can feel her now and she is very sad about how her behavior affected you. She knows about the book, she saw you get the award, and she is again apologizing, for . . . giving your sister the car you wanted."

Charlie didn't even blink. She was still so angry that she was now questioning the room. "Doesn't everybody's mother give them a car ? So what? So she gave my sister the one I wanted, so WHAT?"

The other women looked at me shaking their heads, like, "Nope, my mom never had any cars to give *me*."

"Charlie, you have an opportunity here," I continued. "You can either accept this apology, or we can move on."

She folded her arms and said, "Okay, whatever."

I could feel her mother trying to be as calm and loving as possible as she started to explain some of the things that she as a mother had wrestled with. She cited events that were upsetting for Charlie, and again she apologized. Charlie simply would not hear it.

I silently told the mother, *She is not ready for this.* Charlie was now in a full-blown meltdown, so I put up my hand and said, "Charlie, please stop! Your mother says you were born on August sixth and that she loves you."

Charlie gasped at the exact date of her birthday. She finally calmed down and began to cry. I heard later through the grapevine that Charlie talked about that for weeks.

The wounds between parents and children are tender in life, but in death they can be gaping and raw. There is no right or wrong way to grieve. There is nothing one can do but let the wildness of those wounds find calm. You can't force a person to be rational and you can't wake up a person who is pretending to be asleep. You have to wait. The dead know how we feel, and if we hurt they know it. It's my job to mediate as I did with Charlie and her mother, but that experience was also Spirit's way of preparing me.

My mother was one of the queens of Judy's Beauty Parlor. She had been traveling the twelve or so miles up the narrow two-lane highway past Shawnee State Park to the one-streetlight town of Shellsburg to see either Pauline or Judy every Friday for thirty-two years.

It was a chatty room filled with women who wanted a break from their housewife lives in exchange for silken waves. They came to get beautiful, but it was more like a group therapy session. They endured the harangue of bristle rollers wound tight and cooked under the blast of a dryer for the opportunity to have their say about life and its challenges. But when Mother couldn't drive those distances anymore, she settled for a shop in town. One Friday morning, Reinette hooked her sensible shoe heel into the rung of the salon chair, fell, and broke her wrist and hip.

After her hip replacement she was put in Donahoe Manor, a convalescent nursing home two blocks away from our home in Meadowbrook.

"It's the old folk's home!" my childhood friend Bonnie would say about Donahoe. Bonnie and I were always producing neighborhood entertainment, charging a quarter for friends and parents to watch bargain-basement slapstick comedy. Sometimes we extended the festivities into the streets, leading a parade of costumed neighborhood kids—destination Donahoe to entertain the old folks.

By the time I was born, both sets of grandparents were dead and there were few visits from relatives, so I looked for guidance from sage strangers among the residents of Donahoe Manor. The blind Miss Dean was my favorite. Her black hair, streaked with silver, was always pulled back in a tight bun, which framed her beautiful, full-moon face. Miss Dean taught me about being blindsighted. She could always sense when I came into the room. She could see me in ways no one else could and taught me how to draw stars with one fell swoop of my hand.

The windows in Mother's room at Donahoe gave her a view of the home that Daddy had built for her, which we hoped would inspire her to heal quickly.

The jovial nurses and physical therapists catered to her every whim. Mother loved doctors and caretakers. She was instructed not to bend over, an order barked by the kindest of nurses to prevent her hip from dislocating and give the socket time to heal. But Mother did what she always did—what she wanted—and bent over to pick up a Kleenex tissue off the floor.

I woke up early, anxious, knowing something was terribly wrong. I called Donahoe. My mother wasn't there, and that meant one thing—she was in the hospital. I called Pat, Mother's housekeeper; no answer. That meant Pat was with my mother. I called the hospital. "Could you please connect me to emergency? I believe my mother came in this morning."

"Oh, are you the daughter in Los Angeles?"

"Yes, I am."

"Well, your mother had a massive stroke and is dying. I'm sorry."

This lack of decorum was bad even for a small-town hospital. "Is there a woman with her?" I asked.

"Uh, yeah," the nurse said.

"Could you please give the phone to her?"

"Well, I don't know if I can do that."

"If my mother is dying, don't you think I better be able to say something to her?"

After a silent moment on the other end, she said, "All right."

"Pat?" I said anxiously.

Pat was crying, "Yes, Marla, it's bad."

"Is she coherent?"

"Her eyes are open and she has some movement," Pat said.

"Can you put the phone up to her ear?"

"Yes, I can do that."

"Mother, it's Marla. Everything is going to be okay. You can let go now. You don't have to fight anymore. You are going to be fine . . . I love you."

I had wrestled with my feelings for so long that I had no idea what I would feel when my mother died. My greatest teacher and adversary was leaving. Pat was still crying, and then got back on the phone and said that she would call me. I thanked Pat for being by her side.

I prayed loved ones would meet her. I prayed for her peace. Pat called an hour later. "I'm sorry, I just got home. She's gone, Marla."

I had no breath, no sense of myself as I asked, "What happened, Pat?"

"I put the phone up to her ear so you could talk to her. Her eyes were open, but when you stopped talking, she turned her head away from the phone and cried. She died right after that."

"Thank you, Pat. I'll fly in on the red-eye tomorrow night."

I picked up Pat early in the morning and as she climbed in the car I said, "Buckle up. We're going to see Mother."

We drove the short distance to Berkebile's Funeral Home. Tim Berkebile was a calm, slender, centered man who was never rattled by death or the grieving loved ones left behind. Mother had opinions about the other two undertakers in town. Tim was cute and I'm sure she liked that.

I walked into the office and said to Tim, "I want to see her."

He was surprised. "She's just been washed, but she hasn't been prepared."

"I understand, Tim. I still need to see her."

"Okay, then." He led us back to a room. "Let me just adjust the lights for you, and I'll be outside when you're finished."

"Thank you."

I longed for the moment when I would finally see my mother calm and serene. I hoped that at the end she had let go of all the pain that had gripped her life and hurt so many. I prayed that her heart had melted and that she was finally at peace.

Pat and I walked in to the dimly lit room with a greenish tint that cast shadows on all the paraphernalia. Everything seemed clean and orderly. *Mother would like that,* I thought.

There was a warm heavenly glow from one light that hung over her body, and I could see the back of her head. Her fine, frosted hair was wet and hung in small ringlets. I remembered, *Oh, yes, she had natural curl to her hair.* All my life I had only seen her hair wet when we were down at the beach or in a chair at the beauty parlor.

She was on a shiny steel table with her shoulders elevated on a block of sorts. I moved to her right side and saw her body covered to just above her breasts by a crisp white sheet. *She would like that,* I thought. And then I saw her face. My hand flew up to my mouth and I muffled my shriek. "Oh, my God, Pat, she looks mad as hell, like she's not going to take it anymore! Look at her!"

Pat walked over. "Oooo, you're right, Marla. She does not look too happy."

"Maybe she's upset that she's naked or doesn't have her hair fixed or her lipstick on?"

"Oh, I don't know. Marla. Maybe she's upset 'cause she's dead."

I touched her cold bare shoulder, hoping she would see and hear me from some place on the other side of the veil. "Oh, Mommy, oh my goodness, you look so upset, you poor thing. Don't you worry. I'll get you all fixed up. I promise I will take care of everything and you will look beautiful."

This time I could help. Never in all my years as a daughter could I do anything for her in a normal loving way because our relationship was not at all normal. But today I could. This time I would love her in a way she could not resist. I would dress her in her favorite black suit with her ruffled ivory shirt. Underneath, a sturdy bra, good underwear, and no girdle this time. I would find her attractive patent leather loafers, her favorite brushed gold earrings, and the pewter angel necklace I gave her that she named Hope. I would ask Judy to do her hair, then make sure she had her favorite coral lipstick and signature glasses to frame her face. I finally had an important purpose, and this time she couldn't argue with me.

My mother had made it clear about what she wanted when it was her time to be eulogized. "I want Paul!" Not the minister from Trinity Lutheran where we were members for forty some years and where she had just donated a couple hundred bucks for the new wing. Nope, she wanted Paul from one of the other popular churches in town. That's the kind of news that could get Bedford buzzing, stir up pulpit egos, and encourage people to be less than their best by gossiping. *Let God's grace handle that.* A wise note from the Voice. I had always loved Paul and his wife, so I was delighted to honor Mother's request.

Paul and his new wife, Jerri, who had sung in the choir with me at Trinity, invited me into their comfortable home to discuss the funeral. We sat at their kitchen table to discuss the simple ceremony my mother wanted. But as I was talking, I began to see, hear, and feel information. I went blind to my present circumstance. In place of the kitchen where we were talking, I saw Paul as a younger man walking into a hospital room to talk to an older woman. This wasn't like Paul was visiting a parishioner. I could feel that this was someone very close, like his mother. The scene continued to play. I was overcome with grief, but it was not my own. How am I going to explain this one? I asked Spirit to help me share what was happening.

"Paul, Jerri, I'm sorry, but we have to stop for a moment. I know that I had mentioned to you that I now help build bridges of love between the living and the dead, and I cannot go on talking because something is happening. Would you mind if I shared what I am seeing and feeling with you?" They agreed that I should continue.

"I see an older woman. She is lying in a hospital bed and talking about the last time you saw her, Paul. She is telling me that you came into her room and she was mean to you. She wants you to know that she is deeply remorseful for her behavior."

Paul was visibly upset. "That's my mother. She told me to get out when I went into that hospital room," he choked. "She said that she never wanted to see me again. It was horrible, and I have carried that memory with me forever. I can't believe she is apologizing for that." He burst into tears.

"There's more going on, Paul," I said.

I knew that a number of years ago Paul's first wife had taken her own life. It was a tragic event for his family and parish. In such a small town, everyone is affected by such loss. His deceased wife, Pam, was with Paul's mother. Pam said to me regarding Paul, "We have to talk, and it has to be at the house." I relayed her words to them.

Jerri, Paul, and I looked at each other wide-eyed, not knowing what to do. I broke the ice and asked, "What house?"

Paul said that his previous home, where Pam had ended her life a number of years earlier, had never sold. There was no question for me—we had to go there.

It was a sweet home filled with charm, comfort, and a family secret. I walked in and went through every room. I could feel that Pam was in the house and wanted to communicate, but first I had to find her. She was not in the room where she had ended her life, but down in the basement laundry room, and that is where she wanted to talk.

I could feel her upset. She was distraught that Paul had blamed himself for not being able to save her. "I was ill!" Pam said. "You could always help your parishioners, but not me, because there was nothing you could do. I was not well."

I got the impression that she had been bipolar and had tried to medicate herself out of the despair. She was anguished over Paul still punishing himself for not being able to help. She said her actions had deeply hurt the children and she was bereft at what her behavior had done to them. She was desperate to apologize. It was time to heal.

Paul teetered between disbelief and acceptance of the events I saw and described, but I was determined to share what I heard and felt in order to facilitate the healing Pam and Paul needed. God's grace divined this opportunity for healing, and in that benevolent love Pam took this opportunity to use me, a former neighbor, to deliver her message.

Paul ultimately acknowledged what she was saying. They forgave each other for whatever happened all those years ago. Pam was determined to resonate love again in her family and in the house they had shared. I could feel her joy and immediately felt her spirit move beyond us into the light. Paul hugged me and we prayed.

It was all about the love as they addressed the tragic parts of their past in a musty basement laundry room. Love and forgiveness changed not only their relationship, but also the energy in the house. When I was back in California a few weeks later, I heard that the house had sold. Years later, Paul's children and I would talk about that day. They were relieved and grateful that their mother shared her grief, was released from her pain, and had moved into the arms of God. She loved them so.

My mother was laid to rest in the outfit I knew she would like and with Paul offering his compassionate sentiments. That same day, Laura, a dear childhood friend who was a part of my life at Trinity Lutheran and kindergarten through twelfth grade, hung herself.

People die in ways that make no sense to the living unless the living somehow understand the despair. The topic of suicide is often avoided. There is still a widely held belief that those who have attempted or do take their lives are crazy or emotionally weak. Because of those stigmas, many people who suffer from mental health issues who desperately need help do not seek it. Many try to keep it a secret by medicating themselves. Unfortunately, these tragic events are often met with judgment and condemnation, the opposite of what the victims and their families need. It is my experience that Spirit lovingly welcomes those with illness that result in troubled minds. It is not God who punishes them, it is the grief and regret they experience as they see, hear, and feel the pain of the loved ones they leave behind. It is the love for the living that makes the deceased push through the veil and find a way to apologize. It is our love and forgiveness of their actions that helps the deceased forgive themselves and move on.

There is no manual for death, no right or wrong way to grieve. We just do our best to cope.

That night I went to Laura's home and drank shots of Jack Daniel's with her mother, Jane. We cried.

My sister had been there for Mother after the accident and rehabilitation, traveling back and forth from Philly. The least I could do was stay as long as it took to clean out the entire house by myself and prepare the home for an estate sale.

I was lucky that Mother had Pat to help her for so many years. There wasn't much mess. The only place that could even be considered untidy was the attic. I felt guided, almost "told" where to start.

I climbed through the dusty Christmas ornament boxes and saw my father's military footlocker. It was unlocked, so I opened it to find a folded army hat and a couple of loose dress bars in the top section. Lifting it off to reveal the rest of the contents, I found an envelope with my father's service papers. "Date of active service, April 14, 1943." That was also my parents' anniversary; they were married the same day he left for active duty. Then an army-green tin can caught my eye. *Open it,* I heard.

Inside was a series of letters from my mother to my father dated between June and July, 1942. *This is what I wanted you to find.* Was this my father or mother pushing me to read these letters, or was it the Voice that wanted me to pay attention?

As soon as I held the letters I became sad, so very sad. I knew they were filled with emotions that I wanted no part of, and I said out loud, "I can't read these now. I have things to do." I put them aside, wondering when I could ever bear to read them.

With the exception of the things I knew my sister wanted from the house, I gave Pat everything she and her family could possibly use. I gave away pieces of costume jewelry to neighbors who wanted tiny remembrances of Reinette. I placed all of the items that Mother had collected in her eighty-some years down in the basement in rows of importance for the estate sale. Everything else I packed up and took to Goodwill. Those Goodwill ladies didn't know what to do when I delivered twenty-three yard-sized garbage bags of plastic flowers alone in four separate trips. I sold Mother's Lincoln Continental, cut down a rotten tree from the front yard, had the mulch around the plants replaced, worked with a childhood friend who was now a realtor to sell the house, and went to bed each night exhausted.

I would wake in the dead of night hearing messages. *"Hello, hello, Marla . . . Marla, this is your mother, I'm good, I'm fine, I can't believe I'm out of my body, I can't believe what I did to my body!"* Oh, my God, can I take this? This was the first time I had ever been in the house alone. Thumps and bumps I had never heard before, loose change on my dresser rattling in the middle of the night, and whispers from the ethers haunting me along with Mother. It was one noisy place.

I had cleaned out just about everything so that my sister could come in and stage the home for sale when I heard, *Look under the steps.* What? Who is talking to me? The only steps I could get under were the ones going down to the basement.

The laundry chute room was an area no bigger than five by eight feet, sat just under the steps. The musk of my father's scent from sending down a stinky shirt or two still permeated the little walls. *Look under the steps.* What the heck is going on here? This better be worth the hunt.

I found a flashlight and got on my knees, and there underneath the bottom step the light caught something brass. My eyes adjusted. It was a huge artillery tank shell with the head still attached. What the hell! All sorts of things ran through my mind. *OK, Daddy, this isn't funny. How did you get it here? Is it live?*

Pat would know what to do about this. She knew what to do with everything in that house, so I made a panicked call. "Oh, my God, Pat, what do I do with this thing?"

She laughed on the other end of the phone and said, "I've never seen *that* before! Wher'd it come from? How big is it?"

"I don't know, twenty-five to twenty-seven inches—it's HUGE!"

Pat knew every inch of that house and its contents and was still trying to figure out where the shell came from, but I was more concerned with other things.

"Pat! Do you think it's still good? I mean—can it blow me up?"

"Well, if it were me, I'd take it outside and put it far away from the house. Just in case."

"Ok, but if you don't hear back from me, you'll know what happened."

It was ten o' clock at night and pouring rain. I put on the forty-year-old pair of red rubber boots that Pat, Mother, Debbie, and I had all worn at some point in our lives and carried the big honkin' shell up the outside basement steps. I skipped the umbrella, deciding that using both hands was more important than staying dry. I walked a good twenty yards, mumbling, *Daddy, if you think this is funny, it's not. It's just like you to pull some dumb-ass joke on me.* I placed it next to the little brick wall, hoping it could protect our house and the neighbors if the shell went off.

The next morning Deputy Bob from the Bedford Burrow Police came over and escorted the shell away, smiling and laughing all the while. I wasn't sure why I was directed to find that shell. Maybe it was a scare tactic in the middle of all the chaos to make sure I was listening. After all, there *was* something under the steps. Or maybe the shell was a metaphor for the pent-up emotional energy that had built up in our home over the years, so hidden and repressed, and so deadly. Only now, with the explosive emotional release of all of us, either through words or death, could it be brought to the surface and carried away like a harmless, oversized blank.

I found joy in that house the last week I was there. I held mediumship sessions in the living room, bringing together loved ones and their deceased relatives in memorable moments with various Bedford friends. I had a picnic in the living room with friends Joyce, Diane, and Pat, eating with our fingers, drinking wine, and laughing as we told story after story about things that happened in my family.

As a child I lived my life under the canopy of custom luxury drapes, perfect valances, and sheers that blurred the world outside. I moved furniture out of the way to twirl batons, dance, and sing to top forties. I tried to work my way through a piano, clarinet, or trombone piece and carefully trim many a Christmas tree. But this beautiful room, dressed up with soft pastels of gold, rose, sage green, and powder blue, could not soften Mother's bitterness. I realized that this beautiful house perched atop a hill was sturdy enough to weather storms. A landscape of spacious rooms and doorways gave my mind and heart a place to create, craft, and nurture myself. It had been the perfect colonial backdrop my father helped build and my mother dressed up for the turmoil of this fractured family. I loved this home and intuitively understood that it was all perfect—despite the relentless heartbreak.

I prepared to leave my home in gratitude for holding the space for me to grow in, as well as to navigate the challenges of my life.

Don't forget the letters, I heard. I didn't want to do this, but someone wanted me to read them.

I felt like I was eight years old again as I sat on the floor in my sister's bedroom, where I felt safe. Beside me was the now-empty closet, where as a child I would slip behind Debbie's prom dresses and winter coats to hide from my mother. I opened the first letter, which was different than all the others, written on dark beige paper that carried the gold seal of the U.S Army. It was a letter from my father when he was in active duty overseas to his aunt who lived in Mercersburg, Pennsylvania.

> Dear Aunt Grace,
>
> I guess you feel about as lonely as I do now that Henry [Grace's son] has put on the uniform. I hope he never has to go through anything like this. I never dreamed that a person could be made so miserable and at the same time do so many things. . . . Reinette writes to me every day, but I hardly find the time to read the letters, let alone write any.

Although this barely scratched the surface of the despair of a boy sent off to war, it made my heart ache. I was not familiar with my father writing words to express his feelings, and this was the only letter from him that had been saved. The other sixteen letters were from my mother to my father, dated between June and July of 1942, less than a year before they were married and he was sent overseas.

In each letter my eyes grabbed hold of Southern phrases I had never heard Mother say to my father, as well as words that were painfully familiar.

"I know one thing Fries . . . I love you, I really do, more than anything!"

"I'm so upset about all the talk about you going overseas, I think that would really finish me."

"I don't believe you love me as much as I love you, I tell you one thing, you'd better!"

"I haven't had a letter from you, I just cried and cried."

"I don't care about having things, all I want is you!"

"Fries, I so hope your people will like me, I want that more than anything."

"I'll try to be real good and **NOT** TALK UGLY, hear? It will be hard but I'll try real hard. You don't really think I'm so very bad, do you?"

"I love you Fries."

I understood why I had to read them. Her terror, fears, and desperation for love, all magnified by the terror of war, were heartbreaking. Her self-absorbed fear and lack of empathy for my father's situation was deeply disturbing, but her awareness, even before they were married, that something might be wrong with her, was oddly calming. *"UGLY"* was a punishment she could not stand within herself, so she tried to project it out—and onto me. Needing my father's reassurance that she wasn't "so very bad" was the tragic realization that she knew, even in her twenties, that she was troubled.

What could have happened to her in the backwoods of her childhood tobacco farm? Never knowing either of my grandparents, and hearing only a few stories of how she deeply resented her alcoholic farmer father and worshiped her mother, left me wondering. This was another moment in which, even though I was sighted, I felt blind.

I have had time to reflect on the patterns and illnesses of both my parents. The WWI and II generation preceded the self-help and awareness revolution. Therapy and programs like Alcoholics Anonymous, Al-Anon, and CoDA (help for codependency) meetings that could have made such a dramatic change in their lives are now here to assist those of us who survived these troubled American families. Instead of spiraling into despair or having no other option than killing myself, I had to get help, and perhaps my parents, now on the other side, can learn from watching me heal my wounds and transform. This could be the whole point of karma, to allow the dead to now bear witness to the effect they had on their loved ones and others while they were alive. They see, hear, and feel how they affected us. It is up to us to acknowledge their behavior, find ways to heal it, and then forgive it. In turn, they can heal too.

I could not be who I am, lived the life I have lived, or experienced the many challenges and joys I have known without being the daughter of Fries and Reinette. Those are the gifts that came out of all the pain. They had disconnected from Spirit, each other, my sister, themselves, and me. The separation from love is the root of pain. This is what forced me to fight for my life, heal, and forgive those who didn't know any better. It took time and hard work to feel gratitude for those wounds. And it was in those wounds that "sight" had a chance to be born in me so that I might help others.

19

Consummations

"What the caterpillar calls the end of the world,
the master calls a butterfly."
—Richard Bach

My friend and client, Chris Dane Owens, who had lost his wife to adrenal cancer, continued to have sessions with me. Teachings for Chris came in from Spirit in such a high frequency that my living room seemed to go white, and I was blinded with the light of an overwhelmingly loving and intelligent consciousness. "Chris, I am being told that you are thinking about quitting, giving up your efforts to produce TV shows."

"Yes, that's right," he said.

"Don't! Don't give up. I'm being told it's going to work. You will be successful!"

Chris listened to the messages, stuck with his plan, and eight months later he and Jerry Biederman, his producing partner, got a show on the air. Two more shows followed as well as an Emmy nomination.

Chris was also very interested in the UFO phenomenon. He became a voracious student of people who had dramatic stories of "contact" and was especially interested in Whitley Strieber's *Communion*, the book I had read in Cleveland back in 1987 while sitting in a little rowboat.

Chris's day job at Warner Bros. Studio afforded him the opportunity to arrange a screening of a new documentary on the unexplained UFO event that happened the night of March 13, 1997, over Phoenix, Arizona, called *The Phoenix Lights*.

"Marla, I'd love for you to come meet Dr. Lynne Kitei," Chris said. "She is the woman who actually caught the event on video and was compelled to pull together all the information and eyewitnesses to make the documentary."

"Chris, you know me—the whole idea of UFOs confuses me, and after my own experience in Sedona, I'm not sure I want to go down that road again."

"Well . . . I invited Anne and Whitley Strieber," he said.

"I'm there!" I squealed.

Ever since reading Whitley's book ten years earlier I had hoped that I would meet him and his wife someday.

Dozens of people showed up for the screening on the Warner Bros. lot. I leaned into Chris right before the film started. "Hey, where are those Striebers?"

"Marla, they're sitting right next to you." I was shocked. Just two seats away was a cute little woman in a green sweater with short-cropped red hair, and beside her, wearing distinguished wire-rimmed glasses, was the famous author Whitley Strieber. I threw myself over the empty seats and said, "Oh wow! I have been waiting to meet you since 1987! Your book blew me away. I'm so happy to see you!" They looked at me, smiled, and graciously said, "Thank you." I sounded like a total groupie.

Even though the documentary was powerful and educational, my thoughts over the next few days were all about the Striebers and the book. The cover of *Communion*, though powerfully haunting, was strangely familiar. The Striebers felt like colleagues from some faraway institution of learning—interesting, intelligent, curious, deeply unique, and kind. We struck up a friendship that opened a door of information for Whitley, information that, similar to Chris's, came at such a high resonance and frequency that I started to download it in chunks to him over the phone, information that meant nothing to me but resonated deeply with him.

Whitley and Anne were full of humor, smarts, and wonderful stories. I felt like doors had swung open for a new yet familiar group of friends and associates to come into my life. We bonded over Anne's cooking and hot chocolate. I had deep respect for their unique experiences and wanted to know more. They invited me to be their psychic medium expert and co-host for their popular radio webcast, *Dreamland*, interviewing fascinating authors about their cutting-edge books.

My new venue inspired exciting conversations about the paranormal all over the world. People were curious for information and hungry for understanding.

"Hey, why don't you come back to Bedford and let's go UFO hunting! " Diane teased when she called.

Diane and I became fast friends after she and her husband, Bob, were transplanted from Connecticut to my hometown of Bedford for work. She had first heard about my abilities through small-town gossip and wanted to know how to develop her own. Funny, smart, and deeply respectful of my work, Diane would call and we would gab for hours. It had been three years since we'd picnicked in the middle of the living room after my mother had died. I was always able to give her information to assist her and her family, but today was different. Diane sounded anxious.

"Marla, I have had this damn cough off and on for a year and can't get rid of it. Can you tell me what's wrong with me?"

Often I can see a health issue with the help of Spirit. I had met Pamela Stacey a few months earlier in one of my groups. Pamela is a darling, slight woman with great energy, yet very time I looked at her in the group, I saw a shadow over her left chest area. When the evening was over and Pamela was about to leave, I grabbed her arm and said, "Sit down. I'm not finished with you." This surprised both of us. I told her it was time for a mammogram. Pamela realized she was almost two years overdue. The result: cancer in her left breast, caught phenomenally early, treated, and a full, cancer-free recovery. Pamela's oncologist, who marveled that they caught it so early, was a Catholic doctor in a Catholic hospital. She asked how Pamela had found out about her cancer. "I took a deep breath and told her about my experience with you, Marla," she told me. Pamela said that the doctor's eyes widened as she told her about the message, and after hearing the full story, the doctor's only comment was, "God works in mysterious ways."

But when Diane asked me about her cough and I looked at her to "see" the way I see things, I saw a black wall. I had never encountered that before. I then heard a very stern, *Tell her to go see a different doctor.* "Diane, for some reason I'm prevented from seeing anything, but I am told that you need to go to a different doctor—now."

"I know, Marla, I can't stand this guy. He doesn't listen to me. He just gives me these dumb inhalers."

"Diane—go see someone else!"

"Okay," she laughed, "Oh, and congratulations on the radio gig!"
"Keep me posted," I told her. "I love you, Diane."

A few months later I flew to New York to visit with friends and to take a class offered by a Dr. Laura Thibodeau. She was a loving, calm, and talented medium who invited me to join her in mediumship demonstrations at the META Center in the heart of New York.

Spring was beginning to bloom. I was walking the streets of Manhattan with my old friend Jim Corti, laughing and enjoying the warmth of the sun, when I got a call from Diane.

"Marla, I have stage four ovarian cancer."

The possibility of her imminent death gripped me. In the silence of the news we cried. Diane was as strong in her spirit as anyone I knew. We would rally together and do whatever we could to make a plan for the rest of her life.

What were these psychic gifts for if Spirit would not reveal the most crucial of information for a close friend? I could tell a complete stranger some lifesaving facts, but I was prevented from seeing Diane's illness.

"I will do chemo for my family," Diane said, "but I'm tired. I think it's time for me to go. I think I *have* to die. I have a feeling my family won't change unless I am gone, Marla."

Her prophetic wisdom was hard to swallow, but the next few months would teach us how to prepare for her leaving. "Marla, you are going to have to help Bob," Diane said. A deft piece of irony, since in most of our conversations, after talking about how much she loved her family, we would always talk about Bob, how much she loved him and how she was having problems communicating with him. But Diane was right, her death did change everything and Bob was completely devastated. Bob and I worked together over the phone for a number of years to help him integrate his terrible loss. He now lives and loves much differently, and their children have grown to make beautiful families of their own. No doubt Diane has been watching and loving this family even in death.

It was a sobering moment when I realized that Spirit does not always want me to see things, because there is a process, a plan, and purpose to death. Diane was right.

The "knowing of things" is never about ego satisfaction. It is actually harder when the information is about someone so close to me, someone I love. Being "right" is just about information. I had to find a way to be grateful for *not* knowing, even when it was all so painful, and also *for* knowing, because that can be painful too.

It's funny, but what we try to hide or protect ourselves from often becomes the very thing our life is about. Until we face those hidden secrets and fears, they seem to hold us hostage. But the fact is, we are not hostages—we are accomplices, consciously or unconsciously plunging head first into the many quandaries in which we find ourselves.

Spirit, this Larger Consciousness System we call God, shows up to help us if we are willing to listen. Spirit uses whatever it can to get our attention—dreams, visions, illnesses, messages from friends, insight through meditation and prayer, and even someone who is able to "see" like me.

I was so grateful that Spirit/THEMS gave me a chance to start a new life. In hindsight, it took time to understand that Spirit's initial message to me when the marriage was falling apart, *We want you out of this. We want the best for you ... trust us,* really was the 'insight' that Spirit had my back. Pain is the change that makes us reset our lives.

My old college beau, Bill, who was pushed to ride across the country on his bicycle, was a divine catalyst of healing for both of us, hurling me back into the dysfunction of my family. I had to dig deep into a part of my life frozen in fear, break apart the pain that my father's alcoholism had done to us all, and find a way to forgive not just Daddy and Bill, but also myself for deeply loving these beautiful, fragile men who were part of a disease I could not fix. I surrendered to Spirit and asked for my heart to be changed.

Spirit had cleared the way for all of us to find love for ourselves and begin the process of forgiving each other and moving on. Now on my own and free to focus on me, I was driven to find answers to the questions: How do our lives get set up? Why do we have these families? And what the heck am I supposed to do now?

20

Providence

*" The belonging you seek is not behind you ... it's ahead. I
am no Jedi, but I know The Force. It moves through and sur-
rounds every living thing. Close your eyes, feel it.
The light ... it's always been there."*
—*Maz Kanata,* Star Wars VII: The Force Awakens

By 2010 I was part of one of the most exciting international
paranormal communities. My web radio gig as the
psychic medium expert and co-host for Whitley Strieber's
Unknowncountry.com's *Dreamland* gave me the opportunity to
interview leading authors about their work on UFOs, psychic
phenomena, consciousness, near death experiences (NDEs),
crop circles, alternative healing, conspiracy theories, and past
life regression, to name a few. In turn, I was thrilled to share
with the world some of the most influential talents who had
trained and supported me.

Three pioneers in consciousness paved my path to a place I
had wanted to go for many years, The Monroe Institute (TMI),
a nonprofit research and educational organization dedicated to
exploring and enhancing expanded states of consciousness, located outside of Charlottesville, Virginia.

My controlled remote viewing instructor and friend, retired U.S. Army Intelligence Sergeant Lyn Buchannan, first

piqued my interest in TMI when he shared how the programs enhanced his awareness and psychic abilities along with those of other military remote viewers. Lyn and his remote viewing training gave me the confidence that psychic functioning was possible for everyone, could be taught and was easy to learn. I interviewed Lyn on *Dreamland* about his book *The Seventh Sense* and his surge in popularity due to George Clooney playing a slicked-up version of Lyn in the movie, *Men Who Stare at Goats*. The movie, a somewhat humorous attempt to describe the serious nature of military remote viewers, was pretty wacky, but Lyn confirmed that 85 percent of the movie was true.

One of Joe McMoneagle's books, *Memoirs of a Psychic Spy*, inspired me to hunt down Joe and get him on *Dreamland*. Joe is one of the top remote viewers in the world. His career spans thirty-four years of providing professional support to numerous intelligence and defense agencies. Twenty of those years has been within paranormal operations as remote viewer No. 001. Joe not only taught at Monroe, but also fell in love and married one of Bob Monroe's stepdaughters, Nancy (Scooter) Honeycutt, who is currently the managing director of the Institute. Joe, like me, had a difficult mother and challenging childhood, which he believes contributed to his psychic sensitivities. I was so excited to have Joe on the air that I enthusiastically flubbed my intro of him five times before I could contain my appreciation. Whitley, who was producing the show, patiently put up with my groupie gusto as he re-recorded me.

I also interviewed Tom Campbell, author of *My Big TOE* (**T**heory **o**f **E**verything), a one-volume trilogy unifying philosophy, physics, and metaphysics. Tom had a long career as a scientist and physicist and has been at the heart of developing U.S. missile defense systems. Tom began researching altered states of consciousness (without the use of drugs) with Bob

Monroe at the Monroe Laboratories in the early 1970s. For the past thirty years, Tom has been focused on scientifically exploring the properties, boundaries, and abilities of consciousness. As a scientist and expert in consciousness, he has taken his work around the world in workshops and amassed hundreds of free hours of his talks on YouTube, making him a global education sensation. I not only had the pleasure of interviewing Tom, but also studying with him and collaborating on YouTube teleconferences and workshop panel discussions.

Through his scientific lens, Tom describes what I do as a psychic and medium as "accessing information." This view trims away the ideologies, fears, and possible misconceptions of where this information comes from. Tom's theory that we are in a virtual reality challenges those who are anchored in materialism. His recent physics experiments, variations of the double slit experiment, have been published in a peer-reviewed online physics journal with Houman Owhadi, Joe Sauvageau, and David Watkinson as co-authors (*International Journal of Quantum Foundations*, vol. 3, 2017). If these experiments work as Tom has predicted, what is now considered paranormal will simply become normal, that is, a fully explainable natural part of human existence.

For me, Tom's message about the Larger Consciousness System reframes God in a bigger way. It does not reduce God into a specific belief system, but instead expands our consciousness to everything that this benevolent source encompasses to help us grow. His ultimate message, "It's all about the LOVE," is the goal. As he writes in *My Big TOE*:

Improving the quality of consciousness, advancing the quality and depth of awareness, understanding your nature and purpose, manifesting universal unconditional love, letting go of fear, and eliminating ego, desires, wants, needs or preconceived notions—these are the attributes and the results of a successfully evolving consciousness (p. 744).

Whatever vocabulary or framework we use, we are all on the same path of evolving our awareness of who and what we are, why we're here, and why it matters.

Lyn, Joe, and Tom, three highly educated, psychically aware men who were put in the front lines of intelligence and defense, have inspired, guided, and assisted thousands of people who are looking for more answers about the abilities of our hearts and minds. All three were part of the history of what The Monroe Institute offered: expanded awareness—and then some.

I was on my way to Monroe!

Let me start with a caveat. You are stepping into territory that could be challenging or impossible for some of you to believe, while others might find it juicier and more interesting than tabloid TV or politics, because it is real. It is a part of all of us.

As Rod Serling said before every episode in the first season of *The Twilight Zone*: "There is a fifth dimension beyond that which is known to man. It is a dimension as vast as space and as timeless as infinity. It is the middle ground between light and shadow, between science and superstition, and it lies between the pit of man's fears and the summit of his knowledge. It is an area which we call the twilight zone."

During the last leg of the flight between Atlanta and Charlottesville I struck up a conversation with my seatmate, Marsha, a sweet, kind woman who lit up when I talked about where I was going. We swapped stories about the paranormal and before we parted she said, "I took some psychic classes, Marla. I know this mediumship work is real. If you see my husband, Barry, over there, please tell him I love him." Marsha's eyes welled up as she told me that her husband had taken his own life. I hugged her and said, "Of course I will."

The van from the institute awaited those of us who flew in from places all over the world. We enjoyed the comfortable one-hour trip through the lush Blue Ridge Mountains of Virginia to the sprawling grounds of Monroe. As soon as we drove up, it felt like home.

Eighteen of us convened for the Gateway Voyage, the first program for all new attendees. We were a mixed bag of unique personalities between the ages of twenty-eight to eighty-three—executives, moms, students, engineers, healthcare workers, and a retired military man who now designed furniture. We all came to explore.

We stayed in the pine-paneled Nancy Penn Center with facilitators Penny Holmes, Bob Holbrook, and Robert Sandstrom. Each of our comfortable rooms included an individual Controlled Holistic Environmental Chamber, or CHEC unit. The CHEC unit was our personal bed in a wall where we not only slept at night, but also, with headphones in place, carried out our guided meditation exercises. Blackout curtains could be used to darken the CHEC units and pillows and a cushy comforter could be molded to our bodies to make us as comfortable as possible.

Music, verbal guidance, and subtle sound effects are combined with Hemi-Sync® signals in the guided meditations. Hemi-Sync® is a patented, scientifically and clinically proven "audio-guidance" technology refined by over forty years of research by Bob Monroe and his team. Using binaural beats, the result of two slightly different tones being played into each ear, the brain starts to synchronize the differences in tones. This eventually creates a totally new brainwave frequency, leading the brain to various states of consciousness ranging from deep relaxation to expanded awareness and other extraordinary states. This was a different way of approaching what I knew happened in mystical Shamanic drumming circles. These beats had been part of my soul since the first time I felt the drum rhythms of the Bedford marching band resonate in my chest.

Each exercise began with the same preparatory phrase, "I am more than my physical body." I would come to learn what that actually meant as I pulled down the black-out curtain to sit in utter darkness and snuggle in with my headphones for my first session.

In these interactive exercises I could slow down the images I saw in my head, ask for guidance from nonphysical energies who were available to assist us, and be awake enough to report and record what I was seeing and feeling on my iPhone. The instructions and frequencies on the guided meditation transformed me to an altered state of consciousness within minutes.

The first thing I saw was ... nothing.

Then, blue smoke began to ooze in my mind, and out of that void came a voice ... "I am here for you."

What? Wait! Who was that?

Then more fuzzy blue and chatter, voices trying to talk to me. But I wasn't interested in the voices—I was anxious to *see* something. I was frustrated. My control issues came up, and that was really stupid, so I took a deep breath, let go, and just listened to the instructions.

A mechanical hand appeared, like a robotic android hand. I saw it performing surgery on a heart. *Well, that's interesting,* I thought. I wonder why that heart was damaged and what the hand could be doing to repair it. And then I realized, my God—that's *my* heart. It continued to work. I felt an ache and a twinge in my chest and stopped the exercise by taking my headphones off and opening up the curtain. What the—!

It was a cloudy, calm day in the mountains of Virginia and I just had my heart operated on in an altered state. Was this a metaphor? Or had something actually changed around my heart?

After every exercise we would go to the den to debrief. We watched the faces of the dazed, surprised, and awed as one by one we shared with our facilitators and participants what the heck happened in our experiences. In the next few days our energies changed, our frequencies altered, and with each exercise and intention all of us were transformed in what seemed to be the best way for each of us.

At the crack of every Blue Ridge Mountain dawn we were awakened by a voice recording of Bob Monroe with an inspiring morning meditation. This set the tone for a day of expanded awareness and gratitude. We had the choice of taking a stimulating yoga class, a hike, or simply relaxing. A couple of sweet local women homecooked our breakfasts, lunches, and dinners, providing choices that met all our dietary needs including some wicked peanut butter cookies.

In one exercise we were guided to understand and work with our own energy systems for healing called Dolphin Energy Healing. We imagined a small dolphin traveling through our bodies to an area that was in pain. Even though our facilitators shared their own experiences and showed us a pamphlet of testimonials about this "dolphin energy," my skepticism kicked WAY in.

I did have chronic problems in my piriformis butt muscle from a Taekwondo injury two years earlier. It was so painful that I stopped my martial arts practice after my red belt testing. I wondered if Flipper could find his way to that!

I surrendered to the exercise. Heat started to build as I saw my little dolphin swirling around the area, and then I watched in my mind as this little guy chomped on the scar tissue. He chomped and chomped, and I started laughing when it began to tickle. I rolled out of my CHEC unit onto the floor in laughter. I got up, went downstairs, and was just thrilled that I had imagined such a thing. But as I sat down to talk about my experience, I realized that my pain was gone.

We all integrated gratitude for whatever we were about to receive in each exercise. When I felt blind, I would relax, and then I could see. I trusted. There was not only a loving physical team helping us in this program, but also an invisible benevolence on many other levels of consciousness also willing to assist us.

I decided that Monroe was an adult version of Hogwarts. Some people, like me, reported that pain in their bodies had disappeared. Others met deceased loved ones, talked to enlightened beings, and were given messages about work and family. Some had out-of-body experiences, or OBEs, in which they flew to other parts of the property and reported on who and what they saw. Others had fears challenged, patterns adjusted, and sometimes we just fell asleep, or as the trainers called it, "clicked out," working on some level without being aware of it.

Were these experiences real or just my imagination? I wanted more proof that what I was experiencing was not just the group consciousness of a bunch of people with overactive imaginations. Whatever was going on was happening to all of us, and it was transformational and profound.

In the next program I took, called Lifeline, things really began to get interesting. Franceen King, Joe Gallenberger, and Andrea Berger would be my facilitators up at the other site for training at the institute called Robert's Mountain Retreat, or RMR. Robert Monroe's mountain is like a stairway to heaven—glorious.

This time my CHEC unit was in the Annex, a building separate from the main house. I loved my new little home nestled up high in the green of the trees. We all met in what was formally the Monroe family home. The pastel peach dining room, void of any family furniture with the exception of a stunning crystal chandelier, was the perfect place for everyone to convene to debrief after our exercises.

As a medium I was used to deceased people seeking me out or pushing their living relatives to find me and engage in communication, but in Lifeline we were taught to "retrieve souls." We learned how to locate, contact, and find souls who were waiting to move on and didn't know where to go, didn't know they were dead, were confused after a devastating event and needed assistance, or for whatever reason did not want to move on. It would be our job to lead these people to "the park" of level twenty-seven, a higher level of consciousness where they could be met by loved ones, get assistance, and move on in their new consciousness. In order to make sure I documented what I was seeing, hearing and feeling, I brought a spare iPhone to record.

With no idea of what was going to happen, I surrendered to the exercise and clicked on the voice recorder for my first "retrieval."

I am alone in front of an empty nurses' station in a hospital wing. The space is color-saturated in blue, like film noir. The clarity is incredible. I can see the counter, computers, files, and cabinets. I can even feel the coolness of the plastic chair I'm sitting on. It is nighttime and completely silent. I have bilocated to another reality. "Now what do I do?" I ask out loud.

I heard, *Be patient.* As I relax, I get even more details of my surroundings and everything is in sharper focus. *Look down the hall.* The hall is illuminated in bright light and at the far end is a man who I just met at the Institute, Eben. He is dressed in a white doctor's coat. I wonder why he would be here in my exercise. He motions for me to come down the hallway to him. He leads me to a door and opens it. There, in the brightly lit room, sit six children between the ages of five to ten. A little girl says, "Are you an angel?" I am stunned that she sees me and I don't know what to do, so I ask, "You can see me?"

"Yes . . . you are glowing," she says.

A little boy with a sweet round face says, "My name is Robbie. Are you my mom? Are you an angel?"

"No," I say, "but I will take you to a place where you can be with other family members and you will be cared for." They trust me.

A wave of sadness moves over me. I can't think about why they don't know they are dead, or other elements that conjure questions. The point is that I am here to learn and to assist them, not to judge. Eben is calm and centered as he helps me lead the children to focus level twenty-seven, the heavenly park where they can be met by loved ones. I have the children with me. When I reach this vast heavenly park, the children are all met by people they recognize.

As I am still in this retrieval exercise, a man who looks familiar walks toward me. Oh my God—it's my father! He's younger, healthy, robust, and very happy to see me. I'm shocked, having thought he might be on the level where people who had addiction problems seem to convene. But no, apparently he had done some work to move out of his addiction consciousness and he is here to meet me. My dear friend, Diane, who had died from cancer three years before, runs up to me and gives me a big hug. I can feel her and her love for me. She is beaming, healthy, happy, and laughing as she says, "I'm a greeter here."

I am so excited to see them, but I am doing an exercise and the audio promptings are telling me what to do next.

"I love you guys and am so happy to see you, but I have work to do!" I said to my dad and Diane.

As soon as I take a deep breath, I am back in another retrieval.

I am now in what looks like a police station interrogation room. I am sitting at a table talking to a young African-American man who is crying. He can't be more than twenty years old. He is wearing a white sleeveless basketball shirt and long red shorts with a white stripe on them. His basketball shoes are new. He seems inconsolable as he cries out, "I'm in a lot of trouble—I'm so sorry! I know I killed that guy—I had the gun in my hand and it just went off!"

Another man who is considered a "helper" in this experience says, "Young man, you are so very remorseful for having caused a death, but what you don't realize is that you too are deceased. Someone shot you in this altercation and you, too, have died."

The boy looks at me. His face is open and calm as he asks, "Really?"

"I'm new at this," I tell him, "but I'm the one who will be taking you to a place where you can get some help and meet other loved ones."

He seems dumbfounded, but relieved that he is not alone, and then I hear, *It is because of his remorse that he will process this quickly.*

I am out of that retrieval and immediately find myself sitting on the ground in a cave with a beautiful light source illuminating the area I have landed in. I laugh out loud, finding the snap between the hospital, police station, and now a cave remarkably fast. How did my mind do that?

"Okay, now what?" I ask.

I see a thick rope extending from between my feet over the edge into a hole. I hear, *Pull on the rope.*

So I do. It's not difficult, but there is weight. Something is definitely attached to the end. With one more pull the rope brings up a man with an electrical cord wrapped around his neck.

"Are you all right?" I ask. I realize that was a dumb question.

One of his eyes opens and he says, "Well, I'm dead." Even in an altered state there's humor.

"What happened?" I ask.

"I killed myself."

"Why?"

"I had been sick for a long time. I felt my wife and daughter were better without me, but I now know that is not the case."

"What's your name?"

"Barry, I'm Marsha's husband."

This was the husband of the woman I met on the plane on my way to Monroe. I tried to stay focused.

"Oh, Barry, Marsha told me to tell you she loves you!"

"I know," he says. "That's how I found you. I love her and my precious daughter too. Please tell them I'm sorry!"

As I lead Barry to the park, a tall man with glasses comes and embraces him. Barry falls to his knees and sobs in this man's arms. Weeks later, when I called Marsha to talk about this experience, I found out that Barry hung himself with an electrical cord, and the man who met Barry on level twenty-seven fit the description of Barry's boss, who had passed on a few months before Barry.

These retrievals were deeply moving. The idea that Barry could appear because of the love Marsha had for him helped me start connecting the dots. Many of the deceased with whom I had connected over the years said the same thing, that love gave me the ability to see, hear, and feel them—*their* love, as well as the love of those they left behind. Those who had killed themselves were no exception—I found them through the love and forgiveness of the living. These visions could be the imagination of a mind rich with imagery and story, but part of my work was proving who these people were. Confirmation of very specific details, like seeing the electrical cord wrapped around Barry's neck, corroborates the reality that consciousness survives the death experience.

Emmanuel, one of my Monroe classmates, walked up to me after one of our exercises and said, "Do you have a friend named Diane? A tall, attractive blonde with short hair and blue eyes?"

"Yes, I do." I said.

"Well, I found her on level twenty-seven at the reception center greeting people!"

"Yes, you're right," I said. "That's exactly where I found her earlier today!" We laughed with delight.

People who had never talked to dead people were having the time of their lives, and so was I.

That night in Bob Monroe's cabin we were all treated to a presentation by neurosurgeon Eben Alexander. No wonder he showed up in my retrieval to help me. Eben shared the story of his near-death experience in which he was thrown into the after-life by bacterial meningitis and lay comatose for a week. His account of what happened during that coma and his subsequent life-altering experience made Eben living proof of an afterlife. His book, *Proof of Heaven,* had not yet been published when I met him; however, I knew it would teach millions that science was being impacted by the spiritual. (Eben's book, released in October 2012, became a #1 *New York Times* bestseller.)

I had no idea what was on the schedule, but I woke the next morning with an anxious, daunting feeling, as if my body was registering, in a precognitive way, what was about to happen. Our next exercise was to reclaim aspects of ourselves that we had lost. We were told that we might encounter previous life-times and that this was a way to help us integrate and understand our life process. We would also receive guidance from unseen, benevolent helpers if we needed assistance. Knowing as I did that we can communicate with the dead was one thing, but how our subconscious can take us to places that could be considered other realities was fascinating. Freud and Jung would have a field day with this, I thought. Maybe they or some other grand teacher would show up and give me some pointers.

As the auditory process began I pushed the record button on my iPhone. I wanted to make sure I didn't miss anything.

I am a dark-skinned child sitting in the shade, leaning against some structure. A dirt road is in front of me. I am starving. I can see flies all over me. My belly is distended. A hand comes down to my mouth and feeds me milk with some kind of meal mixed in it. I am overjoyed, but the sun is on me now and I am hot. I know I will die. I can feel everything and still be detached to the process. I ask out loud, "Why do I need to experience this?" I hear from a helper, *You need to understand that you have died many times before. Being a starving child is what 'being without' teaches, and how suffering is a human condition that teaches compassion.*

The dying is peaceful for some aspect of me as this child, but the living was so painful. This experience is over, but not the exercise. I take a swig from my water bottle and enter another experience.

I am in a dirty, dimly lit room, strapped down on a table. A doctor stands to my left with a nurse behind him. I can feel the restrictions on my legs and wrists from the straps. I am not me, Marla; I am a dark-haired, ten-year-old Jewish girl. I am in a Nazi concentration camp.

The doctor exposes my left arm under the light and says, "I am going to open up your vein and put something in it that will make you either very sick or kill you."

"Please do not do that!" I beg as this young girl. As I'm talking I can feel myself becoming the doctor. I see things from his perspective and feel how disassociated he is from the girl. I feel the hate and disgust in his heart. He does not see the girl he is working on as a person, but as a thing, an experiment to work out his own pain. I can feel myself as the girl again, terrified that I am going to be hurt. I keep bouncing back and forth feeling each person's experience. I feel the emotions of both the victim and the perpetrator. I want to change this so they too can feel what I am feeling.

"You don't understand," I say as this girl. "I am you. You are me. We have the choice to change this—please do not hurt me."

I start to cry. He and the nurse ignore me as they prepare my arm. I know that I am going to die and that I will be going home to the place where I came from. I know that this life, though ending, will teach me something important. And I want the doctor and nurse to also be left with something different.

I look at them and what comes out of my mouth surprises even me: "Your hate cannot destroy my love."

I want to give us all an opportunity to change and heal this. As I lay dying I say, "I will take all of you with me to a place where we can all get help and heal." As my spirit comes out of my body, I try to take the doctor and nurse to the park on twenty-seven, which is now becoming more real to me, like a garden starting to bloom. I am not sure if they have come with me. It is my intention for all of us to heal.

I took off my headphones and pulled back the black curtain. The sun hit me and I was Marla again. My heart was pounding—it was so real, so enormous. Something dramatic had shifted in ways I could not comprehend. All I knew at that moment was that I had been broken apart and put back together. I left my CHEC unit to debrief with the instructors and then went for a hike.

Walking up and down the steep gravel mountain road kicked my butt just enough to move all the intense emotion out of my body. The phrase I said as that young girl in Poland kept resonating through my mind "Your hate cannot destroy my love." I had been through a version of hell and found compassion for my abusers. I was them and they were me during an integration and transformation on a very deep level. I wondered if my mother was watching from wherever she was on the other side. I prayed that she too could be a part of this healing.

Karen Malik, Bob Holbrook, and Lee Stone would facilitate my next program, X27 (Exploring Focus Level Twenty-seven). Lee, a wise, bespeckled redhead, had his instructive eye on me as the facilitators discussed how we would move to level twenty-seven and meet with the "entry director." There we would find out why we were born this time. Hearing this I immediately started to gasp for air. "I can tell you already that this is terrifying for me," I told my fellow students before we left for the exercise. "I've had a lot of anxiety about my birth and I'm scared shitless—look at me! I feel like I'm already back in the womb feeling the cord wrapped around my neck."

Lee just put his hand on my shoulder and said, "See you in a few."

Not the most comforting note to walk away on, but Lee was an older, confident facilitator, and a therapist. He had watched many a TMI participant go through all these exercises and survive them. I was sweating and afraid when I put on my headphones.

I am on a bridge. The light is bright but diffused like sun oozing through fog. A woman with short blonde hair walks toward me. She is calm, graceful, and dressed in white. Oh, my God—she's a better version of ME! I had been told I have a higher self, a more conscious aspect of myself than the physical Marla, and here she is—and I *love* her outfit.

"This is your opportunity, Marla," she says. "We have been waiting for this. You have asked for this experience, and that is why you are here today. You are my greatest purpose."

I am taken back by her affection and attention. "Thank you," I say.

"Let us embody the experience of meeting with 'the council' and find out why you agreed to come back, what you wanted to learn, and what you need to do for the rest of your time on earth in this incarnation. No need to be frightened, for you are here—that means you have already accomplished much."

I know what it feels like to have someone mirror back a part of you that is honest and delivered for the highest good. The best therapists had done that for me, and I tried to do it for my clients, but I never thought it would show up for me in this way. I know I can trust her, but I still feel anxious.

"I'm getting uncomfortable," I say. "I'm scared, but I don't know what I'm scared of. My neck is beginning to hurt." My tears are uncontrollable.

"Just let the pain go, Marla. You don't need to relive the cord wrapped around your neck or your painful birth. It was not pleasant for you, the disconnection from us." Her words, *the disconnection from us*, vibrate in my head.

We leave the bridge and arrive in front of an open, buff-colored, marble hotel lobby. People are coming and going and my higher self knows everyone. She is gracious as she says hello and hugs people. We walk to another bridge and she speaks to me again. "I am to take you to the Planning Center to meet the entry director." We come to a tall, silver, octagon-shaped building. There is a white door and she opens it. It looks like a lighthouse, round on the inside, with a tall tower and a crystal at the top.

"This is nice," I say. "I like the openness. I feel much better."

My higher self says, "The entry director is in a form that will make you feel comfortable." Then she is gone. There is a man behind the table dressed in a white shirt, relaxed khaki pants, and sandals. He looks like a modern-day Jesus.

"Welcome, Marla. Please sit down."

Everything is simple, very clean, white and grey. There's not a smattering of color except for the well-trimmed, reddish brown hair and beard of the man in front of me. The guided meditation coming through the headphones reminds me that this is a process—observe the interactions, especially anything that is surprising, and listen acutely to what is being communicated.

The modern-day Jesus leans back in a chair and says, "We were all working together. You helped assist others in the process of being born again. We made a decision that it was time for you to have another physical experience, to be challenged, to overcome, learn, and teach.

"You agreed," he continues, "and decided you should be a female without the enormous responsibility of children so you could focus on the work you agreed to do." The guided meditation tells me to observe the steps and process of coming into the physical body. He gestures to a vertical stack of what look like CDs, about twenty feet high. "This is a library of some of your lifetimes."

I am trying to process everything I have just seen and heard. I have helped others be born again? We all worked together? I reach to the stack of lifetimes and choose a CD. On the cover is the title, "Roman Warrior," and a picture of just that, a Roman soldier in battle. I begin to feel what that lifetime was like, so I quickly put it back and reach for one that is light blue and titled, "Gentle Maiden with Many Children." Another one calls out to me, and even before I can read the title I see myself on a ship in turbulent seas. The tile reads, "Seafaring Captain."

I look to the modern-day Jesus who says, "This has not been your most challenging life experience, but in this life you have been restricted from the depths of love that you knew before, from the connectedness that you felt with all of us. You miss your true family of origin. The disconnection from us has been so hard for you. You understand what you have missed in your soul and that is why you are able to help others find that in themselves."

I ask him, "Are you Jesus?

"Call me 'the Council.' We are too vast for you to see what we are. The man and son of God called Jesus is part of this vast-ness. And since you have not yet left your body in the transition of death, it would be too much for you to process."

Again the guidance from the TMI meditation is instructing me to ask specific questions. What lessons am I to learn? What do I need to see about myself ? Before I can ask, the Council says, "Would you like to review part of this life?"

"Yes, I would, thank you."

The room darkens like in a movie theatre, but there is no screen. The room disappears. I am now in a place filled with brilliant color—trees, grass, blooming flowers, and a porch I knew so well. I am in the back yard of my childhood home.

I hear the Council say, "Your mother wished for something more. She prayed for a gift to change her life. You heard her and agreed to be born to that family because you felt you could make a difference."

"I'm sorry—I'm getting very emotional," I say.

"This is where you have been mistaken about your life, Marla. You never felt you *made* a difference."

I am sobbing, because what he is saying is profoundly true. "Why is this so painful?" I ask.

"Marla, you were removed from your real family—us. Some who reincarnate forget, but you carried the pain of that separation into this life. The light and frequency that you brought into your home caused your family members to react to you in ways that were very … visceral. You longed to feel the same love connection you had with all of us."

I see a beautiful little three-year-old girl running through the yard, playing and laughing.

"Is that me?"

"Yes, and as you can see, there is nothing wrong with you. In fact, you are divine."

A wave of relief pours through me.

"It was difficult for you to assimilate into your mother's body. Everything she put in her body affected you: the food she ate, her smoking, as well as her thoughts and feelings. This is what is so challenging for souls becoming human—adapting. You were born perfect and joyful, no matter what your family said or did. You were their mirror, a reflection of love and a catalyst for their personal pain and suffering. They had the choice to overcome this or not. As a child you did not have the tools to know what to do to help them when they became fearful and angry, emotions that they did not know how to process."

"When people have so much pain and they cannot transform or contain it, they take it out on others. Your mother did not seek help for her pain. She chose to discharge her pain onto you and others to try to relieve her own suffering. It is hard not to take her reaction to you personally. You wanted to make a difference, but you misunderstood, thinking you had to *be loved* in order to make that difference. Marla, you *were* the difference."

I am sobbing and my heart feels like it is going to explode.

"Their reaction to you was an opportunity for them."

I am so moved. I do my best to stay composed as the Council continues.

"The separation from love makes the yearning to come back to be in the group, the whole, more intense. When you don't have it in the family you were born to, it makes it more important to find it for yourself. This is why you came back, Marla, to learn this and bridge this understanding for yourself and others. This terrible pain has now been lifted from you. It is but a memory."

The Council smiles and says, "You are on the right track. Just follow the guidance. Do not be concerned."

"Oh, thank—thank you," I say.

As this exercise comes to a close I walk out of the Planning Center and Lee, my instructor from the class, shows up in this experience! He greets me by putting his hand on my shoulder and saying, "That wasn't so bad, was it?" I stopped the exercise, took off my headphones, and crawled out of my bed unit, exhausted and filled with gratitude. I looked in the mirror at my face, smeared with tears of relief and joy, a reflection of the new openness in my mind and heart. I walked over to the house for the debriefing.

Lee was the first person I saw. Before I could open my mouth to tell him he was in my experience, he walked up to me just as he did in my exercise, put his hand on my shoulder, and said, "That wasn't so bad, was it?"

My work with Dr. Brian Weiss taught me about past lives and the richness of the cycles of life that we live. But to really feel that we have lived many other lives, chosen our families, and have always been so deeply connected to the divine felt like a huge responsibility and a relief at the same time. The family I chose was providence. The shift in knowing I made a difference, whether I was loved or not, was life changing.

I had one more lesson to learn on this adventure. We were told that we have a "special place" on level twenty-seven, a home base we find comfortable and to which we can always go. I was ready to find mine.

I put on my headphones and reached the park on twenty-seven.

I am walking through a clearing and into the woods. It seems like midafternoon, when the sun bursts between all the leaves and warms everything with a golden glow. There is a cabin, a place already made for me. I liked how beautiful and rustic it is, made of smooth and well-crafted woodwork. It has a porch that stretches across the entire front. I step up and walk in.

"Helloooo?" I call.

There, in a comfortable wingback chair in front of a massive bookcase, sits a man who seems familiar. I have seen his face before, but I do not know him.

"I'm John Mack," he says, "and I'm here to prepare this place for you to help you integrate your process with awareness. Therefore, what you take from here can translate on earth to assist others." He gestures to the bookshelves, which contain books on space, extraterrestrials, planets, stars, and UFOs.

I look at him and ask, "UFOs?"

He smiles and says, "UFO means Unidentified Family of Origin. The credible part of the UFO consciousness is about establishing contact in a soul and mind space to accumulate the knowledge of other worlds, other life forms, and other galaxies. We connect with them for learning and to hold all things of love and similar loyalties. This is part of your family of origin."

I was delighted. It was surprising to get a lesson on this subject. To think that the UFO conversation was also part of me and all of us was very interesting.

I would later find out that John, who was deceased, had been a psychiatrist, Harvard professor, and Pulitzer Prize-winning author who later in his career researched the alien abduction phenomenon. That courageous work, which included writing books such as *Abduction: Human Encounters with Aliens*, threatened his standing in the psychiatric community.

I thank John for his gracious introduction to my special place and proceed to explore.

I come across a large, empty room with big windows. A woman with glasses dressed in a blue suit jacket and midcalf-length skirt is setting up the room as if she is a teacher preparing for an important class. She wheels a blackboard into the middle of the room and starts writing on it.

Death = Life. Life Eternal. Life—before the physical.

She looks at me and says, "I'm Elizabeth Kübler-Ross, and we have some work to do."

All I know about Elizabeth is that she was known for her work on death and dying. I have not read her books, so I ask, "Do you want to explain this to me?"

"The fear of being controlled and hurt is the fear of death," she says. "Part of this misconception comes from the time when religious establishments started to control the people, punishing them in the name of a god. This needs to be changed so that death can be viewed as another phase of life. In my second book I talk about something I want us to extrapolate on. Look at chapter thirteen. Use your interpretation of this to assist others. Your communication with those on the other side helps people understand that life is eternal. I'm going to assist you with this."

Is this really Elizabeth? How does she know me? How does she know what I am doing? She shows up in this experience and wants me to expand on something she has written about and offers to help me do it? My God. My exercise comes to an end but a whole new life is beginning.

I had been blown apart by my experiences and put back together with the glue of the hearts, minds, and visions of the Monroe guides and participants. These experiences did not just transform all of us in the group, but also many others as they rippled through the lives of all of our families, both the living and the dead.

I returned home and spent weeks integrating.

I did what Elizabeth told me to do. I ordered her second book, *Questions and Answers on Death and Dying*, and as instructed, turned to chapter thirteen, which was titled "Personal Questions." It didn't take long to find what she wanted me to see, a question posed to Elizabeth along with her answer.

Question: In all your research on death, what is your personal belief on what happens after death?"

Answer: Before I started working with dying patients, I did not believe in a life after death. I now do believe in life after death, beyond a shadow of a doubt . . . I believe that our bodies die, but the spirit of the soul is immortal.

Elizabeth was famous in the realm of death and dying, but she was also a bridge connecting people to information. Being connected to her words, words that validated what I had learned about myself, made my purpose as a bridge even more clear.

As Elizabeth said from the other side, "We have more work to do."

While reflecting on my Monroe experiences, I wondered about my heart and the robotic android hand that came to tweak me. I don't think the problem was that I had refused statins and opted for diet and exercise to modify my genetically high cholesterol. No, something else about my heart needed to change. I'd learned that the heart had its own intelligence. Plenty of scientific studies concluded that intuition was not only about perception by the mind alone, but also involved in the entire psychophysiological system.

When I was in Brazil the psychic surgeon telepathically said, "Heart and thymus," before he got down to business and operated on me. At various times in my life I saw doctors about some heart pain I had been having. The doctors said nothing was medically wrong but that it was just anxiety, nothing a little Zoloft couldn't take care of. I probably wasn't ready to accept that the mysterious heart pain was my body warning me that heartache was coming.

Yet my heart felt great when I could connect to the dead and *feel* their love. A heart attack cut short the life of Kathy Graf's husband, but in death his love was so strong it pushed his wife up a hill and pulled me into his heart to express his love for Kathy. Chris's wife, Nancy, who had sent the electronic message after her death, filled not only me but also a room full of people with her love for Chris. Mike's father, Fred, showing up on a commercial shoot to talk about his new grandson was so heartwarming that I no longer wanted to act.

I could feel the love of every deceased person who wanted to say hi, who wanted to come back for a few moments and give a message, advice, or some extraordinary detail to prove to the family that even in death he or she was alive. Love was at the core of every communication, and so was forgiveness.

Those who struggled with mental illness and took their lives or died during an event that caused harm to themselves or others were deeply remorseful. Once they understood the pain that their choices made they took responsibility for their actions, and once they made restitution they could move on. We are not thrown into hell by a wrathful God—we create our own heaven and hell on Earth as well as on the other side. Pam, the minister's wife who killed herself after being tortured by an illness, deeply regretted her actions and what they had done to her family. When she was able to apologize to Paul and was forgiven, she peacefully went into the light, and even the house finally sold.

Rebecca's love for her fiancé, Randy, (even though he was responsible for her death) was the force that allowed her to punch though the veil to talk to Randy's daughter, Mindy. The prayers and forgiveness from Randy's family gave Randy strength to forgive himself, therefore releasing him out of his hellish, self-imposed mental prison.

At the luncheon with friends, my deceased father came in over a Caesar salad. He expressed his terrible sadness over his addiction to alcohol and his deep remorse of not protecting me from the hands of my mother. He revealed that he saw me standing by his casket, knew I had prayed for him to receive help, and was grateful. Fifteen years later he showed up at Monroe—healthy, happy, and on a higher level of consciousness. I now wondered if my mother could feel the difference in her soul from my prayers, or benefited in some way from all the work I was doing with Spirit and Monroe. Knowing she had been assisted in some way would certainly help my heart.

After all of the therapeutic studies, life coaching, personal development classes, life lessons, and loves, I thought I had healed enough. But when my marriage blew up and the entire alcoholic family template I had buried so deeply reappeared in my life in the form of Bill Bonnard, I realized that there was an incredible larger consciousness, a more grand, benevolent, personal awareness and understanding at work. Yes, God, which I had given so many names, was guiding me into a deeper understanding of love and forgiveness. We were working together. So once again I surrendered to what was coming.

I had been in Taekwondo for five years, kicking, punching, and nun-chucking all the pent-up upset in my body when I met Meena, a dark-haired beauty with a little voice and gentle demeanor. Meena had been experiencing a situation that I, too, had struggled with. Meena had all the right moves as a second-degree black belt trainer, but found herself defending her life against a boyfriend who ended up stalking her. Meena and I grew to respect each other. She came to my office for a session and we found out she was a very gifted medium-in-training. A year had passed since I had been to Monroe. I felt a transformation so powerful that it touched both the living and the dead, a transformation that reverberated through lifetimes. I had been working for a few years on this book and was prepared to publish it when I heard the Voice: *We want you to talk to your mother.*

It was the day before a blue moon, the anniversary of Sonny biting off the end of my nose, when I invited my student Meena to come for a class.

Meena had grown more confident. Her voice was deeper and she was in acting classes, of all things. I was proud of her. She made herself comfortable on the sofa and we started to work.

Meena immediately connected to a woman who was fun, energetic, and wanted to laugh. "I have a woman who says, 'I am so proud of Marla for writing her book. Please tell her I understood why she could not see my illness, tell my family I love them, and please mention Monroe. I was a greeter.'" That was my friend Diane, whose cancer I could not see before it was too late, and whom I and my Monroe classmate found greeting people on focus level twenty-seven. It felt like she was right there in my office, alive and happy. We talked about her family and how well they were all doing. Visiting with her was joyful and amazing. Diane had known my mother in life, so I asked her if she had seen my mother on the other side.

Meena paused and said, "Diane says, 'Your mother is on a different level and I can't see her.'" I knew Meena and I had to find her.

Meena wasn't sure what to do, so I handed her a piece of paper with my mother's name on it. This was a way Lyn Buchannan had taught me to connect to a person who might be challenging. Immediately Meena's demeanor shifted. "Oh Marla, I feel sick to my stomach. It's your mother—she's upset ... oh, my God."

"What! What's wrong, Meena?" Her face contorted and she pursed her lips just like my mother used to.

"Meena, stay calm and tell me what you see."

Meena stared straight ahead, transfixed.

"Oh, Marla, I can feel it, I can feel it—on my lower back, my thighs, stomach, legs, and private parts! She is showing me what she used to do to you!"

"Stay calm, Meena, detach from the pain."

"Your mother tells me that this rage would overtake her, an unstoppable anger with no end that she took out on you like you were just an object."

I never imagined this moment. But I also realized that Spirit had set up this situation. I tried to stay present to help Meena, Mother, and me through this.

"Mother, we are here to help you. Would you like to be with your family, your mother?"

"I feel her softening," Meena said, "It's like she is a little girl with wonder. She's reluctant, but she is telling me how she felt loved in the meticulous way you took care of her after she died, dressing her for her funeral, getting her hair and makeup done right, and choosing her special blouse and necklace. She wanted to believe that you forgave her, but she will never forgive herself for what she had done. She doesn't feel fit to deserve love or forgiveness or anything but the hellish existence she is in now. She wants to be with her family, but she doesn't think that's possible because that would involve happiness, something she will not allow herself."

"Mother," I said, "I want you to know that I am who I am because of what you did to me, but on some level we agreed to do this together. I have transformed all of that, Mother, and now I help others. You were ill, and now we have an opportunity to help you."

I leaned in, looked deeply into Meena's eyes, held the intention that I was connecting to my mother's soul, and said with all my heart, love, and conviction, "Mother, I love you and *completely* forgive you for everything."

We sat in silence for a moment, and then Meena said, "Your mother now knows you are there to help her, and that you have always been trying to help her."

I saw the light in my mind's eye, the bright golden light that I often see when it's time for a consciousness to move on. "Mother, there is a portal of light opening for you so you can see how to move out of where you are. All you have to do is step into the light. Can you do that?"

"Yes," said Meena, "she sees the light, and there are two adults and a smaller person she recognizes reaching out to her." Meena says the names John and David. "Now she is taking their hands—she is stepping into the light. Marla—she's gone."

It felt like all the air had been sucked out of the room. Everything was silent. Nothing moved but the tiny shadows of the bamboo that gently twinkled on the walls.

Meena and I had slipped into my mother's personal hell and gotten her out.

"It was incredible to see and feel your mother's energy change when she took the hands that reached out to her and stepped into that light," Meena said quietly. "After everything she had done to you to hurt you and your life, she could not imagine that you would come back to help her. But then you reached out to her. You gave her the hope she could never see for herself."

"Oh, my God," was all I could say.

"There is another presence here," Meena continued. "Two wise men, elders, are saying that you and your sister will now talk. They are telling me that your sister's birthday is next week." The elders were correct about my sister's birthday and it was time for my sister and me to communicate after so many years.

I walked Meena out of the building and hugged and thanked her for being a part of one of the most amazing experiences of my life. I was so proud of her, and grateful. As Meena turned to leave she said, "Marla, you just accomplished something you knew you were destined to do and have been trying to achieve forever."

Part of me was drained of the self I knew. I lay on the sofa for three days wondering about this new feeling. All the anxiety that had been with me my entire life was gone, like old gasoline siphoned out of my chassis and replaced with a higher octane. I never realized that those who are troubled in death can still affect us, and when they shift in consciousness, we all transform.

The details that my student so beautifully delivered was another reminder of the profound significance of the healing that comes with this work. After talking about this experience with other facilitators and friends, I began to feel refueled. I called Meena to check on my amazing student and process more of the details of the session.

"Meena, how are you?"

"I was leveled for three days," she said.

"Me too! How strange."

"This was even more significant that I first realized, Marla. Your mother knows all about your book. It is as though what you wrote made her face for the first time what she had not been willing to look at."

My experiences with talking to the dead had taught me that the karmic process we all go through includes experiencing—after we have passed—what we did while alive and how it affected ourselves and others. The dead also feel, see, and hear us as we go on living. I was stunned that my emotional authenticity of feeling, speaking, and writing this book would have an effect on my mother. The idea that 'I gave her the hope she could never see for herself' was the greatest gift for both of us. I didn't need to hear the words "I'm sorry." Her acknowledgment signaled an opportunity for change, and that was critical to the process of true forgiveness.

Through many tears I said, "I can't comprehend the enormity of all that yet. I am just so deeply grateful that you helped us."

"What about the names John and David?" Meena asked. "Did they make sense to you?"

"Mother used to tell a story of planting two trees on either side of the driveway entrance to her home in North Carolina and naming them after two boyfriends she dearly loved. One of them was John. She also shared that the baby she lost before my sister was born would have been named David. I am not sure who the other adult was, but I hope it was her mother. She loved her so."

It was all about the love. I wondered, just like my clients do, what would happen next after such a mind-blowing experience. What unexpected situation or person would come into my life? And how would this healing ripple out into the lives of others?

Three weeks later I received a manila envelope in the mail from my sister. It contained a precious little lace dress with a pink camisole, olive green trim, and ribbon. It was the dress I had worn in first grade on stage as Cinderella. Why or how she had kept it all these years and was now returning it to me was simply—wonderful.

Those of us who carry the shock of physical or emotional abuse and trauma in our systems do what we can to survive it; however, the internalized abuse does not disappear on its own. It becomes a foreign body, a grain of sand, a chronic irritant lodged in our delicate psyche. We unconsciously respond by trying to rid ourselves of that pain and anxiety by medicating ourselves, acting out, or swallowing that assault by creating layers and layers of protection. Over time we create an emotional wall disconnecting us from God and the people in our lives.

The unattended pain can become like a tumor that makes us ill or, if acknowledged and addressed, a precious pearl.

It is our responsibility to recognize this and do something to help ourselves. My trauma and drama forced me to get help. The danger I experienced at times was a way for me to face fear, stand up for myself, and take on forces that taught me to speak the truth and strengthen my spirit. Fear tries to trick us into believing we don't deserve love. We must find ways to love ourselves, and that courageous act is the most generous thing we can do because only then can we truly love others. Every experience, including the most painful ones, with family, friends, loves, and foes has shaped us into the people we are. I pray we choose to create pearls.

Death changes us. In the midst of the pain, we often forget that the anguish we feel is equal to the love. If we allow it, that pain can buff us smooth, crafting us into something our soul needs to feel, experience, and be. We will never be the same, but in time we will be stronger having lived through the loss and honored death with living and loving.

Prayer is not just about begging for help when your life is not going the way you want. Prayer is another generous expression of love. It is an intention, an expressed desire to *see* what we need to do or understand so we won't feel so *blind*. Prayer is our way of sending love and being love as we request help from God. Prayer is the powerful resonance of light and love. It assists the living and the dead. Our prayers are always answered, not necessarily in the way we want, but exactly how we need them to be.

When we take responsibility for our behavior while we are alive, it not only helps everyone around us, but also the dead. When the dead accept responsibility, the living are able to feel the freedom, too. The pain of life and death can be transformed on both sides of the veil through love and forgiveness. Our blindness is only temporary!

The connection and guidance I found from the Voice, Jesus, the Holy Spirit, the Force, the Larger Consciousness System, or THEMS—my loving collective term for what most of us call God—has been the greatest blessing of my life. The same blessing of love awaits everyone. Look for it, intention it, meditate on it, and pray for it.

The light, my friends, has always been there, and always will be.

About the Author

Marla spent twenty-five years as a successful TV and stage actress, and since devoting herself to her current work she has appeared as a psychic medium on A&E, Bravo, History Channel, SyFy, TV Land, and Gaia TV's "Beyond Belief with George Noory." Radio audiences have heard Marla on George Noory's "Coast-to-Coast," Lisa Garr's "Aware Show," and dozens of podcasts. Marla is a co-host of "Dreamland" on Unknowncountry.com and most recently she appears on YouTube teleconferences with physicist and author Tom Campbell, blending physics with metaphysics to understand the "science" of how Marla works, making the paranormal "normal." She appears in cities and towns across the country presenting "Messages with Marla" to small and large groups, educating people about their own intuition, connecting them with deceased loved ones, and potentially providing information about any aspect of their lives for their greatest good.